HARDWIRED BEHAVIOR

Neuroscience research over the past twenty or more years has brought about a significant change in our perceptions of how the brain affects morality. Findings show that the mind and brain are very close, if not the same, and that the brain "makes" the mind. This is bringing about a change of focus from examining mental activity ("mentalism") to the physical activity of the brain ("physicalism") to understand thinking and behavior. We are discovering that the physical features of the brain play the major role in shaping our thoughts and emotions, including the way we deal with "moral" issues. This book sets out the historical framework of the transition from mentalism to physicalism, shows how the physical brain works in moral decisions, and then examines three broad areas of moral decision making: the brain in "bad" acts, the brain in decisions involving sexual relations, and the brain in money decision making.

Laurence R. Tancredi, a psychiatrist-lawyer, is a Clinical Professor of Psychiatry at New York University School of Medicine and the author or coauthor of numerous articles and several books on topics in law, ethics, and psychiatry, including *Dangerous Diagnostics: The Social Power of Biological Information* (1994) and *When Law and Medicine Meet: A Cultural View* (2004). Tancredi has a private practice in New York City and works as a forensic psychiatric consultant. He has consulted in dozens of legal cases involving a wide variety of psychiatric issues, from the effects of toxic environmental substances on brain function to criminal cases involving assault, rape, and homicide.

HARDWIRED BEHAVIOR

WHAT NEUROSCIENCE REVEALS ABOUT MORALITY

Laurence R. Tancredi

New York University School of Medicine

CAMBRIDGE UNIVERSITY PRESS
Cambridge, New York, Melbourne, Madrid, Cape Town, Singapore,
São Paulo, Delhi, Dubai, Tokyo

Cambridge University Press
32 Avenue of the Americas, New York, NY 10013-2473, USA

www.cambridge.org
Information on this title: www.cambridge.org/9780521127394

First published 2005
Reprinted 2007
First paperback edition 2010

Printed in the United States of America

A catalog record for this publication is available from the British Library.

ISBN 978-0-521-86001-7 Hardback
ISBN 978-0-521-12739-4 Paperback

To my parents,
Samuel and Alvesta Pera Tancredi,
for their support and encouragement.

Contents

Preface

My intention in writing this book has been to generate discussion about the findings of neuroscience research over the past few decades and their possible effects on our understanding of humankind's moral precepts. Extraordinary advances in neuroscience have accelerated the breakdown of the idea that a dichotomy exists between mind and body. This erosion of a long-standing belief has many implications for the medical diagnosis and treatment of neurological and psychiatric illnesses. Not least, it forces us to reexamine basic notions concerning the human condition and our construct of morality.

During and since the publication of this book in the fall of 2005, some of the most interesting researchers and thinkers have been writing on the neuroscience of morality. Franz De Waal at the Yerkes National Primate Research Center and Emory University has conducted research on moral development in primates and published several books in the last decade, including his most recent, *Primates and Philosophers: How Morality Evolved,* describing his research. He proposes in his work that human morality emerges from social instincts that we share with other primates, in particular chimpanzees, bonobos, and apes. Joshua D. Greene at Harvard has demonstrated in his fascinating research, which has been published in the scientific literature, the pivotal role of emotional influences on moral judgments.

Marc D. Hauser's *Moral Minds: How Nature Designed Our Universal Sense of Right and Wrong* introduces a unique theory regarding the brain's center for moral decisions. He posits the existence of a moral grammar that involves universal rules and cultural exceptions to these that result from nurture as well as nature, and that allows for an instinctive tool for building moral systems. This concept is similar to MIT professor of linguistics Noam Chomsky's idea of a "universal grammar," which is an inborn cognitive capacity for developing language and applying systematic rules for its usage.

Richard Joyce's *The Evolution of Morality* addresses the origins of morality, questioning whether it is the result of environmental pressures, inheritance, or a fabrication of culture to serve the need for order in society. He concludes that scientific evidence supports the notion that morality in humans is innate, and he sets the foundation for philosophical research in the biology of morality. His views are consistent with those of Marc Hauser and other neuroscientists.

Clearly, our focus is shifting from an emphasis on mental processes – particularly the strong emphasis on free will and intentionality – to recognition of the very important role of the physical brain on human thought and behavior. We are learning that social morality begins in the brain, for without the brain there would be no concept of morality; the brain allows for interaction among individuals within the community, and this interaction leads to the construction of a framework for moral order. Individual responsibility, therefore, must be reconsidered in the light of biological brain processes, which may under certain conditions exert a deterministic influence.

The events of 9/11, the abuse of Iraqi prisoners by American soldiers, the uncontrollable sexual desires and greed of some members of society who infract the rights and personhood of others – these are among the many examples of "immoral" behaviors that have captured the attention of the public over the past decade. The question of whether these behaviors reflect biology rather than conscious intent has been debated in many forms and in many venues. Have new scientific findings destroyed the relevance of free will, placing it in a context of biological forces that may often operate outside of the conscious control of the actor? This book is an attempt to quantify the current debate from the neuroscientific point of view without neglecting the ancient precepts of "morality" that have guided humanity throughout its history.

Hardwired Behavior begins with a framework for understanding community notions of morality in our culture. Proscribed or negative behavior – including deception, personal and mental abuse, and manipulation for the benefit of one party over another – are common precepts of morality in society that originate in ancient philosophies and religions and reflect immoral actions still proscribed by today's major religions – the Judeo-Christian tradition of the West, Islam, and the religions of the Far East. Yet the new developments in neuroscience are altering our concept of these moral guideposts, converting many of these proscribed behaviors into problems of brain biology. This new understanding of morality, therefore, may be more representative of a framework reflecting the hardwiring of the brain as it has slowly modified over many centuries of inching evolutionary changes.

Hardwired Behavior addresses brain biology from two perspectives: the factors involved in the synchronizing of regions of the brain directly involved with moral decision making, and the influence of biological conditions (such as enzyme irregularities and hormone effects) that indirectly affect moral decision making. In discussing these two dimensions of brain biology, I have resorted to discussions of cases, some of which (as in the case history of killer Ricky Green) involved serious defective brain wiring that led to the development of highly undesirable "moral" traits.

Even though imaging technologies, such as functional MRI, allow us to map the regions of the brain during thinking and emotions, the state of development of these imaging technologies is far from delivering a thorough understanding of thought and emotions. The future will bring about refinements in imaging technologies, and more detailed study of the brain will show how its parts work together like a symphony within a network to produce conscious thoughts and feelings. In addition we will in time study people with imaging technologies not only on an individual basis as we do now but also while they operate within the dynamics of a group setting, the primary organization of society.

Taking these biological factors into account, as well as the likelihood of major breakthroughs over the next seventy-five to a hundred years, this book concludes on a futuristic note – one involving eugenics, a concern that goes back to humanity's earliest moral precepts as articulated in ancient philosophy, in the Ten Commandments, and in the Seven Deadly Sins.

Acknowledgments

In preparation for writing this book I have reviewed the relevant scientific literature from many specialties, most particularly the neurosciences, genetics, psychiatry, psychology, primatology, and the social sciences. I have focused predominantly on what is known at this time from neuroscience research. But I have also explored the implications of the course of neuroscience research in terms of likely findings for the future.

During the months that I worked on this project I relied on the advice and support of colleagues and friends. Myrna Weissman and Nora Volkow played an important role early in my thinking about neuroscience developments and possibilities for a book on the biology of morality. Others have helped me cull information and think through particular issues. In this regard I want specially to thank Paul Schipior, Andrew Slaby, and David Weisstub.

I am very appreciative to Lisa Kramer Taruschio, who read early drafts and helped with sentence structure and clarity of expression, and to Linda Thomas for providing me with excellent images of the brain. I also want to thank Jane Nevins for her input. Anne LaFarge, Amy Hempel, Eric Houston, and John Polto read the final manuscript from the viewpoint of nonscientists, and provided me with many helpful suggestions.

Karen Gantz Zahler, my agent, played an essential role in making this book a reality. Finally, I want to express my appreciation

Acknowledgments

to John Berger of Cambridge University Press for his ongoing belief in this project, to the entire Cambridge staff, and to free-lance editor-typesetter Michael Gnat for his quick and very detailed editing of the book.

Neuroscience and Morality

Neuroscience advances during the past few decades have been nothing short of astounding. Our notions about how the brain works and the relationship between mind and brain have been radically changed as we have come to understand how parts of the brain function to provide a wide range of human functions – from short- and long-term memory to the production of fear when certain areas of the brain (most particularly, the amygdala) are activated, and to how the brain's cognitive centers influence and are influenced by regions of the brain that produce emotions.

Many traditional notions of the "mind" as it reflects a dichotomy between mind and body are being revised. Evidence that the brain "makes" the mind is strengthening with indications that brain and mind are not two entirely different realms, but rather that the physical brain has the major role in creating and shaping our emotions and thinking.

With these ideas in mind, I began wondering about the impact of the brain on moral thinking. Because the brain is basic to decision making, it must play a powerful role in our thinking regarding moral issues, and consequently in the way we treat each other in our society to maintain order and uphold fairness, individual rights, and equity. Through my research on these issues as they involve a wide range of behavior, I learned that much thinking and some research have already gone into the impact of neuroscience on morality. Our view of morality has already been altered by new understanding of brain biology, and at the rate that new discoveries are being made, that view will change even more in the future. With these changes will come the understanding that we can intervene at the most fundamental biological levels to affect moral development. Herein lies the primary dilemma posed by these new advances: The modifications in morality empowered by neuroscience will lead to hard choices on how we as a society want to handle these changes, how we want to deal with each other, and the untoward potential consequences of a biologically engineered morality.

Moral Precepts

When I started to think about the biology of morality, I cast around for a frame of reference, one that would help me convey how our culture identifies and classifies right and wrong. My first instinct was to look to religion; all religions have well-defined notions as to what is "good" and what is "evil," and with minor variations religions are in agreement about serious immoral acts. Murder, stealing another's property, and infidelity are forbidden by nearly all the world's religions. These notions of right and wrong have provided a set of rules for human conduct, particularly involving personal relationships, and form the infrastructure of a socially constructed system that exerts, at the very least, informal controls over individual behavior.

According to the Judeo-Christian tradition – which has been the foundation of social morality and laws in Western cultures – from as far back as Genesis humanity has been forced to confront evil. When Adam and Eve disobeyed God and fell from grace, this tradition holds, they changed the nature of Man. The Old and New Testaments caution us each to work every minute of our lives to be faithful to the integrity of our soul, which reflects God's wishes for goodness.

An important dimension of our grappling with our potential for "evil" is self-awareness. Of the ancient philosophers Socrates was reputed to be the first to espouse the value of "Know thyself" as a guiding principle, and over the centuries this "self-knowledge" has not been limited to recognizing our desires and unique abilities. It has required searching within ourselves for knowledge of our "dark" side, our predisposition for evil. Worldly considerations and our emotions may lead us to the ways of "evil" but – theoretically at least, in the Socratic view – we can gain control over these tendencies by understanding our deepest feelings, passions, and needs.

To heed Socrates' advice in our day and age in culturally diverse societies is daunting, to say the least. I suggest that we examine instead the moral precepts developed as guides by humankind in the postclassical world. These precepts may have once been religion-specific, but today they apply generally to civilized societies and, despite their once religious pedigree, have a modern ring to them. They are in fact the moral values that we generally embrace – secular descriptions of our modern moral consensus.

The "moral" proscriptions on behavior appear in one section or another of the Old and New Testaments. In the Jewish faith, the Sixth through the Tenth Commandments, and in later Christianity's Seven Deadly Sins, certain behavior that we might term immoral for all human society is proscribed. The Deadly Sins is a listing believed to be the work of Saint John Cassian, a monk who lived in Egypt and France during the latter part of the fourth and early fifth centuries.[1] Cassian wrote two principal works of rules for governing the monastic life,[2] which included eight books devoted to what he called obstacles to perfection – impurity, covetousness, gluttony, anger, ennui, vainglory, pride, and dejection. Pope Saint Gregory (the Great), who lived from the middle of the sixth to the early part of the seventh century, has been credited with refining the list to the Seven Deadly Sins (or "capital vices").[3] His list was closer to the modern one and did not include some of the terms, like "ennui" or "dejection" (though "ennui" might be interpreted as distantly related to "sloth").

These moral precepts fundamental to Judaism and Christianity have permeated Western culture, serving as the basis of countless literary works over the centuries. Dante in his *Divine Comedy* conceived of moral infractions as transgressions against "love," and grouped them according to three broad classes: wrath and pride;

infractions that created "insufficient" love, such as sloth; and finally lust and greed, inducing "excessive" love or undue desire for material goods.

Geoffrey Chaucer in *Canterbury Tales* and Edmund Spenser in *The Faerie Queene* explicitly addressed these moral infractions. Spenser created visual images of individual immoral acts like gluttony and lust. In the early nineteenth century, the novelist Jane Austen devoted much of *Pride and Prejudice* to the impact of her leading male character's pride on the society around him and to the biased reactions of the woman (Elizabeth Bennet) he had grown to love. More recently Stephen Sondheim and George Furth, in their play *Getting Away with Murder*, constructed characters to represent the Seven Deadly Sins. An entire series of murder mysteries by Lawrence Sanders takes its titles from these sins.

In relation to contemporary secular society, each moral transgression anchors an evil. Within this framework we go from mild or seemingly insignificant nuances of infractions to the most profound offenses, such as those described in the Ten Commandments. Nearly every act that we may deem immoral relates to one or another of these breaches. Wrath or anger, for instance, can be petty, manifesting itself in social slights against another person, such as not inviting someone to an important social event because of unresolved past grievances. It can also be the basis of harmful psychological and physical acts. At the very extreme, homicide and even suicide find their sources in anger. Lust can also fall along a spectrum from a private interest in pornographic magazines and salacious movies to the imposition of one's sexual desires on another person, such as taking advantage of one's superior position to demand favors. When combined with anger, lust can lead to serious criminal behavior and sexual psychopathy – rape, assault to exact sexual pleasure, and even homicide.

Behavior that might easily classify as "greed" or avarice also falls along a spectrum from mild to serious. Mild greed might be an unwillingness to donate one's money to assist a socially important cause. On the more extreme level of greed are the many white-collar crimes of corporate executives skimming off millions for themselves at the expense of employees who suffer devastating reductions in their retirement savings and the prospect of serious financial problems as they get older. In many cases this is done with the contrived appearance of legitimacy; in others, money is confiscated or embezzled by those in a position of trust. Perhaps even more reprehensible is when greed goes beyond acquiring money and goods to involve the physical destruction of innocent people, as when the clerk in a convenience store is shot for a few dollars in the till.

Do Moral Precepts Arise from Social Concerns?

The Ten Commandments and the Seven Deadlies are handy and simple references whose fame has spread far from their original sources: Moses (if you will), a Catholic saint, and a pope. And that begs a question: If Moses, Saint John, and Saint Gregory hadn't articulated them, would someone else have? I think so. Morality deals with people and how they relate to one another. One can engage in immoral acts by oneself, like shooting up heroin or snorting cocaine, but one is not immoral alone. One's actions – even if essentially victimless – affect others in society.

Social scientists have theorized for years that morality has its roots in primitive societies, claiming that the ways people treated each other determined whether they would survive or fail in the natural world. Men had to learn to work together to obtain food and protect their families against predators and natural disasters. In the formation of the family unit and of societies that would focus on the common good, rules of conduct emerged to ensure that communities would work in harmony and that dissension would be minimized or completely averted.

Basic human emotions, such as the territorial imperative (the need to control land and other property, as well as defined and predictable relationships, particularly with mates),[4] and the desire for love, affection, and respect had to be recognized and carefully factored into the structure of community. A male who aggressively sought out another person's property and disrupted that family unit by seducing the other man's wife would create enormous tensions, not just between the two males, but within the community at large.

These tensions would be destabilizing and could lead to serious disorder and the weakening of the bonds in the community.

By the same token, it is important to recognize that these "sins" involve behaviors that created an evolutionary advantage during certain early phases of man's development. They served the ends of individuals and to some extent groups. For example, greed and aggression (which activates the same reward pathways as drugs of abuse) led to ruthless leaders. The compulsion to eat, reflective of genes that lead to obsessive behavior, had the advantage of holding people over during periods of famine. Women having "extramarital" affairs resulted in children, which increased genetic diversity. Even homicide, during periods of limited resources, ensured the survival of some over others; perhaps, arguably, the stronger physically and emotionally would succeed.

The creation of "community" did not happen overnight; it developed over many millennia. People came to understand that emotions like shame, guilt, disgust, and fear of abandonment could be used to induce the individual to practice self-control for the common good.[5] Hence, according to many social scientists, agreed-upon morality came to serve as the device to use these emotions to control individual behavior. Over time, some system of rules for behavior had to prevail if a community was to prevent its own disintegration.

Today, research in evolution, genetics, and neuroscience is showing that what appeared to evolve from social need had in fact far more complex origins. It now seems more likely that human biology had to be of a certain type for society to be shaped in particular ways.

A new science, evolutionary psychology, emerged in the 1990s to focus on explaining human behavior against the backdrop of Darwinian theory.[6] This science considers how the biological forces of genetics and neurotransmissions in the brain influence unconscious strategies and conscious intentions, and proposes that these features of biology undergo subtle but continuous change through evolution.

Though it is indeed a social construct, morality gets its timelessness and universality from the human brain. The community's demands for cohesiveness and continued existence – its own ideas of what is appropriate human behavior – brought into play certain qualities that were already present in the human brain.

We have some evidence to support this view. We know that the limbic structures of the brain, often referred to as the "old" brain, are the physical circuitry for our emotional responses – fear, disgust, guilt – to the environment. These structures work in concert with the prefrontal lobe to attach emotions to specific behaviors. When we have done something that we feel was terribly wrong – like failing the final examination in mathematics in college because we stayed up the night before at a party – our prefrontal lobe considers the facts and checks them against a particular set of emotions. We feel shame because we have been trained from childhood to understand that our parents and friends will look disparagingly at our failure. Over time we internalize that emotional response and automatically feel shame whenever we are not successful.

Similarly, guilt can be induced by certain kinds of behavior that our family and society see as bad. When we cheat on a test because we are ill prepared, or simply can't understand the complexity of the problems being presented, we naturally feel guilty about it.

We are not constructed to have consistent reactions of guilt or shame to specific types of behavior. Changes in attitudes and mores about human conduct will bring about adaptation in us to conform to what is going on in the environment. Certain thoughts and actions have always resulted in feelings of guilt, shame, and fear. Most significant of these are incest and homicide. Many kinds of behavior, however, are perceived differently by society now than they were even a hundred years ago. For example, attitudes toward premarital sex and infidelity have changed again and again and radically through the ages, depending upon a given society's mores. What was totally unacceptable a mere hundred years ago in our society, for example, may today be treated with a "get over it" attitude or by divorce.

Support for the evolutionary and biological thesis of social morality comes from our understanding of natural selection and evolution from primates and other animals.[7] Darwin recognized that social instincts exist among animals and believed that the development of a moral conscience was related to well-developed intellectual powers.[8]

Thomas Huxley,[9] one of the major proponents of Darwinian theory, and more recently Richard Dawkins,[10] felt strongly that morality had to be learned, as a person was born to be basically self-interested, or selfish. Huxley went so far as to claim that human nature was fundamentally evil, with morality essentially a human invention. He saw it as a system to control competition and selfishness.[11]

Recently conducted research by many evolutionary scholars – most particularly the cognitive ethologist Frans de Waal – has questioned the validity of Huxley's and Dawkins' views. Since the early 1900s biologists have been aware of how evolution favors mutual assistance among animals.[12] In *Good Natured: The Origins of Right and Wrong in Humans and Other Animals*,[13] de Waal writes about his discovery that primates engage in many acts, such as sharing food, that are antecedents or building blocks of morality.[14] Sharing (which is not limited to apes)[15] may take the form of "reciprocal altruism," where even though giving is contingent on receiving, there may be a time lag before the favor is returned and the benefit to the recipient may require a significant cost and risk to the giver.[16]

De Waal and his colleagues have also shown that apes and even monkeys hold negative acts in mind as well and are capable of revenge.[17] Violations of the social code, such as when a chimpanzee cheats another chimpanzee by not returning a favor, can result in what has been called "moralistic" aggression. Furthermore he has found that nonhuman primates are capable of conflict resolution, consolation, and expressing empathy, sympathy, and even community concern.[18]

Neuroscience and Moral Precepts

The fact that morality in humans evolved from other primates and depends on the brain for its universality and stability does not negate the importance of social forces in its creation, or the role of "free will" in its execution. The moral proscriptions in the Judeo-

Christian tradition are our articulation of responses etched in the biological structure of the brain. We have the ability to understand how these proscriptions developed and to recognize the importance of regulating them for an ordered society. Furthermore we can alter our behavior to square with our understanding of the wrongness of certain behavior, and we can thus exert control over our emotional responses to provocations.

Recent neuroscience discoveries are adding twists to this equation. We are getting a handle on brain biology as it relates to specific moral precepts, and in time all of them will be seen as originating, to some degree, in biology. This understanding might suggest that under certain conditions "immoral" behavior is not necessarily the product of willful acts. By controlling behavior, brain biology might be responsible for some of the extreme manifestations of these bad behaviors. In that case, some individual "sins" may not be "sins" at all.

Three of the Seven Deadlies, for example, have already been shown to be affected by biological factors in varying degrees, and in some cases the individual may have little power, or "free will," to prevent them from happening. These three are gluttony, sloth, and lust.

Gluttony is a complex concept, but we have made some progress in understanding it. To a large extent, the "immoral" character of gluttony flows from the notion that this behavior consists of excessive consumption, waste, and a basic unwillingness to exert self-discipline. It is this tendency toward excessive self-indulgence that most likely resulted in gluttony's inclusion as one of the Seven Deadly Sins.

With regard to the most conspicuous display of society's notion of gluttony – obesity – the two conditions are not always compatible. Many causes of obesity have nothing to do with lack of control or excessive self-indulgence. Metabolism, which is genetically determined, can result in weight gain despite efforts toward control of excessive eating. Studies have shown that obesity may involve either of two brain systems: the system that sends hunger and satiation messages to the brain or the system associated with the reward circuits involved in drug (cocaine, heroin, marijuana) addiction.

Gluttony is on its way to being seen as part of the spectrum of addictive diseases. Research is already showing that gluttony and obesity may involve abnormalities in specific areas of the brain. With the use of positron emission tomography (PET scans), researchers have shown within the past few years that the human brain is highly sensitive to food and that the presence of food increases brain metabolism in specific areas.[19] Increased metabolism in the right orbitofrontal cortex correlates highly with self-reports of increased hunger and desire for food, just as it does for drugs in those who are addicted.

Sloth, or pathological laziness (another of the Seven Deadlies), is closely aligned to depression. A person experiencing serious depression has no desire to do anything. Some people suffer a "retarded" depression, which means that they think and move slowly, are unable to concentrate and focus on information, and may experience some memory loss. This is clearly a biological condition, as we know that in depression major neurotransmitters – in particular serotonin, dopamine, and norepinephrine – have been decreased in amounts in the synapses of neurons located particularly in limbic structures. Though an individual may appear willfully lazy, often he (or she) is suffering from an underlying depression and is biologically limited in his ability to become active and productive.

The third "sin," which relates to the Sixth Commandment against adultery, is *lust*. The biology of testosterone and its impact on structures of the brain – such as the hypothalamus – of vulnerable individuals, mostly men, has been the focus of much research on sexual behavior. Again, extreme behavior seems to be aligned with addictive propensities in the brain. The power of "lust" varies among individuals. Some people have minimal sexual desires. This may be due to less testosterone, or to differences in the brain biology that responds to hormones. Others may have overactive libidos, whereby they become obsessed with sexual thoughts and indiscriminately engage in sexual behavior. The two extremes may reflect biological differences. The person consumed with lust may be powerless to exert free will and control his or her behavior. When lust is combined with anger it can result in violent acts – rape, assault, and even murder.

With more research we are likely to find that other behaviors proscribed in the Ten Commandments or in the Deadly Sins are also influenced by biological factors. Such findings do not suggest that those afflicted with strong biological pressure are without responsibility for their behavior. But in some cases the biological influences may be so intense as to preclude restraints of behavior through free will. Neuroscience findings that are supporting the power of biology have been forcing a reexamination of the morality of much behavior, as well as the importance of handling abnormalities through medicine rather than guilt, shame, and criminal sanctions.

This is not to discount the relevance of "free will"; but under some circumstances its importance does diminish. In the same vein, I am not saying that there is no such thing as "immoral behavior" simply because we can demonstrate its specific biology. The idea of a moral transgression is a nontechnical compass pointing to behavior that can injure oneself or one's society. Biology is unlikely to supply all the answers necessary to erase the uncomfortable notion of immorality, but evidence is building that brain biology will make major advances in that direction.

In this book I examine the history of our general ideas about morality and its development through childhood; show how modern neuroscience research is shifting the focus to the brain as a physical organ shaping moral responses; and illustrate the outcome of defective "brain wiring" in the development of undesirable moral traits. Finally, a view through the crystal ball into the future will explore how the shift to "physicalism" will lead to hard choices about how we deal with each other, and will discuss the potential for political control to create a homogenized moral society.

2

Morality and the Mind

*Men ought to know that from the brain, and from the brain only arise our pleas-
ures, joys, laughter and jests, as well as our sorrows, pains, griefs and tears.
Through it, in particular, we think, see, hear and distinguish the ugly from the
beautiful, the bad from the good the pleasant from the unpleasant. It . . . makes
us mad or delirious, inspires us with fear, brings sleeplessness and aimless anx-
ieties. . . . In these ways I hold that the brain is the most powerful organ in the
human body.*

Hippocrates (c. 460 BC–c. 377 BC), from "The Sacred Disease"

One of the most astonishing things in the history of the brain is
the seesawing between mentalism (focus on the mind as separate
from the brain) and physicalism (emphasis on the primacy of the
physical brain). As early as 400 BC, Hippocrates acknowledged the
brain as the center of human emotions and thinking. During the
ensuing centuries this viewpoint moved like a pendulum from that
position to one espousing the dynamics of mental processes. Now,
it appears, we are returning to a belief in the primacy of the brain.

When I began my practice in the late 1970s, psychiatry was in
transition. A different model was replacing psychoanalytical explanations for mental and emotional illnesses, which had focused on
the impact of infant and childhood development, particularly interactions with parents and siblings, for creating adult neuroses and
psychoses. Research on behavioral genetics and brain neurotransmitters was bearing fruit, so that by the 1990s there was increasing

acceptance of the notion that serious mental illness had its origins in biological dysfunction.

Blaming abnormal genes and neurotransmitters for depression, anxiety, panic, and even schizophrenia had become more commonplace than blaming victims and their backgrounds. No longer were expressions like "snap out of it," which created the impression that we control our mind and emotions, being offered to a seriously depressed or suicidal person. The zeitgeist had changed. With the publication in 1993 of *Listening to Prozac,* everyone became aware of the power of antidepressants and the general view that psychiatric illness involves brain biology.

As a psychiatrist I have seen many patients who suffer from a wide variety of mental and emotional problems, from serious depression, bipolar disorder, and panic, to marital disharmony and inability to function on the job. As with those who are mentally healthy, many of these patients presented moral quandaries. Several years ago I treated one such patient, a 35-year-old married lawyer, for depression. He presented an impeccable image. His shoes were so well shined that they looked like mirrors. It wasn't until after several visits that he confided in me that he abused cocaine while frequenting houses of prostitution. He admitted that his wife was completely unaware of this hidden side of his life. When I confronted him with the moral dilemmas his activities produced, most particularly the infidelity, lying, and betrayal, and exposing his wife to the possibilities of developing a serious illness, he seemed indifferent to these issues. His concern was only that she not find out about what he was doing because she would likely retaliate and cause serious problems for him. He seemed incapable of understanding or chose to ignore the morality of his behavior.

I had similar experiences with other patients, causing me to wonder if our understanding of morality at this time in history is similar to our knowledge about mental and emotional illnesses before the biological revolution in psychiatry. Could it be possible that we are assigning too much power to "free will" and blaming the perpetrator, who may instead be a "victim" of his or her own biology?

The accepted wisdom about morality is that we learn what is good and what is bad from parents, teachers, and religious leaders.

But we are also told that our ability to abide by these "moral" rules is seen as reflective of our character or personality: People of good character possess moral strength or integrity;[1] they would not cheat or take advantage of others; those who are immoral have bad character.

An individual confronted with a moral choice processes in his (or her) mind reasons for his decisions and actions. A person of strong character places his wants and desires in perspective by recognizing what others want; when he carefully balances competing factors he is most likely to make a moral decision. The mind of the individual, his intention, controls his character, which thereby determines how he will handle competing interests. By being self-indulgent and indifferent to the harm of others, the 35-year-old lawyer showed he had a weak character. He considered the options and impact of his decision and came out in a self-interested way. He had a choice and could have taken a different route.

This conventional way of looking at moral decisions focuses on the mind of the actor. Each of us operates to some extent under the influence of self-interest,[2] but we have the power to be sympathetic to others, and to choose against our own interests in keeping with social and moral standards. The accepted wisdom is that we have free will and control over our minds. Therefore, when we engage in an immoral act, we choose to do so.

With few exceptions, this belief has dominated much of Western European tradition for centuries. Exceptions have been made for mental illness as a condition that may influence a person's capacity to make a moral choice,[3] but generally people are seen as intentional and responsible for their actions.

Moral Development in Children: Three Mentalists

Three towering figures took up the question of how morality develops in children. These three – Sigmund Freud, Jean Piaget, and Lawrence Kohlberg – were "mentalists" in the sense that their focus and object of study was the mind, not the body or brain. Virtually by themselves they shaped our fundamental views of moral development. Freud, the first of these, began spelling out his theories during the early twentieth century. Through his explication of the unconscious and early childhood experiences that shape adult behavior and thinking, he set the stage for Piaget, who constructed a framework for understanding the stages of development in the way children learn how to think and judge ideas and facts. Influenced by Piaget's staging of cognition, Kohlberg applied this dynamic to how children learn about morality.

Their theories still underlie contemporary cultural notions of child rearing, influencing experts like Drs. Benjamin Spock and T. Barry Brazelton. Each of these thinkers in psychomoral development contributed incrementally to the understanding of how the mind works; how intentions, desires, and intuitions as well as the power of socializing factors such as sympathy, empathy, sociability, and integrity guide us and shape our decisions.

Freud, Piaget, and Kohlberg tried to understand human thinking and behavior by assessing what was in the mind of the individual. They saw intellectual and moral development as requiring instruction. They explored what family and environmental factors affect the mind in early development, and set out ways to usher the young to higher levels of moral maturity.

The great theorists of the mind have given us ways of thinking about human behavior that serve as building blocks for a more scientifically accurate view of the species. All of them, especially Freud, saw in general terms the value of biology in human functioning.

Though he started out as a bench scientist in Vienna, Freud was denied academic opportunities for working in physiology (today, neurobiology) because he was Jewish. This forced him to shift his attention to another area that did not require resources such as a laboratory. He focused instead on the influences of early childhood development on forming the personality of the adult. He did not believe that humanity had an inherent moral sense, but instead saw the necessity of repression of sexual and aggressive instincts to create social-mindedness. How we learn to make choices, he felt, came from a balance of the forces of the unconscious, particularly instincts and desires (the "Id"), against those of the "Ego," which is the conscious part of us that relates to the environment to bring about adaptation.[4] To Freud, understanding the mind by examining its contents and early social development was the key to understanding the power of unconscious and conscious factors in shaping character.[5]

Following many of Freud's ideas, Piaget also emphasized the child's mind, although the name of his theory, "genetic epistemology," suggests a prominent, if unknown, role for biology. His theory described the seemingly programmed way children grow and develop in their cognitive capacities, the faculties for recognizing and handling moral issues. This system of cognitive growth, he claimed, occurred in four major stages.[6] Each stage builds on the cognitive skills mastered in the preceding one, leading to the final stage, which he referred to as "formal operations." This occurs between eleven years of age and the end of adolescence, and is manifested by abstract thinking and deductive reasoning. Through adaptation, or the ability to interact with and adjust to the environment, the child learns how to take in new experiences from his or her environment and to shape knowledge to reality.[7]

Following the idea of stages laid down by Piaget, Lawrence Kohlberg further refined moral-development theory with detailed descriptions of the stages of evolution in moral judgment.[8] Kohlberg focused on moral reasoning and the developmental changes that occur through a sequence of stages that serve to change or reorganize an individual's way of thinking.[9] With each stage of reorganization – which, as in Piaget's system, integrates the insights from previous stages – the child achieves more understanding and the ability to handle a diversity of viewpoints regarding moral conflicts.

Kohlberg constructed three levels of moral development.[10] The first, the *preconventional* level manifested most frequently in children under ages 9 to 11, but also in adults, is where the "don'ts" are seen as responsible for punishment. To the individual at this level, social rules and expectations are not internalized: They are imposed on the child by others.

The second, the *conventional* level observed in adolescents and adults, involves understanding and upholding the rules and values of society. At this level the individual identifies with the rules and expectations of others in society. An illustration might be an adolescent girl who knows it is wrong to smoke marijuana behind the school gym, and chooses as a result not to because of a desire to follow parental and societal rules.

The third and final level is the *postconventional* level, where social rules are critically examined against the backdrop of universal human rights, duties, and general moral principles. According to Kohlberg only a small number of adults reach this level of moral development, where a person's values are defined in terms of principles he or she has chosen.[11] Protesters during the Vietnam War illustrate this postconventional level, for they were clearly going against social and political "rules" to support their positions on what is a "just" war.

The staging concept was seen by Kohlberg as universal. He and his followers claim that anyone studying moral development in children through interviews and evaluations of the logic of a child's thinking will inevitably arrive at these three levels.[12] Furthermore they contend that, under normal circumstances, developmental change consistent with logical analysis will be upward in direction to increasingly sophisticated levels, with perhaps some differences in the content of thinking. For example, using Kohlberg's model in her examination of moral decision making in women, Carol Gilligan showed differences in the content and process of thinking between women and men. She saw men as more focused, directed, and deliberate, whereas women she saw as more encompassing and broader in the range of issues they consider in arriving at a moral decision. She also followed Kohlberg's pattern of shifting upward to higher levels of sophistication.[13]

Attachment: A Basic Element of Morality

In keeping with "mentalism," theories about attachment support the idea that morality is a social construct, a set of rules that is intended to maintain order and cohesiveness among a group of people. Where the power of these rules and our desire to follow them comes from has long fascinated moral thinkers. Psychological research suggests our moral impulse is related to an infant's need for attachment to parents. A child's craving for love, warmth, and human contact sets the stage for moral development. To ensure that a child continues to receive benefits from his or her mother, there is a powerful incentive in the child to imitate and please the adult.

John Bowlby, one of England's leading psychologists during the latter half of the twentieth century, showed in his pioneering work on attachment that an infant begins to demonstrate attachment behavior toward a caretaker within the first month of life.[14] This behavior intensifies with increasing proximity to the object of attachment, usually the mother. In return the mother becomes "bonded" to her child, and this ensures that the child will be secure and benefit from the mother's mentoring. Such behavior occurs in humans, primates, and many animals.

Bowlby believed that "attachment" behavior has a Darwinian (natural selection) evolutionary basis, ensuring that the young will be protected by adults.[15] Those incapable of attachment would fail to survive. It is particularly beneficial for humans and other species that have extended periods after birth of nurturing their young. In humans there is a long period when nurturance is necessary if the child is to develop the ability to form relationships and to have the cognitive capacity for complex intellectual thought.[16]

Attachment and bonding facilitate the passage of moral understanding and behavior from one generation to the next. According to Bowlby, attachment leads to sociability (although much developmental neuroscience now suggests sociability is hardwired), and sociability drives us to create and shape moral understanding. A child's desire and need for attachment, or for affiliation, and the mother's caring response and bonding provide the dynamics for the son or daughter's adherence to parental values. To maintain the attachment, the child will do whatever he or she thinks is necessary to please the parents.[17] Even though a child possesses a complex brain that is capable of constructing alternative beliefs and actions, the fear of loss or disengagement from a parent usually ensures that the latter's values will prevail.

This relationship between parent and child regarding core values is the bedrock for societal values and sociability. The transmission of morality enabled by the dynamics of attachment from generation to generation ensures consistency of basic values in a culture.

Of course, this also encompasses vast diversity. We know that cultures differ to some extent on what they consider immoral, as they do in what they consider insane. In some cultures polygamy is allowed; in others it is strictly forbidden. The social acceptance of "deviant" sexuality, such as bisexuality or homosexuality, varies among cultures. Respect for dead members of a group also seems universal, and in nearly all cultures eating parts of a deceased's body would be strictly forbidden. Yet, we know that in certain tribes in New Guinea the brains of dead relatives, ancestors, are eaten as a show of respect.[18]

Even such a taboo as incest is actually defined differently in different cultures. Sex between parent and child is forbidden in all cultures, as it is between brother and sister, but in ancient Egypt brother and sister relationships were allowed in the royal family. In contrast, the incest taboo in some cultures may extend as far as to second-order cousins.

Merging Nature and Nurture

Though seen as a feature of "mentalism," attachment is being understood increasingly as a dimension of "physicalism." Attachment does not simply result from learning. We know from studies that the capacity for attachment must be present in the brain of the child or it will never occur. It is possible to determine one's temperament at birth, which suggests that the newborn's basic response to his or her environment is set in the brain.[19] Children born, for example, with severe autism are virtually incapable of forming bonds with adults or other children. Also, children who have been socially deprived from birth reach a certain point in their development when they lose the ability to attach and be bonded.

The theories of moral development with their escalating stages of maturation also involve more than just environmental or instructional exposure. Piaget, Kohlberg, and Freud helped us understand the way children reason at various stages of their personal development, and the psychological process that allowed for this achievement. But they didn't address the physiological changes in children's brains that allowed for their movement through these stages.

Though geniuses in their theorizing about human thought and behavior, these three researchers were nonetheless limited by the biological knowledge of their time. Hence they lacked the sophisticated means for understanding how the brain functions. The tools for investigating the brain did not exist. During most of the first half of the twentieth century, genetics was primarily a descriptive science, meaning that information was obtained by observing in animals and plants how traits (predominantly physical characteristics) were transmitted through generations. DNA's structure was not discovered until the 1950s, and the correlation of specific genes with thinking and behavior have only recently begun to bring about interesting results.

These changes during child development, as we are now learning, had to involve basic biological changes in limbic structures and the frontal lobe, as well as instruction from the environment. As with attachment, the child must have the innate capacity to understand emotionally and cognitively at each of these stages.

This shift from "mentalism" to "physicalism" forces us to focus on the dynamics of nature versus nurture in trying to comprehend how the brain functions, particularly with regards to morality. Those who believe in the supremacy of nature over nurture see genetics and brain biology as the important factors in shaping an individual's personality and abilities. In contrast, the proponents of nurture see most of a person's abilities and behavior as due to cultural learning. Even though they may accept the presence of genes and brain biology, they see humanity as a product of learned culture, which is passed on from one generation to the other.

But this distinction between nature and nurture no longer seems relevant because of scientific discoveries. Basic human dynamics are being shown more and more to be based in biology. The biological capacity to react in specific ways may be transferred genetically or result from changes in the biology of the brain brought on by very early conditioning. What seems most likely is that there is usually in operation a combination of *selection* factors, or the genetic capacity for transferring the trait, and *instruction,* which refers to an environmental event that may trigger the innate capacity present in the genes (see Chapter 6). This latter dynamic appears to operate for most behaviors, as it appears that the transmission of a genetic tendency is not in itself sufficient to ensure the presence of a trait. Rather, gene transmission must be followed by some "instruction" as the child ages.

From Mind to Brain: Completing the Circuit

"Physicalism," in the broad sense of characteristics that are innate to humankind, has a long and distinguished intellectual history, although the technology to bring it to the level of brain biology is only recent. Philosophers and thinkers from Aristotle[20] to Saint Thomas Aquinas[21] claimed that man's nature was to be social. Aquinas argued that human sociability is an example of "natural law" or of man possessing an innate tendency to be rational and social. In keeping with this position, man would be disposed by nature to rely on his reasoning and social instinct to abide by the moral law. Natural law emerges from the awareness of ordering in nature, of laws that underlie the physical and mental dimensions of man. Moral law, therefore, is simply an expression of this tendency for social order and reason, qualities perceived of as inherent to man.

The concept of natural law dominated Western thought for centuries. Some philosophers added nuances to the basic principle. For example, Adam Smith believed that sympathy was another motivation behind behavior.[22] It was not just that people had the tendency to be self-interested, although that was an important element.

The modern world was influenced by the scientific revolution of the nineteenth century, in particular the scientific method, which promoted questioning given "truths" and organized the pursuit of knowledge into the formulation of a problem, the obtainment of data through observation and experiment, and the construction and testing of hypotheses. This scientific approach brought about major changes in our perception of morality. Natural law, or anything resembling a naturally endowed moral sense, was discarded as fundamentally wrong.[23] The focus turned to what could be empirically tested and understood. Paradoxically, the way we are now looking at the brain and mental processes is a story of conflict and reconciliation. The new brain biology is likely to resurrect natural law, though perhaps in a different form than that of Aquinas and the Middle Ages.

The twentieth century was a period of intellectual ferment with thinkers such as Karl Marx, Sigmund Freud, Jean-Paul Sartre, John B. Watson, B. F. Skinner, and E. O. Wilson proposing very strong new views of humanity and its behavior. Marx saw morality as having no independent meaning, characterizing moral thoughts as "phantoms" created by the mind.[24] His philosophy essentially saw little benefit in allowing moral considerations to affect personal and political objectives.

Others influenced by the zeitgeist of diminishing the relevance of moral sensitivities took the position that values were not derivable from facts and, therefore, at best existed in the realm of personal preferences. Some went so far as to assert that since moral arguments and values cannot be scientifically verified, they are essentially expressions of feelings with no objective validity.[25] Jean-Paul Sartre claimed we have to choose our own values. However, he provided no guidelines or other methods to assist us in making moral choices.[26]

Freud did not believe that people inherently possessed a moral sense. His psychoanalytical approach to human behavior focused on unconscious desires, instincts, and bodily forces that he felt influenced the mind at the conscious level. He placed a strong emphasis on the presence of sexual and aggressive inborn forces, or instincts, that he felt drive people to decisions and actions. According to Freud, morality is imposed from outside of the individual. It is necessary for the survival of civilization that base instincts are controlled or repressed. It is through this repression, and not out of a natural tendency to be "good," that morality is learned and that people develop a conscience, or as Freud called it, a "Superego."[27]

The behaviorists, in contrast, rejected the relevance of a conscience. John B. Watson, the founder of behaviorism, claimed that psychology should not concern itself with mental states, including the unconscious. He advocated strongly that introspection was of no use and should be given up. The primary center of concentration, he felt, was overt behavior, observing how people behave in different settings.[28] B. F. Skinner, his most famous follower, was even more insistent that understanding the mind is meaningless. He belittled the idea that we have "free will," for he saw the mind as having no effect on action. To Watson and Skinner human behavior could be predicted without reference to mind by conditions that precede and follow actions. Furthermore, Skinner went so far as to maintain that a conscience did not exist in human beings.[29]

The idea that biology was basic to human behavior and the workings of social groups didn't reappear in a major way until E. O. Wilson published his book *Sociobiology* in the mid-1970s.[30] This work detailed the activities of social animals, investigating, among other things, insect colonies and wolf packs. Wilson, an expert on the ecology of ants, centered his attention on the complexity of instincts in the ant society. He was captivated by the fact that ants behave in a characteristic fashion with a degree of sophistication that should necessitate transmission from one generation to the next through learning. However, he found that learning does not occur; rather, ants function primarily from instinct. A striking example of this is that worker ants do not breed, but delegate the function of reproduction to a queen. This was confusing to Wilson, since it is a general principle in biology that animals strive to reproduce their own.

It was a British zoologist, W. D. Hamilton, who provided an acceptable answer to this dilemma. He found that the nature of genetic relatedness explained why ants, and other insects such as bees, were satisfied not reproducing and were social: They were more genetically similar to their sisters than they would be to any offspring they might otherwise have had.[31]

Influenced by this and similar work,[32] E. O. Wilson in his last chapter of *Sociobiology* suggested that social patterns in humans involve a collaboration between nature (genes) and nurture. He was putting forth the viewpoint that the biological understanding of social animals may have its correlation in human society. This nature argument created a furor among his colleagues who were proponents of the perfectibility of humans through social action. They characterized him as a "right-wing extremist" and discredited his idea.[33] As a consequence the thrust of argument shifted in favor of nurture, with the belief that human behavior evolved as the result of learning and environmental exposure.

Recent discoveries of neuroscience, however, are once again supporting the thesis that genetics and biology are important for understanding human thought and behavior. In some respects we are coming full circle back to some of the principles of natural law, with perhaps one exception: The new biology recognizes the importance of environment in influencing even basic biological structures in the brain. The line between genetics and environment is blurred. The presence of a gene or a biological tendency, as we will see, may not be sufficient to direct brain development or behavior. Often this development depends on input or stimulation from human culture.

We are essentially entering an era of what two prominent neuroscientists, Steven Quartz and Terrence Sejnowski, refer to in their book, *Liars, Lovers, and Heroes: What the New Brain Science Reveals about How We Become Who We Are,* as "cultural biology"[34] – that is, that culture has a dynamic role early in life in shaping brain biology. In their work they have shown that the human brain continues to grow after birth rather prominently for at least two years until the fontanels (the "soft spots") on the skull are closed. During this period the input of culture through instruction and other environmental exposure acts directly to enhance brain growth and function.

3

Beyond the Mind Zone

The shift in our focus from mind to brain did not happen overnight. It represents the outcome of a growing body of research accumulating on the biology of the brain over the past thirty years. Neuroscience discoveries are calling into question the long-held idea first proposed by René Descartes, the French philosopher, that the mind is separate from the brain. The mind was felt to have its own world, a mental life, without influence from the brain. In contrast, the brain has been thought to be the physical organ operating on a mechanistic level to sustain the mind, but not directly affecting the mind.

The old view is that the brain is composed of stand-alone components much as an automobile engine has parts like spark plugs or a carburetor. The new view based on neuroscience research is making it increasingly evident that a close association exists between the brain's physical status and a person's mental processes. Although we have yet to discover biological evidence that when a specific physical action or biochemical reaction occurs in the brain it relates in some consistent way to a specific form or dimension of mental activity, the mind–body association is close enough that many researchers in neuroscience believe that a dichotomy between mind and brain does not exist, but that they are one and the same.

Some early research conducted by Benjamin Libet of the University of California at San Francisco not only supports this position, but suggests that under many conditions changes in the cerebral cortex occur before one is even conscious of a particular feeling, decision, or movement of the body.[1] This observation makes a strong case for environment and experience training the neurons to react in certain predefined ways.

In a landmark experiment using electroencephalography (EEG), Libet tracked the sequence of cerebral activity, conscious awareness of intending to act, and the time when a free, voluntary motor act is actually conducted.[2] The brain wave patterns EEG records are called event-related potentials (ERPs). While their brain activity was being measured, Libet's subjects were instructed to make a conscious decision to move a limb. Before making this decision, they looked at a clock to determine the moment the conscious decision was made to move and reported this to the researcher. The objective was to correlate the exact moment of the readiness potential from the brain waves with the time of conscious awareness. He recorded a wave of brain activity (readiness potential, RP) that occurs anywhere between 500 and 1,000 ms (i.e., milliseconds) – half a second or so – before we actually consciously decide to move our arm or hand.

Libet discovered that, based on the readiness potential, the subjects' brains were active around 300 ms before the moment when they made the conscious decision to engage in the act. This implies that the cerebral initiation of what becomes a free voluntary act begins unconsciously or before there is any subjective consciousness or awareness that the decision to act has already been activated in the cerebral cortex.[3] Hence the suggestion is strong that the brain initiates the process toward a movement before the "mind" or consciousness is cognizant of the decision.

This is not to say that such an initiation came utterly out of the blue, or that the brain made the decision without any input from other sources. It may be reasonable to assume that the brain had been activated by prior experiences. The "unconscious" may be picking up sensory signals that bring about activation of clusters of neurons in part of the brain that had been similarly activated during prior analogous conditions. This cerebral initiation is responding to "stored representations" of what may be environmental contingencies, in this case the setting and perhaps the instructions the volunteers had received from the researchers.

Research conducted at New York University by Michael Platt and Paul Glimcher[4] with monkeys fortified the Libet findings that the brain becomes activated before one becomes conscious of what is happening.[5] They worked under the assumption, consistent with decision theory in economics, that the probabilities of gain (or reward) an animal can anticipate from specific behavior affect relevant areas of the brain.[6]

Conducting research on three monkeys, the researchers discovered that the individual neurons of the lateral intraparietal area (located in the inferior parietal lobule, a region toward the back of the sides of the brain, below the top) have preferences of specific areas of the visual world. Through a series of experiments involving neurons in this brain region, they learned that these neurons "know" a lot about their receptive fields from previous experience – for instance, the probability of succeeding in obtaining a particular reward (such as a treat) and something about the potential size of the reward.[7] In other words, neurons regarding a particular act are not passively responding, but rather in some cases actively assisting in the decision to engage in a particular act before the animals consciously decide what to do.[8]

Though some argue that nonhuman primates lack the ability to act upon a cognitive decision-making process rather than more basic sensorimotor learning, recent studies are strongly questioning this position. Evidence is growing that primates and some other animals are self-aware and capable of conscious decisions.[9]

Essentially the research of Libet and that of Platt and Glimcher suggest that two classes of input are key motivators of action. These inputs are *current sensory data,* which means the best estimate of current elements of the environment, and *stored representations* of events, which are assumptions that the brain makes based on experience. This research challenges the classical reflexive mechanisms regarding sensory–motor connection. In contrast, these researchers suggest the brain compiles an inventory of possibilities from which to make a decision.

Extending these results to general psychological principles, the findings of Libet and of Platt and Glimcher seem to demonstrate – though perhaps somewhat speculatively – the presence of something similar to unconscious processes.[10] In everyday human decisions an analogous set of events demonstrates to some extent the impact of unconscious processes – or "stored representations" on decisions at a future time. During psychotherapy one often learns of an unexpected situation actually occurring in a patient's life.

About two years ago a married woman who was a high-powered senior executive of a large manufacturing company came to see me because she felt guilty that she had entered into an unplanned extramarital relationship. She claimed that eight months prior to seeing me she had been at a corporate meeting and met a younger junior executive whom she found attractive. He had seemed interested in her, as he'd kept finding reasons to talk to her about minor issues involving the business. She had sensed that he was trying to get to know her, but told herself that she would never get involved in an extramarital affair. On numerous occasions she'd continued to see him at company meetings and social occasions, yet maintained that she would never have an affair. Still, a month before coming to me, he had approached her, and she had readily submitted.

In other words it is possible to work out a powerful intention without the slightest awareness that we are doing so – even if we assert, as did this woman, that such an event, an affair, would never happen. However, at the moment of the transgression, an unusual desire, titillation, or some underlying, unrecognized, long-term interest takes hold, and the person gives in. It is probably the case that this possibility was laid down at the initiation of contact, at the very moment the two met and the woman said "never, never" to herself.

One could relate this anecdote to the studies of Libet, and those of Platt and Glimcher: The brain is a very cooperative trainee. It is being informed of an outcome that has the possibilities of rewards; it becomes sensitized, responds to a stored representation of environmental contingencies. By finding the man attractive, the woman began a "rehearsal," which was intensified with every interaction, until the thought that could not be entertained had given rise to activation in parts of her brain before she was consciously aware of it. She might have had the chance at the moment of conscious awareness to veto the behavior that led to the liaison, but she did not exercise her power to do so.

Such pinpoint studies as those by Libet and by Platt and Glimcher are new, and much is yet to come. But we are becoming increasingly aware of biological conditions, some from birth, that induce a wide range of behavior. One of these, Williams syndrome (discussed in the next section), involves genetic abnormalities that cause those afflicted to be highly sociable without approach inhibition. Many other biologically generated conditions are strongly influential on behaviors, and in some cases capable of trumping an individual's rational control.

Is the Brain Hardwired for Morality?

Physicalism has direct relevance to our understanding of how moral development came about. If moral rules weren't a product of social ideas handed down through generations, would we be in a state of anarchy? Not likely, because the underlying foundation for morality appears more and more to be in our biology, hardwired in the brain.[11] Think of a thick slab of metal on which is cut a pattern for an intricate artistic design, such as a New England winter scene by Currier and Ives.[12] This slab of metal acts as a blueprint, a template that allows the design, with the addition of ink, to be transferred to paper. In a similar way, the brain is a template. Genes first, then early interaction with cultural experience, etch a pattern that influences thinking and behavior.

I am not the first to describe the brain as a template. Noam Chomsky, a linguist at MIT, introduced in the 1950s the idea that language development and formation begins with biology. Chomsky proposed that the brain has an innate circuitry for syntax.[13] He was struck by the fact that all languages shared similar characteristics. His theory, referred to as *transformational grammar,* held that the brain comes equipped with a set of rules that operate on the underlying structures of sentences to produce specific sentence sequences. Since his early work many linguists, working with biologists, have found evidence to accept the premise that language has a dominant biological base.[14]

The power of biology, particularly genetics, may be similar for behavior and sociability, which is one of the essential elements in moral development. An unusual medical condition suggests that we really do come equipped with a sociability "template," a necessary condition for trust and the development of moral understanding. This condition, Williams syndrome – a rare genetic disorder found in roughly one of twenty-five thousand live births – has been the subject of fascination to neuroscientists for years.

Suppose that, as a creative exercise, you were asked to imagine a character unfailingly and unreservedly approachable and friendly. Your reaction to the assignment might be, "Impossible! Unrealistic! It's simply not human nature." But in fact, in Williams syndrome, nature demonstrates precisely such a character.

Aside from the identifying physical features of the disorder – short stature, malformation of the heart, and distinctive facial markings – the afflicted Williams children also possess unusual cognitive and behavioral capacities. Indeed, despite neurocognitive deficits, particularly in visuospatial ability and mild to moderate mental retardation (IQ varying from 40 to 100), these children frequently show normal linguistic competence, the ability to recognize faces (paradoxical in light of their compromised visuospatial perception), and a profound love of music, sound, and rhythm.

Even more interesting than these cognitive abilities, however, are the remarkable personality characteristics of children with this disorder. They are strongly attracted to people and social situations. Some of this hypersociality may be related to their heightened ability to recognize faces – but it may also be related to an accompanying feature that is most intriguing: They lack what is known as "approach inhibition"; that is, Williams syndrome children respond warmly and positively to everyone. They seem unable to differentiate between those who are well-intentioned toward them and those who may harbor evil intentions. They exhibit what appears to be an inherent trust.[15]

Lack of approach inhibition has been seen in other medical conditions. When presented with facial photographs of unfamiliar adults, individuals with damage in a specific part of the brain, the amygdala, are unable to judge approachability and trustworthiness. But these individuals have incurred an injury to the part of the brain responsible for conditioned fear; no such brain injury has occurred in children with Williams syndrome. Some studying the latter phenomenon have speculated that the visual and cognitive pathways in the brain of Williams syndrome children may be smaller than normal. However, this hypothesis, if true, provides little insight as to why their personalities have this unique quality of trustfulness.

That Williams syndrome presented a genetic abnormality has been known for many years, but the precise nature of the abnormality has only recently been discovered: hemideletion in the long arm of chromosome 7; at least fifteen genes have been deleted. Application of a new multilevel approach, behavioral neurogenetics, to the personality manifestations of this disease has yielded interesting results. The approach includes not only genetic screening, but also an examination of brain structure and function, as well as of neurobehavioral processes (developmental milestones such as language, play, and motor skills).[16] The findings have shown a causal relationship between the genetic abnormalities and behavior – most particularly, the lack of approach inhibition.

In early childhood we are taught to be cautious when meeting someone for the first time and to attempt an evaluation of his or her honesty and intentions. By the time we reach adulthood, having experienced many social interactions, we have learned to be "street smart," developing a type of informed intuition that helps us to decide quickly whether a person is a friend or foe. Now it appears that genes, more than the experiences of socialization, are responsible for this capacity.

How We Know the Brain Directs the Mind

Our knowledge of how the human brain influences both the process and content of thinking has come basically from four types of study.[17] Clinical research on patients who have been afflicted with brain lesions (injuries), has provided considerable information on locations in the brain that are responsible for cognition, memory, feelings, and behavior. Discrete lesions may be associated with specific cognitive problems, which would imply that the physical integrity of these areas of the brain is necessary for normal functioning. Much of this research has been conducted on victims of traumatic accidents, and on patients suffering from strokes or degenerative disorders affecting their brain.

A second type of study that has enhanced our understanding of the brain is that conducted on patients with psychiatric and neurological disorders in whom brain abnormalities exist that impinge on cognition and emotional control. It has been possible to track the pathways of neural networks that have been changed by these disorders and to determine what detailed areas of the brain are compromised in their performance.

Researches of genetic differences that are manifested in variations of memory, cognition, and mood have become a third important approach for "searching for" the biology of reasoning and feelings. Discrepancies in genes (particularly gene combinations) as a basis for differences in brain biology are beginning to reveal how the brain develops and to suggest where to look to uncover the impact of these on personality.

Finally, *neuroimaging* – the use of highly refined technologies such as magnetic resonance imaging (MRI), single-photon emission computed tomography (SPECT), and positron emission tomography (PET) – provides the means to compare normal with abnormal individuals. These technologies produce computer-generated pictures of the brain, with indicators – such as a color gradient (red and yellow signify high activity; blue and green, low and no activity), in the case of SPECT and PET – that allow for measurement and comparison. Thus neuroimaging has introduced a completely different approach to understanding what is happening in the brain. For example, color differences in scans comparing a "normal" brain and one of an abuser of "recreational" drugs, such as cocaine or heroin, reveal abnormal blood flow or aberrant metabolic rates of specific areas of the brain induced by the drug. This information may be very important in determining what section of the brain is not functioning under select circumstances.

Neuroimaging, such as MRI, has been used to study what areas of the brain "light up" when a subject does something specific, such as: thinks of something new, like a new word; experiences deep feelings, such as would emerge from looking at an aesthetically appealing work of art; or tries to impose control over behavioral impulses. Complex emotions like grief, empathy, uncontrollable anger, fear, sadness, guilt, and shame are being shown to arise in specific areas of the brain and to engage other brain areas that affect motor and intellectual functioning.

Although neuroimaging, at its current level of technological development, has not achieved a thorough understanding of thought and behavior, such technologies (also including fMRI and CEEG, among others), when used in studies involving several or more subjects, nonetheless provide important information on brain activity and the relationship between an image reflective of thinking and emotions, and behavior.[18] In the future, neuroimaging studies of individuals operating in group settings will considerably enhance the value of findings about brain activity and behavior.

Behavioral neurogenetics is a newer interdisciplinary research design, including neuroimaging, genetics, and neuropsychological testing, that has begun to correlate different research findings to provide a fuller picture of the brain biology of specific conditions. For example, recent neuroimaging and genetic studies have revealed specific brain images that correlate with discrete gene dysfunction to produce a child who is very likely to become highly violent and antisocial as an adult.[19]

What's exciting about the breadth and diversity of functioning and sources of discovery about the brain is that all of them have implications for understanding morality – because virtually every moral issue draws on almost every part of the brain. Even more fascinating is the seemingly endless ways these regions and elements of the brain can interact in almost limitless forms and guises, with regard to a variety of moral challenges.

4

The Moral Brain

Although morality is a social construct, it would not exist without the brain. This complex organ consists of many structures that work in synchrony to produce feelings and thoughts, the ability to make decisions and to act on these choices, and most important, the capacity to relate to others in society.

The two broad regions of the brain are the emotional brain[1] and the frontal lobes. Within these regions are three faculties that compose the elite machinery geared toward facilitating social interaction and maintaining order through social morality. These three structures are the amygdala; the inhibitory networks, which include principally the anterior cingulate cortex, the hippocampus, the hypothalamus, and the prefrontal cortex; and the mirror-neuron system.

The Emotional Brain

Our major emotional equipment consists primarily of four so-called limbic structures in the brain, each of which seems to have a specialty: the amygdala (which serves as Guard Dog), the hippocampus (the Governor), the anterior cingulate cortex (the Mediator), and the hypothalamus (the Master Regulator) [Figure 1].

The *amygdala,* the brain's "Guard Dog" (one on each side of the brain) surveys and rapidly assesses what is happening in the outside world through connections with the sensory cortex and frontal

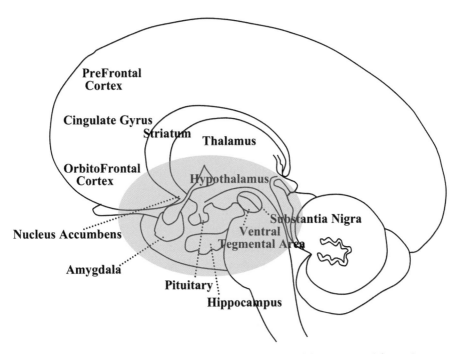

Figure 1. Artist's schematic diagram of the emotional brain, viewed from the left side, showing in the pink-shaded region the primary limbic structures: amygdala, hippocampus, hypothalamus, and part of the anterior cingulate gyrus frequently associated with that region.

lobes, and then applies emotional meaning to environmental stimuli. Its scope of control includes a full range of emotions from disgust, dread, envy, and frustration to deeper feelings experienced in states of embarrassment, jealousy, and even affection and love.[2] But its biggest responsibility is for fear, particularly conditioned fear acquired from exposure to a traumatic or scary event.

The amygdala is believed to have an important role within the repository of learned information concerned with conditioned fear; it is also the agent of the expression of that fear once learning has occurred.[3] After the amygdala processes our emotions, like fear,[4] it directs the mind to act in specific ways for our survival, such as by attacking or escaping in the face of danger, by obtaining food when smelling an appetizing odor, or by pursuing an attractive sexual partner.[5]

The amygdala also acts essentially as a memory structure for stored emotions. In this role it influences our unconscious choices. Emotional memory situated in the amygdala helps to drive behavior. For example, when we see fruit that we like, this activates dopamine pathways that facilitate memory of that experience in the amygdala – setting up a conditioned response that can be activated subsequently by the smell or taste of the fruit.

The *hippocampus* (one on each side) frequently complements the amygdala by helping to focus the brain on sensory stimuli and to generate emotions, linking these to memory, images, and learning. By connecting memory with emotions to influence the amygdala and the hypothalamus, the hippocampus, in its role as the brain's "Governor," works to regulate the arousal and quiescent reactions of the autonomic nervous system and other key parts of the brain.[6] The hippocampus is also involved with several aspects of memory, mostly "declarative memory," or context-dependent memory, such as recalling facts and events.[7] This type of memory consists of two components: a familiarity element that sees recent facts or items as recognizable, and an episodic component that remembers the context in which facts were learned.[8] The hippocampus is involved in transforming new memories into long-term memories.[9]

The *anterior cingulate cortex* (ACC), the brain's "Mediator," has an advanced degree in problem solving[10] and dealing with uncertainty. Although located bilaterally (one one each side) near the prefrontal cortex, this part of the brain is often seen as one of the limbic structures. Studies have shown that in addition to being involved in problem solving, the ACC is also implicated in emotional self-control, conflict resolution, and error recognition.[11]

As to self-control, the ACC dampens the effects of strong emotional reactions; it controls the effects of distress on the individual by reining in the amygdala to temper negative emotions.[12] In doing so, the ACC provides for civilized discourse, conflict resolution, and fundamental human socialization.[13]

It also impacts on the prefrontal cortex, which is involved cognitively in implementing control, by influencing the cortex to exert greater control when the ACC detects conflicts between plans and action.[14] Along this same line of activity, this cortex is part of an error recognition and detection system that also involves the prefrontal lobe.[15] When something goes wrong between expectations or plans and the expected reward, the ACC is activated and with the prefrontal cortex (especially the orbitofrontal cortex) as well as the insula (a triangular lobe at the brain's center) acts to create a visceral response,[16] or warning that things are not right.[17]

Two final points of interest about the ACC: First, its involvement with uncertainty and decision making would relate to its role in conflict and cognitive control. In this capacity the ACC is more closely linked to the prefrontal cortex than it is to limbic structures.[18] Second, the ACC has a distinctive class of neuron, large and spindle-shaped, and this class is believed to be involved with modification of distress and social competence.[19]

The *hypothalamus,* the oldest of the limbic structures, is known as the brain's "Master Regulator" because it controls the counterbalancing quiescent and arousal systems. As a result, the hypothalamus is concerned with survival-related behaviors like sex,[20] food consumption, aggression, and rage. It operates through control of the autonomic nervous system (heartbeat, blood pressure, temperature, thirst, hunger, hormone secretion, and even energy).[21] which is linked by the hypothalamus to higher cortical structures. By controlling internal stability (homeostasis), the hypothalamus can influence emotions like fear, dread, disgust. and pleasure.

The emotional brain draws on structures that developed early in human evolution. Hence, emotions are more primitive than the cognitive skills such as analysis, problem solving, and planning, which are located in our executive centers. These centers, in the frontal lobes, evolved later in the history of our species and mature later in each of us. The executive centers have the job of deciding how to respond to the signals being sent by our emotional systems.

The Frontal Lobes: The Seat of Understanding

Within the front section of the skull, just above the eyes, are the two frontal lobes, a right and a left. Within each is a small specialized area in the very front referred to as the prefrontal cortex [Figure 2].

The frontal lobes – and particularly the prefrontal cortex within them – are the areas where the brain essentially acts upon its knowledge and that contain the regions of the brain responsible for executive functions.[22] The prefrontal cortex is believed to be the center of our concept of self, most particularly our sense of ownership over self, our unity of attitudes and beliefs, and our body-centered spatial perspective.[23]

According to Elkhonon Goldberg in his book *The Executive Brain: Frontal Lobes and the Civilized Mind,* the frontal lobes "are the most uniquely human of all the brain structures."[24] Indeed, these lobes have often been credited with empowering humanity to create civilizations containing art, science, culture, and social institutions. Thus it is within these lobes – in this area of the brain – that we find the seat of intellection, of cognitive functioning, of personality and identity, and of the integration of emotions and thought.

The prefrontal cortex, on the other hand, has often been referred to as the brain's "command post." Virtually every functional part of the brain is directly interconnected to this cortex,[25] which plays a fundamental role in internally guided behavior.[26] By internally guided behavior we mean actions that are influenced by intentions, decisions, and plans that originate in the individual's brain, rather than in external sources like software programs, an athletic team's game strategy, or an academic program.

The prefrontal cortex is connected to four principal areas: the premotor cortex, the posterior association cortices, the cerebellum (behind the top of the spine), and the basal ganglia. These four areas of the brain are responsible for motor control and movements. In addition, the prefrontal cortex is connected to the dorsomedial nucleus – an area of the thalamus responsible for integration of stimuli or inputs in the thalamus. The prefrontal cortex is also connected to the hippocampus, the amygdala, and the hypothalamus.[27] Moreover, this cortex connects directly with brain stem nuclei that activate arousals such as a "fight or flight" response.

Most important, the prefrontal cortex, especially its anterior segment, plays a major role in human cognition.[28] As one of the "attention association areas" of the brain (the parietal association cortex

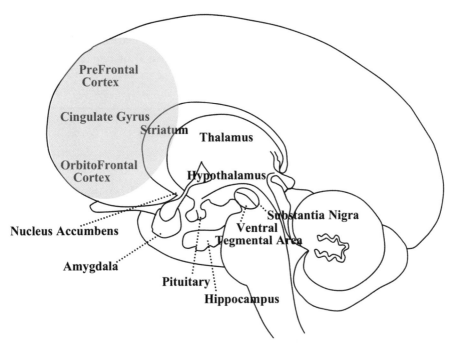

Figure 2. Artist's rendition of the location of the frontal lobes viewed from the left side, showing in the blue-shaded region some of their major components, particularly the prefrontal cortex, which includes among other parts the orbito-frontal cortex and part of the anterior cingulate gyrus.

is also involved with attention), the prefrontal cortex is critical for managing the bodily movements and complex behaviors necessary to achieve specific goals. The prefrontal cortex is also connected with other association cortices – such as the parietal (which may need to be deactivated to enable attention), temporal, and occipital association areas – which allows it to integrate information. For example, the prefrontal cortex would manage the integration of intellectual skills such as language and motor skills in the hands, skills necessary to use a computer properly. This organization of goal-oriented actions and behaviors include the purposeful control and focus of thoughts toward resolving a particular issue or achieving a particular objective. The specific functions of the prefrontal cortex for achieving this end include every phase of behavioral planning, from integrating perceived information – including imaging the mental features of a task[29] – to associative learning, decision making and guidance, and finally to the control of reward-based behavior.[30]

Mirror Neurons: Completing the Machinery of the Moral Brain

Besides the structures of the brain, such as the amygdala, and the inhibitory networks – primarily the hippocampus and the anterior cingulate cortex – there are neurons of a type that are essential for understanding and imitation. Both of these functions form the "mirror-neuron mechanism" that explains the human faculty for learning by imitation, which is at the basis of human culture.[31] These neurons in humans involve a network, which is formed by the temporal, occipital, and parietal visual areas, as well as two additional cortical regions that are predominantly motor.[32] These last two regions are the inferior parietal lobule (rostral part) and the precentral gyrus (lower part) and the posterior part of the inferior frontal gyrus.[33] Together, these regions constitute the mirror-neuron system in humans.

The mirror-neuron system, among other functions, is pivotal to the representation of sequential information, and to imitation. The latter has two components: substitution of a motor pattern similar to the one spontaneously used in response to a given stimulus, and sequence learning, that is, the ability to learn a motor sequence that is directed toward a specific objective or goal.[34]

The machinery geared toward facilitating social interaction, therefore, fits a specific pattern of response: The mirror neurons "learn" from observation of the patterns of others how to behave morally in social situations. When a challenge occurs to moral decision making, the amygdala revs up inducing a range of emotions from fear and anger to disgust. The inhibitory mechanism – the hippocampus and hypothalamus as well as the prefrontal cortex – step in to ameliorate the response. This allows for clear-headed deliberation and a reasoned moral decision on how to handle the matter.

Sometimes the amygdalar response, if very intense, may overpower the inhibitory network. When this occurs the decision maker is no longer able to be objective, which may lead to an immoral decision and behavior.

What Happens with a Moral Dilemma?

But if something as challenging and rewarding as moral choice were merely the product of three areas of the brain – even three such remarkable ones – it would be fairly humdrum. These three areas are where the heavy lifting is done, but the exhilaration of moral decision making might best be likened to a climax of a symphony of our highest brain capacities.

Take a moral dilemma that could happen in any family: A favorite uncle wants to borrow money from you, but the trouble is that he is a compulsive gambler. In three years he has gone through nearly a million dollars, depleting all his savings. His life and marriage are just about on the rocks. So is his relationship with his only child, a seventeen-year-old daughter who has no resources to finance her college education.

As you sit there looking at him, figuring out your answer, no fewer than twenty of your brain structures and their circuits are madly at work:

Your long-term memory (stored in the cerebral cortex) dredges up recollections of your many talks with your uncle, as well as time spent together attending Yankee games when you were a child. Recent conversations (part of your short-term memory and stored in your hippocampus) with him about your aunt's chronic kidney disease also surface to make you feel sorry for him and his family.

Sympathy for him gets a strong boost as your visual cortex and mirror neurons (including the superior temporal sulcus, the fusiform gyrus, and the amygdala) process your uncle's facial expression and his embarrassment over needing money. The amygdala is also activated when you experience a twinge of fear as you perceive that your refusal of his request could cause a rift as damaging to his family as the path he is on.

Fueled by disappointment and anger, your ambivalence activates your premotor cortex, which rehearses throttling him. At the same time your frontal lobe and anterior cingulate cortex step in to stifle the throttle impulse. The problem-solving function of these structures understands that some addictions are impervious to intervention; you thus reason that you might just as well give him the money and keep his affection.

Your prefrontal cortex, on the other hand, steps in to take command and sorts out how to deliver a gentle, loving "no." This winds up activating other regions of the cerebral cortex – visual (occipital cortex and superior temporal sulcus, superious colliculus), auditory (temporal cortex), language (Broca's and Wernicke's areas) – as your prefrontal lobe reviews all the sensations you've received and develops a plan of response. In the process of reconstructing or imagining what to do and possible outcomes of your actions (what neuroscientists refer to as "visualization"), the exact same structures and areas of the brain are revved up and used just as they are when you actually do what you imagine yourself doing.

Finally, you will experience his reaction to your "no." This will activate your sensory systems (auditory and visual), limbic structures – in particular the amygdala (emotional reaction to his affect), hippocampus (connecting memory to emotions), as well as anterior cingulate cortex (self-control), and hypothalamus (bodily response such as sweating, increased heartbeat) – and the frontal lobes.

Fortunately, both you and your uncle are blissfully unaware of these processes. Uncle wants his money, you want the peace of mind that comes from doing the right, or moral, thing. In any case, like most human beings, we are more interested in the end result than the process.

Neuroplasticity

Dealing with this family incident illustrates the complexity of moral decisions. Many structures are involved and must work together with a high level of precision. The possibility of something going wrong is ever present. Abnormalities in one of the structures or in the circuitry will disrupt the symphony, resulting in a less desirable outcome. As we've seen in the previous chapters, aberrancies can be the result of genetics as well as of injuries to parts of the brain during any period of a person's life, from the fetal stage to infancy and through adolescence and adulthood.

Being moral, therefore, isn't easy. This is why moral training – early and often – is essential. Our brain structures are not immutable; they are susceptible to change for the better and change for the worse. What's important is what happens deep down at the level of the neuron – in a process called *neuroplasticity*. By neuroplasticity we mean the ability of neurons at the synapses to forge new connections, thereby essentially bringing about a rewiring of the brain.[35]

Neuroplasticity results not only in the setting down of new pathways through the cortex, but also the remodeling of neural networks.[36] A famous example of this is the case of the "amblyopic" kitten. We know that if we cover one of a kitten's eyes just after birth, at a certain point in time removing the patch will not result in the kitten seeing out of that eye. External stimulation is necessary early in the life of the animal for the nerves of the eyes to develop and make critical connections in the ophthalmic cortex. When this does not occur by a particular time, the kitten has permanently lost the ability to see out of that eye. The nerves form alternative pathways. This work was part of the Nobel Prize–winning research of David Hubel and Thorsten Weisel.

Going down the dangerous route with drugs, gambling, sex, or other addictions is a matter of neuroplasticity. What often starts off as an innocent experiment – drinking alcohol, or smoking pot – can develop over time into compulsive, addictive behavior. The brain changes, adapts because of the development of new circuitry, and induces more and more of the bad behavior.

I remember in the late 1970s walking across Washington Square in Manhattan, when I saw a man in his early twenties with a glass cylinder about one inch in diameter through a hole in his earlobe. I was struck by the capacity of the earlobe to stretch and allow such a large hole to develop. I realized that it took time to go from a pinprick to an inch in diameter. The metaphor of this struck home.

Although there is strong evidence of a biological or genetic predisposition to alcoholism and other addictive behaviors, once a susceptible person is exposed to alcohol or a drug, addiction must follow a similar type pathway of neuroplasticity, or change in the brain. Small changes lead to bigger changes, until the end result can be something as dramatic as a one-inch-diameter hole in an otherwise small earlobe.

We've seen the power of neuroplasticity both in restoring physical abilities where injury has been disabling, and in dramatically improving psychological health for those who suffer emotional and mental problems. In the area of physical rehabilitation neuroplasticity has been demonstrated to work for a wide variety of problems. Perhaps the most dramatic has been in the treatment of strokes. Within the past few years Dr. Edward Taub at the University of Alabama has developed a novel technique that utilizes the brain's capacity for neuroplasticity. When a particular limb is affected by a stroke, he immobilizes the functioning limb, thus forcing the patient to use the injured limb, resulting in brain rewiring and ultimate restoration of the damaged limb to a functioning level.[37]

Recent studies have also demonstrated that verbal therapy (i.e., psychotherapy) brings about significant positive changes not only in the clinical condition of the patient but also in neural pathways. A study comparing brain blood flow changes with interpersonal psychotherapy (ITP) versus a medication (venlafaxine) showed that ITP alone increased blood flow in the limbic area of the brain, whereas ITP together with the medication affected the blood flow in the basal ganglia.[38] A more recent study comparing cognitive behavior therapy (CBT) with antidepressants showed that CBT not only brings about similar clinical recovery for those suffering from depression or anxiety, but that it actually causes changes in the frontal cortex, the anterior cingulate cortex, and the hippocampus.[39] A rewiring of the brain occurs with verbal treatment as well as with medications. Moral training, which can involve processes similar to CBT and ITP as well as lectures and reading, therefore offers the opportunity to bring about beneficial neuroplastic changes.[40]

The good news: Just as finding oneself down the moral tubes is a matter of neuroplasticity, so is getting up again and shucking off the bad habits that can destroy one's career and relationships and possibly result in serious antisocial acts. Neuroplasticity is what we can use to build moral strength through positive experiences and training. Unless we are one of those with a serious biological defect – genetic or acquired – our brains are able to reshape themselves at virtually any age to improve our physical and psychological conditions. Neuroplasticity can be our best friend if we've gone wrong and want to reform.

5

Bad without Conscience

At the age of twenty-nine, Ricky Green had been charged with the serial killing of two women and two men.[1] He had sexually mutilated his victims and had attempted everything from beheading one of them to lacerating another's internal organs. Green was no mundane killer – his homicides betrayed a psychological condition far outside the crimes of passion or self-defense that the police deal with on a regular basis. I was called in to work on Green's case and to give an evaluation of his mental profile in the lawyer's hope that it would influence the sentencing phase of his trial. Psychopathy – a severe form of Antisocial Personality Disorder – immediately suggested itself to describe the particular nature of Green's crimes.

The word *psychopath* describes a person who lacks a conscience, the ability or sensitivity to shape a moral issue and to understand the significance of such issues, and to experience empathy. Psychopathy is derived from Greek, meaning "disease" of the "psyche" or mind. The French used to refer to people lacking conscience and the ability to conform to social norms as "moral idiots."[2] *Sociopath* is another term frequently used to describe these individuals. This term reflects a viewpoint prominent during the 1950s–1960s that environmental hardship, particularly poverty and discrimination, as well as family dysfunction induce abnormalities in socialization, which create moral "outlaws."

The psychopath is a subset of the antisocial personality in that such individuals frequently do not meet all of the criteria for this class,[3] but meet other criteria very strongly. Without being fully anti-social, the psychopath nonetheless displays extreme abnormal behavior – a life of deception, violence, and harm – and is more prone to acts of extreme immorality that even antisocials cannot surpass.

A long debate has surrounded the psychopath, with some feeling that psychopathy is "constitutional," the very nature of a person, one's "way of life." Others argue that the psychopath is bred, or even inbred genetically within families and subgroups. Still others take the position that these individuals have free will, and somehow have made choices that resulted in becoming a psychopath. Recent research indicates that the psychopath has a malfunctioning brain, likely due to defective wiring, which leads to undesirable moral behavior. They lack the ability to shape moral questions, or to behave in a morally acceptable fashion, and finally to exhibit what we consider "free will." Although researchers are madly trying to find out about the mechanisms for these capacities, the effects of malfunction is still informed speculation.

Did Ricky Green make a cool-headed choice to go against society's mores, or was he driven by a compulsion so strong that it overcame his inhibitions? Or was he an antisocial personality who had failed to form those inhibitions in the first place? The answer could have determined Green's entire future.

Each case is a unique puzzle, and this one was especially challenging. I had never dealt with a criminal who had such a long and extreme history of violence, and I was concerned that Green might use my nervousness to his advantage – a talent psychopaths frequently possess. We have all seen films like *Silence of the Lambs,* where a criminal plays mind games with the detective. Though far-fetched, these representations are based on a modicum of truth, as the ability to manipulate others emotionally and through quasi-logical arguments is indeed an identifying characteristic of psychopathy.[4]

In *The Mask of Sanity,* Hervey Cleckley, a prominent forensic psychiatrist in the 1970s and 1980s on the faculty of the Medical College of Georgia, described sixteen attributes of psychopaths.[5] This list was revised in the 1990s by the University of British Columbia psychologist R. D. Hare to include twenty attributes, fifteen of which are personality traits such as pathological lying, conning, impulsivity, and glibness. The remaining criteria are general terms such as criminal versatility, which means the capacity to commit different kinds of crime, such as theft, rape, and murder.[6] Hare recognized two primary factors as constituting his checklist.[7] The first of these were traits associated with narcissism (egocentrism) such as manipulativeness, callousness, and lack of remorse. The second involved traits of instability, irresponsibility, and impulsivity.

Once institutionalized, psychopaths characteristically make treatment difficult by pulling elaborate stunts, such as faking symptoms in order to be transferred to other institutions and offering gratuitous red herrings as explanations of their own behavior. In one famous case, a criminal charged with the murder of a pregnant woman told his clinical examiner that since the woman was pregnant with no husband, the father of the child had more "motivation" than he did to eliminate her. The attempt to use psychological terminology against the interviewer was easy enough to catch, but the case illustrates how vigilant clinical examiners must be in their wariness regarding the information criminals offer about themselves.

The idea, popular within our culture, that low intelligence is a feature of criminals is hideously misleading. If the law finally catches a criminal in the act, it is just as likely that he or she has been "getting away with it" successfully for such a long period of time as to become simply reckless or overly self-assured. Intelligence and manipulative talent are not rare among criminals, and are even frequent among psychopaths. Ted Bundy exuded charm and was of a very high intelligence, but it didn't make him any less merciless as a killer. Ricky Green was uneducated and worked as a radiator repairman in his father's business. A humble profile to be sure, but he was married and described by some to be quite engaging and had managed to persuade people to follow him to remote places, where they lost their lives.

When Green walked into the room, I immediately understood how people could be easily seduced by him, and would follow him wherever he led. Penetrating blue eyes and light brown, short-cropped hair gave a winsome effect, offsetting his more threatening lean, muscular frame. My introduction to Green turned out to be even more stressful than I had imagined: The moment the door locked, Green arose slowly from his chair with arms outstretched, as if to strangle me.

Without hesitation, I looked at him straight in the eyes and said, "You'd better sit down. Now." A typical psychopath, Green was testing me, and I knew it. Green's face registered surprise, and he slowly sank back into his chair. Thus began the first of two long, probing interviews into the brain of a man who, in the course of this chapter, we will come to see as a *biologically* driven murderer.

Sex and Alcohol: Triggers to Violent Crime

Green's first victim, Jeffrey Davis, was a teenager hanging out in the Casino Beach area of Fort Worth, Texas. He had recently run away with his girlfriend, and the couple was spending a few nights in the area until they came up with their next move. Green liked the couple and befriended them, and they ended up spending the night at Green's house. The next day, Green dropped them back off at the beach.

A month later, Davis walked by Green's house, where Green was working on his car. They began drinking beer and driving around. Green told me that he really enjoyed talking to Davis and was getting to like him. He thought he had made a friend. Psychopaths frequently exhibit an inability to form lasting bonds with others, and their personal histories rarely tell of long relationships. Up until this point, Green's behavior toward Davis betrays nothing more than a perfectly normal desire to form human connections and establish relationships with others. But as we shall see, by the time Davis came across him, Green was already so far advanced in his psychopathic process that even his efforts to form relationships – something that could perhaps exert a positive influence on him – would fly out of control and end in disaster.

Davis and Green drove around for a while and drank several beers. Later, while they were sitting together in the car, Davis made a sexual advance toward Green. While relating this part of the story, Green looked at me with visible remorse and expressed in heartfelt tones that the moment Davis made the sexual advance something made him simply "go berserk." Green emphasized that Davis had not tried to force himself on him, but nonetheless he began to beat Davis, and then "something went 'click' in my head and I began stabbing him." Unable to stop himself, Green sexually mutilated Davis and killed him, even attempting to behead him. A normal person in the same circumstances might experience a broad range of emotions at an unexpected sexual advance – from shock, to excitement or rage – and these feelings might be expressed in a wide variety of ways. What separates Green from these normal persons is the "click" he describes here, a switching into an altered state of lost control.

But what if Green was throwing red herrings at me with this dramatic tale? He could have been lying about the circumstances surrounding the murder, perhaps to conceal a conscious motivation to kill Davis that would destroy his chances at a successful insanity plea. To take it a step further, his stereotypically "crazed murderer" behavior at the beginning of our interview could have been an act to convince me of his insanity. Furthermore, the heartfelt, remorseful tone that Green used when describing the circumstances of the murder could have been easily feigned to gain my sympathy. But two factors led me to believe that Green's information in this portion of the interview was fairly dependable.

First, the details of the murder pushed Green out of the category of consciously planned and enacted crimes – if he had only wanted to kill Davis, he could have simply stabbed him. The presence of mutilation, gratuitous violence, and sadism all suggested that Green was truly in an altered state, and, to use his own words, "going berserk." Second, Green's behavior after the murder, more so than his heartfelt tone during the interview, convinced me that he had experienced feelings of remorse. After Davis was dead, Green called his wife, Sharon, and told her what he had done and that he was feeling guilty. He did not heed his wife's offer of help to hide the body, and it would have of course been in Green's interest to hide this heinous crime from his wife. (Indeed, she wound up testifying against him in court.) Instead, his impulse to confess was so strong that he went against his own best interest and called his wife, once he had "snapped out of it" and was facing the moral implications of what he had done.

The presence of remorse does not remove Green from the psychopathic personality group, nor necessarily alter his antisocial classification. But it does suggest that Green had developed a conscience once upon a time, no matter how incompletely or weakly formed, and that somehow this sense of right and wrong was overwhelmed by an impulse that Green himself seemed at a loss to explain. The patterns that emerge in his next murders shed some light on this state.

Steve Fefferman, Green's second victim, was a middle-aged businessman who met Green just months after Davis's death. They also met at Casino Beach, a locale to which Green would return repeatedly to "watch homosexuals and study how they acted." Green was in his car when Fefferman propositioned him to trade money for sex. Seeing an opportunity to make money, Green followed Fefferman to his house. Shortly after arriving there they consumed large quantities of vodka and whiskey. Fefferman performed oral sex on Green, and they watched pornographic videotapes. Fefferman confessed an attraction to young boys and graphically described this attraction and the experiences that resulted.

Paradoxically, while alcohol acts as a sedative on the body, it also relaxes inhibitions and encourages violent impulses.[8] As it turns out, Green had a history of sexual abuse, making Fefferman's graphic stories a source of emotional provocation that, combined with the alcohol, proved fatal. The stories repulsed Green, but unlike others who might express disgust or leave the premises, Green flew into a violent rage and murdered Fefferman, first sexually mutilating him and lacerating his internal organs while Fefferman was tied hand and foot to a bed.

Initially, Green told me that he had no intentions of killing Fefferman, and had gone to his house "just to make some money." Green insisted that three factors led to the murder, all related to sex: Fefferman's sexual advances, his insistence that he would not take Green home unless they had sex, and his graphic stories. As with Davis, once the murder was completed Green felt remorseful and called his wife to confess.

Going with Fefferman to his private premises after a random pickup off the street was an incredibly impulsive and hasty decision for Green. He had not taken any other drugs that day, and was not desperate for money. Going off with this stranger seems difficult to explain. Green did not seem to fear that Fefferman might intend to harm him, and accepted conditions that could have as easily led to his own death. But the violent murderer, unlike the portrayal in the movies, was not the random stranger propositioning another in the night; the murderer happened to be the willing acceptor, as Fefferman unluckily discovered.

We can explain Green's behavior that night by looking back to psychopathic characteristics: During the course of the evening, Green exhibited many types of behavior associated with the psychopath. Starting with impulsivity, or the occurrence of acts that are unpremeditated and lack reflection or planning, Green agreed to Fefferman's random sexual proposition, also exhibiting a promiscuous sexual attitude in his willingness to go with a stranger. (Both impulsivity and sexual promiscuity are characteristics of psychopathic behavior. Psychopaths typically need stimulation that makes them prone to risky behavior.) Once at the house, Green's use of alcohol paved the way for another psychopathic characteristic, the one that resulted in the end of Fefferman's life: loss of behavioral control. Once Green became angry, his inability to stop himself from rashly acting out violent impulses made the difference between anger and murder.

Two types of psychopath distinguished in the literature – though never fully accepted by the American Psychiatric Association – nonetheless shed light on the Ricky Green case.[9] The first set identified is the "predominantly aggressive psychopath," who is prone to fits of violence. The sudden outbursts of violent rage that Green experienced certainly suggest this category. The second subset is the "predominantly inadequate psychopath," an individual who usually engages in acts of petty crime (i.e., pilfering, swindling, etc.), and who lives off of society in this way. Generally such persons are not aggressive. Ricky Green's profile also matches the second subset in that he was predominantly passive. And in both of the cases,

Davis and Fefferman, he needed alcohol in order to become aggressive and murderous.

Antisocial Personality Disorder has long been associated with alcoholism and addiction to narcotics. The relationship between them is called "comorbidity," an apt title given that the term describes a situation where two or more conditions tend to coincide to a very morbid effect. Advanced alcoholism looks a lot like the general definition of the antisocial personality – quickness to anger, irritability, inability to form and sustain long-lasting relationships, irresponsibility, and recklessness.[10] Antisocial personalities have a tendency toward substance abuse, and substance abuse increases antisocial behavior. It's a chicken-and-egg debate to ask which came first; the important question is more centered on exactly how they interact.

We now know that prolonged alcoholism changes the biochemistry of the brain, and can create antisocial behavior patterns that are difficult to break.[11] The substantial role that alcohol played in Ricky Green's life is examined later in the chapter – he started drinking beer when he was nine years old – but for now, what's important is the role it played in his murders. Alcohol was the gateway to both the Davis murder (driving around in the car drinking beers) and the Fefferman case – and, as we shall see, with his final two victims. In the end, it led all of Green's murders.

Two women were the next targets. Green picked up Betty Jo Monroe on the side of a highway leading to Fort Worth and took her home with him. They ate and had sex on Green's premises. Introduced as a potential babysitter to his wife, Betty Jo stayed after Green's wife, Sharon, returned home, while Green was off in another room drinking large quantities of liquor. Several hours later, Green approached Betty Jo to engage in sex. When she resisted, Green became enraged, forced himself on her anally over the bathtub, and stabbed her to death. Sharon was in another part of the house at the time.

Green's next victim was an awful echo of Betty Jo. He found Sandra Bailey in a nightclub, and this time he consumed recreational drugs in addition to large quantities of alcohol before bringing her to his home. Again in a rage, he sodomized her while stabbing her to death.

Ricky expressly denied experiencing sexual arousal, usually a component of similar assaults, during any of the episodes. Alcoholism and sex thread through the four murders, tying them together in a profile of sexual psychopathy. Remorse slowly factors out of the picture, as the pattern of killing becomes increasingly cold-blooded, and sexual assault begins to factor in more strongly (the rape of the two women). By the end, Ricky Green was no longer phoning his wife Sharon to confess to her, but entreating her to help him clean up the mess (which she did).

Where did Ricky Green's harmful behavior patterns come from in the first place? And how did they intensify to this degree?

Family Values: A History of Emotional Stress and Drug Abuse

Ricky Green was born in the Fort Worth area into a family rife with sexual and physical abuse and criminal behavior. In many ways, he experienced the worst that life has to offer. Out of four children, three brothers and a sister, one brother died of leukemia at six years of age. When I saw Ricky in 1990, his oldest brother (a possible role model) was in prison for selling and distributing drugs. His younger brother, twenty at the time, had been charged with assaulting a pregnant woman. Ricky's mother, who seemed at odds with the criminal activities of the family, died of a heart attack at the age of forty-four. His father, who owned a radiator shop where Ricky worked during his teens and early twenties, was also jailed for selling drugs.

Green described his childhood in painful language. He was frequently abused physically, subject to his father's harshness from the age of four.[12] Ricky remembers his father as being demanding and difficult with all of the children, except with his younger brother, who was somehow favored and never reprimanded. The sister was subjected to beatings, and Green learned at a later date that his father had engaged in sex with her from the time she was nine years old until she left home at fifteen. His mother was beaten by his father on various occasions. When Green witnessed his father abusing his mother, he was distraught at his inability to defend her.[13] He had an intense fear of his father and was obsessed with the anger and "terror" in his father's eyes. Green was also convinced his father could control people with his eyes. His father raised him very strictly, never letting him see other children outside of school hours. As a result, Green had no friends while growing up.

As a young child Ricky occasionally killed animals. One incident was particularly memorable – he killed a cat because he wanted to see "if it had nine lives."[14] Here we see a normal childhood curiosity manifested in abnormal and extreme behavior. He also enjoyed starting fires, and did so until he was incarcerated for arson in his midtwenties. Another haunting memory was about his protracted bed-wetting, a problem that troubled both him and his brother. Almost nightly he would wet the bed, often during a dream where he was in the bathroom and would only realize upon waking that the sheets were wet. His father responded by becoming angry and frequently beating him, resulting in black-and-blue bruises all over his body, and worsening an already difficult syndrome. Ricky continued wetting the bed until he was sixteen years old.

Abusing and killing animals, starting fires, and protracted bed-wetting are some of the red flags that can pop up in a childhood history, each indicating a particular aspect of antisocial and psychopathic tendencies.[15] The need for aggressive dominance and control, as well as the inability to resist acting out such impulses, clearly shows itself in these behaviors. A psychologist might interpret them as reactions to the stressful emotional environment of the home, but this is again a chicken-and-egg debate. No matter where they came from, two things are known: First, the stressful environment at home most likely altered the neurobiology of Ricky Green's brain, as recent research has substantiated the impact of external stresses on the hardware of the mind.[16] Second, Green's early antisocial acts express an inability to control his undesirable impulses that, whether genetic or environmental in origin, verify an impaired capacity for self-restraint. The deeply physical nature of this impairment is especially reflected in Green's protracted bed-wetting.

When Green spoke of his mother, his voice softened and became almost inaudible. He stressed that he was very fond of her, and he felt that she was a good woman who cared for him. Only once did she enact physical violence on him – a slap delivered when Green refused to help her in the house. Because she was fearful of his father, his mother was unable to protect Ricky from the beatings.

In terms of immediate biological damage, Ricky Green's biography reveals a nearly constant experience of harmful substances. He started drinking beer when he was nine. By the time he was fourteen years of age, he was a heavy drinker and smoked marijuana; by his midtwenties he was taking amphetamines and other drugs. His sexual experiences are similarly alarming and also begin during the formative years of childhood. When he was eleven years old, Green ran away from home and wound up in Casino Beach, a recurring locale in his life, where an older man picked him up. The man kept Ricky at his home for four days, during which time the man had sex with him. Green remembers being anally penetrated, which he found very painful. His father finally discovered him, took him home, and punished him by whipping the soles of his feet. Two weeks later, Ricky was sent to his grandfather's house. According to Ricky, his grandfather knew the man who had picked him up at Casino Beach, and surmised that they had had sex. This knowledge induced his grandfather to force Ricky to perform fellatio on him; for at least three years, from the time Ricky was thirteen until he was sixteen, his grandfather often had anal sex with him.

His father, Ricky emphasized, never had sex with him; nor did Ricky have sex with his brothers. His sister told him that she had sex with their father, and she also claimed that she had sex with Ricky when he was thirteen years old, as well as with his older brother. Ironically, she assured him that he was the better sexual partner.

When he was sixteen, Ricky ran away from home a second time and ended up living with a homosexual in Louisiana. He stayed with him for a while, eventually leaving him for another homosexual, who beat and raped him. When questioned about this second encounter, Ricky complained that he felt used, and that when "the second man got what he wanted he kicked me out."

Still too young to be considered a legally consensual sexual partner, Green met a thirty-seven year old woman, a topless dancer, at the "Oasis Bar." He recalled that at the time he thought she was probably bisexual, and that she was a prostitute who drank a lot and treated him "like a dog." He got involved with her, moved into her apartment for a short time, and quickly realized that she was "using him" to attract both men and women to her, and then exerting domination over him in front of them. Green said that she exerted her domination by forcing him to service her in front of guests, and by hurting him during sex. He said "she knew she had control over me." He let her demean him and hurt him because he naïvely thought this was part of a "normal" sexual experience. When they would visit her family, she demonstrated her control over him by forcing him to have sexual intercourse in front of them, an act her family passively viewed. He thought on occasion of killing her, but after she introduced him to her relatives, he felt somehow a part of the family and couldn't go through with the murder.

This emotional connection to her family proves that Ricky Green was capable of experiencing empathy, and that it could in fact inhibit his murderous impulses. However, under the influence of alcohol and in later stages of his life, this empathic inhibition was clearly outstripped by his violent desires.

At eighteen years of age, when many people are entering their first committed relationship, Green had moved out of the topless dancer's apartment and met a younger woman and moved in with her. Three years later they were married, but the marriage lasted only six months. One evening Green was alone in the house drinking large quantities of liquor. By the time his wife came home, he was thoroughly intoxicated. He told her to sit on his lap, then pulled out a knife and ran it over her clothes, telling her to take them off. They talked for several hours until he passed out from the liquor. When Green woke up, she had packed her belongings and left. Green stated that he hadn't wanted to kill her, but when pressed he confessed that the idea may have been in the back of his mind.

About four years later, in 1985, he got involved with Sharon and lived with her for six months before they married. After the marriage, they lived together for over four years. He remembered that

Sharon had a sweet personality, was a good worker as a telephone operator, and was very protective of him. They did well together until 1987, when she got involved with drugs. Ricky had been mostly into alcohol, but shortly after Sharon got involved with methamphetamines and LSD, he did too. Ricky started using regularly, and related that this time was very hard, because for about a year Sharon would become violent and get into fights with him, especially when they would run out of drugs. He said that he recalls on one occasion trying to choke Sharon while they were having sex. He even tried to choke Sharon's sister, whom he had dated before Sharon. The cycle of drug use and increasingly psychopathic behavior begins to accelerate at this point in Green's life, soon leading to the first murder for which Green was charged – the murder of Jeffrey Davis.

A Killer Interprets His Murders

After he had finished describing his history of murders and relationships, one of the first questions I asked Green was whether he had ever had sexual intercourse *without* the urge and intent to harm. He answered that he would occasionally hustle homosexuals for money and then have sex with them without hurting them. And after Sharon left him, he went on a thirty-day sexual spree and had sex with both men and women, exhibiting an almost manic episode of the promiscuous sexual behavior associated with psychopathy. Notably, during his spree he allowed anal sex to be performed on him. In view of his aggressive sexual role in the past, his behavior is suggestive of an unconscious recognition that his violent rampages were over.

Remarkably, Green related three episodes in which he was very close to killing a homosexual and suddenly changed his mind and lost the intent to harm. The first was a man he picked up and took into the woods to have sex. They both undressed, and he got on top of the man who was facing the ground. Green vividly remembers lifting a knife in the air, and just as he was about to bring it down to kill the man he saw an image of himself, a shadow along the side of the ground. This shocked him into an awareness of what he was doing, and he stopped immediately, stood up, dressed, and left the scene.

The second incident involved a man with whom he had sex in his home, after which he entered his garage and noticed an ax hanging on the wall. He went for the ax intending to kill his sexual partner, but the man started talking about his young child's arrival and visit. Ricky imagined what it would be like for the child to show up and see his father mutilated, and abandoned the idea of killing him.

Green also remembered picking up a homosexual at Casino Beach and eventually stabbing him in the back. For no reason he could understand he suddenly had the desire to help him, placed him in his car, and drove him to the nearest hospital. After dropping him off at the ramp of the hospital, Green drove around the building and watched as the man was wheeled off on the gurney. Once the victim disappeared through the hospital doors, Green parked his car across the street and fell asleep.

These incidents are significant with regard to the question of free will. It would appear that when something forced Green to snap out of his murderous rage, whether it was a shadow on the ground or an empathic awareness of consequence to a third party, a conscience concerning the moral value of his behavior would slip back into place and inhibit impulses to further violence. But instead of being an argument for Green's free will, these incidents of slippage between murderous rage and empathic inhibition indicate an individual whose controls slowly give way to antisocial impulses. Increased drug use and other factors speak to these episodes as transitional moments to the fully psychopathic behavior that Green would exhibit later in life.

I asked him if he had ever hurt any one other than the four victims he was charged with murdering and the man he took to the hospital. His initial response was, "I won't discuss whether I killed others. The police should pay more money to find out who else I killed." Then he admitted that he might have murdered more than the four already described. He said he didn't understand why these murders occurred, since he never liked fighting and didn't like hurting people or being hurt.

"Yet, for some reason, I killed them," he said, while sitting back in his chair, looking unhappy, and rubbing his hands over his face.

On occasions, Ricky felt that evil spirits took control of him. Thoughts came into his head that he could not stop, and they would control him until everything would "explode in my brain." At these times, he doubted his own sanity and feared the total loss of his mind. He also experienced what he described as thoughts flying of their own accord through his head – coming and going out of his control. He said he didn't know why he mutilated people, but that once he started stabbing his victims he felt the pain that he was causing them and wanted to end it, so he would start stabbing faster. This is an interesting case of empathy and murderous impulses competing side-by-side for attention and resulting in an anxious acceleration of the crime.

Green said he often felt like he was walking in a dream: knowing he'd committed the crimes, he still was unable to believe that they had actually happened. On the other hand, he admitted that there were some motivations for the murders. He expressed rage toward homosexuals and prostitutes, and showed little to no concern for their welfare. In fact, he suggested that society would do well to let him out, so that he could go on killing homosexuals. This is a behavior associated with sociopaths, a group with whom Green has several traits in common. Frequently, sociopaths convince others that they are doing something good for society. Green thought that homosexuals spread their "badness" to the world and are a very bad influence on children, creating lifelong problems for them. Here, we see that Ricky himself suggests an interpretation of his behavior in terms of his early childhood experience.

Ricky acknowledged that alcohol had a major role in his behavior. All the murders occurred when he was under the influence of alcohol, and Ricky went so far as to say that alcohol "allowed him" to kill people. When he got drunk, especially with hard liquor, he would "turn into a different person." He said he had blackout episodes from alcohol, and even periods when he would suffer from tremors and visual hallucinations. When he was younger, he said he was sad and depressed all the time and that – while under the influence of beer – he had tried to commit suicide at least three times.

He added quickly that he did not feel suicidal at the time of the interview, though he felt he had lived a useless life with no reason to continue living.

The Texas trial court sentenced Ricky Lee Green to death, and after seven years, on October 8, 1997, he was executed. In his last statement he indicated that he was no longer "a threat to society."[17] He added "I want to thank the Lord for giving me this opportunity to get to know Him. He has shown me a lot and He has changed me in the past two months." Green also added that his punishment was now over, "but my friends are now being punished."

One has to wonder, particularly in the light of what we know about the brain and the forces influencing human behavior, what purpose if any is served by the death penalty.

What Is Nature, What Is Nurture?

The difficulties of sorting nature from nurture as the cause of "bad" behavior are pronounced in the Ricky Green case. Green's history would initially support "nurture" as the cause of his deviant sexuality and murderous behavior. Physical abuse by his father from an early age, sexual abuse by his grandfather, as well as his domination by both male and female sexual partners during childhood and adolescence, would explain his murderous rage at homosexuals and prostitutes. Ricky came out of a dysfunctional family and an abusive childhood where he felt he lacked power to alter his experiences. Frequently, he spoke of homosexuals and whores as preying on "defenseless" children, a group with which Green would undoubtedly identify himself. Though he said he was not naturally disposed to hurt people, when he drank he would emerge as a "completely different person" and had the power to exert his will over others.

On the other hand, personal history is not the whole story, and may not even be the most important reason for his "bad" behavior. Many people come out of so-called dysfunctional families and experience serious abuse without turning into murderers. We know that some use the pain and anger of early childhood experiences to propel themselves into successful careers. Others may simply withdraw from the world and live quiet, unobtrusive lives.

Genetics and the biology of the brain play important roles in determining how a person will *react* to situations similar to Ricky Green's. His family history of sociopathy, crime (his father and brothers), and sexuality (his grandfather's deviance and sexual abuse, his sister's seduction of him) would give credence to a familial genetic basis for his desires and some of his behavior. Ricky Green was both intensely fascinated and deeply repelled by homosexuality, which was evident in how he described being drawn back to Casino Beach since he was in his late teens, the scene of both his homosexual experiences and his violent crimes.

The basis of his murderous rage is a combination of nurture and biology. The mirror-neuron system of Green's brain most likely imitated the behavior of his father and siblings, including the way they handled anger, rage, and lack of control of their impulses and desires. In addition, as a victim of childhood abuse, his later desire to destroy others who are abusive in the same way is certainly related to his early experiences. Experiences such as these can create "successful careers" depending on the individual's reaction to them; for instance, Ricky's vengeful feelings could have turned into a commitment to fighting childhood sexual abuse through an institution or volunteer organization. Certainly Ricky seemed to feel strongly for other children experiencing the same difficult situations that he had to live through as a child.

But biology enters the field as a basis of his murderous rage in two ways. First, his ability to control his feelings and maintain socially acceptable behavior was challenged from birth. Each person has a threshold, the limit of his or her ability to withstand stress and provocation. This is dynamically set by the force of amygdalar responses (leading to fear, anger, and rage) and the power of one's limbic structures and anterior cingulate cortex to inhibit impulses. Green's threshold, as he himself described, was very low. A statement of desire, or any indication of being imposed upon, would cause him to lose control of his behavior. Problems with self-control are often seen in children who wet the bed, which he and his brother did well into their teens. The capacity to restrain oneself has a genetic basis, and was clearly malfunctioning in Green's case from an early age, though it was also strongly aggravated by environmental factors.

Second, abuse and pain in a child who has little or no recourse results in severe frustration and stress.[18] These feelings affect the biology of the person's brain. Here a dynamic exists between environmental factors and biology. Though complicated, this interrelationship among the stressful situation, the feelings of extreme frustration and helplessness, and the biology of the brain may create permanent neurobiological changes. These changes could include a lower stress threshold, decreased ability to control undesirable instincts and desires, and reduced aptitude to change the factors that provoke the intense inner feelings that let rage take over and make the brain "explode." Harming or killing animals in childhood is a hallmark of the inability to control undesirable or sociopathic desires, and it shows up frequently in the personal histories of violent criminals.

Furthermore, recent research indicates that there is an "aggression gene" – a defect in the gene that codes for the enzyme monoamine oxidase A (MAO-A), which metabolizes various neurotransmitters in the brain. When this gene is aberrant and produces low or no MAO-A activity it may lead to aggression and violence. Researchers found that even among male children who have the aggression gene, whether or not they grow up to be violent depends upon their level of maltreatment. The ones who were maltreated grew up to develop antisocial problems.[19]

The stimulus for this research on children was the case study of a Dutch family in which many of the male relatives were prone to impulsive episodes of aggression, violence, and antisocial behavior.[20] On assessment of the MAO-A activity in the Dutch family it was found that the gene was defective and had been passed on genetically to affect the male members of the family. Girls may inherit the defective gene, but they also inherit enough of the normal gene that they are not affected by low MAO-A. The recent study involved following a large group of male children from birth to adulthood. Those males with the genotype for low MAO-A activity who had been abused in early childhood were more likely to become violent and antisocial. In some cases the probability of this was as high as 85–90%. In contrast, boys with low MAO-A activity who had never been abused were no more likely to become violent than were boys with normal MAO-A activity.[21]

This means that genetic predispositions must be somehow activated by the environment in order to become an aspect of character. Genetics, the result of slow mutations over generations, is responsible for the built-in options for the biochemistry of mental processes.[22] But instruction, or the impact of environment, is necessary to stimulate options that already exist. The instruction – child abuse in males with the "aggressive gene" – does not create the fundamental changes that affect the brain; it brings them to the surface. These findings help to explain why not all maltreated children grow up to become violent, and once again emphasizes the interactive nature of genes and environment, or of nature and nurture.

A second area of genetic study is also important for understanding biological forces that may induce violent or aggressive behavior. A single gene was identified that contributes to the brain's responses to emotionally induced stimuli.[23] This gene encodes the production of a protein that is necessary to transport serotonin, a neurotransmitter, after it has been released back into neurons. By removing the serotonin from the synapse, it minimizes its effect on neurons. This transporter gene has two structural alleles (i.e., alternative forms), one with a shorter promoter region, which contains the DNA that determines the gene's expression. The shorter allele produces less of the transporter protein, and thereby allows the serotonin to linger longer in the synapse. Through functional magnetic resonance (fMRI) of the amygdala, the brain's center for emotional commands and conditioned-fear responses, the researchers compared the effects of provocation with scary faces. They determined that subjects with short alleles demonstrated greater activation of the amygdala, and a greater fear response. This study shows that even small variations in genes may affect an individual's emotional reactions to the environment.

This genetic study is consistent with other research relating the amygdala to fear conditioning. A recent study showed that amygdalar response to novelty may have a genetic basis.[24] Children who had inhibited temperaments (a tendency to withdraw from unfamiliar situations) at two years of age maintained these temperaments throughout adolescence and into adulthood. In contrast, children who were uninhibited during infancy demonstrated greater response to novelty and maintained this temperament years later. Even though there may be greater impulsivity and antisocial features in these uninhibited children, there is the upside that they will be open to new ideas and experiences.

The amygdala has a central role in the brain's threat-response system, which is how it impacts on violence. This response system, when triggered by increasing threat, creates a violent reaction.[25] At low levels of threat this system may initiate a "freeze" response. The hypothalamus and periaqueductal gray sections of the brain stem mediate this freeze response. If however, the threat continues the system will induce "flight" attempts. Where flight is impossible, aggression occurs. Hence human aggression may be seen as a reaction to perceived threat that is mediated by the threat-response system in the brain stem.

The amygdala is critical, for it feeds information on the current state of threat into this system. It helps to establish the nature of the reaction, that is, flight or fight. Hence, an amygdala that is hypersensitive to threat, such as might be seen in individuals with the defective gene for serotonin transport, will impact strongly on the "flight–fight" response system and create the brain environment for aggression and violence.[26]

Ricky Green's need for alcohol and drugs further suggests the powerful force of biology. Ricky claimed that all the murders occurred while he was drinking, but this does not mean that the desire to kill did not haunt him while he was sober. Rather, it is likely that he had these ideas – he said thoughts came into his head that he couldn't control (which has biological antecedents) – and then drank to become more uninhibited, so he could follow through with his desires.

So the dynamic went as follows: He had bad role models in his primary family to imitate (mirror neurons), augmented by a relatively ineffective inhibitory system (limbic structures, anterior cingulate cortex, orbital frontal cortex), which he dampened further by alcohol consumption, and an amygdala that had been conditioned by abuse with its concomitant stress to become hyperactive, allowing him to go readily into a rage. He may have also had the gene low MAO-A activity (though never tested) which would have been activated by early child abuse and considerably heightened the effect of alcohol on containing the force of his inhibitory system.

If Green had not suffered from early childhood trauma and abuse, the nature–nurture line could perhaps be drawn more steadily. A recent study indicated that psychopaths who have *not* suffered from early psychological deprivation have lower metabolism of prefrontal glucose than normal people or other types of murderer who did experience psychological deprivation. This would support the idea of a psychopath who is "pure nature," where the "social push" to violence is minimal or absent and brain abnormalities are wholly to blame for their psychotic behavior.[27] These differences are consistent with other studies of psychopaths and murderers. This research has demonstrated deficits in the prefrontal cortex and limbic system that may induce abnormalities such as inappropriate signaling. Psychological tests have shown differences in the development of the prefrontal cortices, particularly the right, in young offenders.[28]

If we could have subjected Green to brain-imaging technologies, we might find that his limbic system and prefrontal cortex were abnormal. Since the late 1980s, positron emission tomography (PET) studies have been conducted on violent and aggressive offenders. These have shown correlations between brain metabolism and the potential for violent behavior. PET studies of repetitively violent offenders revealed decreased cortical blood flow and hypometabolism in their nondominant frontal and temporal lobes, compared to control subjects. Some even showed involvement into the prefrontal region, which affects cognitive understanding.[29] During frontal lobe activation, researchers revealed significant bilateral prefrontal metabolic decreases in persons charged with murder or manslaughter.[30] But even this would not settle the nature–nurture debate with regard to Green, because even these strictly "biological" traits may be developmental, and could easily have been cultivated by Green's traumatic youth and young adulthood.

Recent research is showing that developmental defects, which may be genetic or congenital in origin, or which may occur shortly after birth, can be responsible for antisocial behavior. A long-term study of two children who experienced damage to their prefrontal cortex, particularly the orbitofrontal cortex, prior to the age of sixteen months, revealed the development of long-term irreversible effects.[31] These children as adults had severely impaired social behavior including antisocial acts such as violence and stealing. They also were unable to reason morally about issues. (When these parts of the brain are injured in adults, such as in the famous case of Phineas Gage,[32] who suffered a traumatic prefrontal lobe injury from an explosion while working on a railroad track, the individuals who survive demonstrate some social behavioral changes, but they don't lose their knowledge of social conventions and moral rules.) This study shows that injury at a very early age can prevent the development of social conscience and adherence to moral rules. The researchers speculate that early damage of the prefrontal cortex may create a personality similar in antisocial behavior to the classic psychopath, a personality type that has been shown by fMRI to have serious abnormalities in affective processing.[33]

The importance of the frontal lobe in control of aggression cannot be underestimated.[34] In fact, the frontal lobe, particularly the orbitofrontal cortex, has extensive neuronal projections to autonomic (i.e., involuntary-action) control centers (which regulate essential bodily functions), particularly in the hypothalamus and periaqueductal gray matter. It is believed that the orbitofrontal cortex, through its projections, has control over impulses from the amygdala. When this cortex is damaged or not functioning, the risk is greatest – particularly in those with abnormalities of amygdala function – that aggressive behavior will develop.[35]

The relationship of nature and nurture is not as simple as the usual opposition between them would make it seem. We have seen that genes, developmental abnormalities, brain injury – especially of the frontal lobe – and environmental insults such as child abuse can induce antisocial behavior. Given the high probability of aberrancies in Ricky Green's biology, as well as his dysfunctional family and personal histories, his behavior was heavily influenced by biological factors. These factors, as we've seen, affect not only how the brain processes information, but the scope of one's ability to think about moral considerations. The very content of thinking, therefore, is affected by the brain. As we have seen, psychopathic characteristics are not a list of behaviors and causes that line up neatly like a chart of symptoms and germs. They interact – frequently comorbidly – as we have seen in the way psychopathic behavior weaves in and out of Green's life, becoming stronger as environmental and genetic factors fuse together to create the adult biology of a criminal mind.

6

The Biology of Choice

Throughout the ages, medical scholars and clinicians have been intrigued by rare syndromes that express one or more human qualities to an exaggerated degree and that are neither readily understood by the scientific knowledge of the time nor, seemingly, within the control of the individual afflicted. Most medical scientists today believe that these statistically highly improbable conditions, if understood, could create major "paradigm shifts" in our thinking about human biology, thereby leading to new, rich avenues for medical research into questions of brain function, individual control and "free will."[1]

In psychiatry some of these phenomena, like the "idiot savant," are still very mysterious – as, for that matter, are geniuses like Mozart, who started composing music at three years of age. I remember attending a meeting several years ago when an idiot savant – he was essentially illiterate and scored very low on intelligence tests – listened to a recorded Bach composition by Glenn Gould and proceeded, with no training, to sit down and play it flawlessly on the piano. I was amazed, and remember wondering at the time whether this capacity for imitating music might be hardwired in the savant's brain.

Unusual syndromes affecting an individual's control of his or her behavior are fascinating not only because we don't fully understand the scientific reasons for their development, but also, and perhaps more important, because they make it obvious that choice entails biology as well as intention and thinking in the abstract. These neurologically described conditions manifest complex, goal-directed actions that have been shown to lie beyond the will power of the individual.

One such "motor release phenomenon" that has been of particular enthrallment is what has been referred to as *utilization behavior.* When objects are placed before patients with this condition, they will react accordingly. For example, if a hat is placed on a table, the patient will put it on. A second hat will result in the same action, and so forth. Similarly, such patients will drink a glass of liquid placed in front of them and continue as more glasses are added. A social form of this condition is *imitation behavior,* whereby the patient uncontrollably imitates another person's behavior despite admonitions to the contrary.[2]

Related conditions that are equally curious and manifest lack of control on the part of the actor have been described in the literature. One of particular note is referred to as *anarchic hand syndrome.* Patients with this condition cannot exert power over their hands, which engage in outrageous acts like taking the food from another person's plate or suddenly hitting the man in front of them in the theater on the head.[3]

There is controversy over whether the neuropathology described in both anarchic hand syndrome and utilization behavior can be viewed as evidence of a lack of free will. On the one hand, the nature of the pathology could suggest that these behaviors are essentially "authorless"; certainly they are not "willed" actions.[4] On the other hand, it may be that we do not yet fully understand who, or what, constitutes the true "author" of such actions. One has to place these data in the context of the work done by Libet,[5] and separately by Platt and Glimcher[6] (discussed in Chapter 3), which focused on brain processes in normal individuals. Both these studies demonstrated in different ways that the brain begins to become active in relevant areas before the individual is consciously aware that an act should occur.

Libet showed that the readiness potential (RP) precedes by at least 300–400 ms the moment when the actors subjectively experience the desire or intention to act.[7] Platt and Glimcher showed that sensory judgments seem to be made through the gradual accumulation of signals in the neurons of the sensorimotor pathways, which leads to favoring one behavioral choice over another.[8]

Subsequent studies have confirmed some of these findings. Using fMRI, researchers at Oxford showed that participants in a study reported the time when they first became aware of the desire to lift their finger as an average of 200 ms before the time of the movement.[9] The researchers went on to study where brain activity occurred when subjects first sensed the intention to move (I) and when they actually moved the finger (M). Blood flow data showed that during the "I" phase, when subjects became aware of their intention to move, three brain areas were activated – the dorsal (i.e., top) prefrontal cortex; the intraparietal sulcus (a narrow groove on either side of the brain, below the crown); and the presupplementary motor area (in the medial [i.e., central] wall of the frontal lobe). The question, in comporting with Libet's work, is this:

> If the readiness potential, which represents an internal model of the desired movement, "revs up" nearly a second before the action, why is the actor, or individual, aware of this desire only at roughly 200 ms before the action itself occurs?

The research opens up the issue of whether intentionality in fact is understood retrospectively – whether there is an *illusion* of "watching" oneself act.[10] The researchers point out that "attention to intention" even milliseconds before the movement may be the means by which conscious control of actions becomes effective, and possible.[11]

Many contemporary thinkers like Daniel M. Wegner[12] and Daniel C. Dennett[13] are highly vocal about the potential illusionary nature of "free will." Wegner, in his provocative book *The Illusion of Conscious Will,* takes the position that human behavior is the result of "deterministic or mechanistic processes."[14] He disregards personal explanations of our intentions to act. Rather, he suggests that conscious will might be merely a "cognitive feeling" similar to the way sadness or happiness are feelings. He finds *subpersonal* mechanistic explanations – those based on biological processes of which the person is not aware, such as biochemical changes and electrical activity in parts of the brain that precede awareness and the individual's conscious desires and intentions – more valid descriptions of human behavior. This belief would be in keeping with the research, described above, by Libet and others, showing that the brain has a type of automatic activation that precedes awareness on the conscious level. This is to suggest that forces within the person, which are shaped by a combination of biological and genetic tendencies and the emotional effects (memories) of past experiences, will cause a person to act.

For example, if one has been attacked and mugged during adolescence, one will react a certain way should a similar set of conditions emerge during adulthood. The first mugging establishes a context in the brain, a set of environmental conditions and emotions – a memory – that emerges to activate the parts of the brain when similar stimuli occur thereafter.

Wegner's theory is also consistent with Antonio Damasio's notion of *somatic markers* – those deeply informed feelings or "reminders" of the interests of the body in our decisions and actions.[15] In effect Wegner sees conscious will as a somatic marker of "personal authorship," which he says validates the self.[16] In the sense that our feeling of committing a particular act provides us with the conscious sensation that we have willed the action, this notion is not unlike the findings of the Oxford researchers, who open up the possibility that intention is retrospective. In other words, once we are set upon the course of engaging in an act, we look back and provide an intention to justify that engagement – unless, of course, the act is planned well ahead of time.

Recent research adds to this possibility by showing that, under normal conditions, brains work alike. There is a synchronization of activity within the individual brain and strong correlations among the brains of participants in a given activity.[17] This would suggest that the research by Libet and others is not simply limited to a small group of research subjects, but rather is applicable to human beings generally. In effect, the automatic processing that serves to activate specific cells in areas of the brain before we engage in a particular action is most likely a phenomenon that all of us experience.

How We Confront Moral Issues

Moral issues arise when we must make choices, often between satisfying a powerful personal drive (status, money, or pleasure) and a less compelling drive that may even go against one's own interests in order to achieve socially desirable consequences. For example: An attractive, young, recently divorced woman meets a former boyfriend and his wife at a cocktail party in Manhattan. His wife is unaware that her husband was involved with the divorcée. During the conversation, the young woman perceives that the man is still very much attracted to her, as she is to him. She senses quickly that she could get him back, or at the very least have an affair with him.

The moral dilemma is clear: Her desire for intimacy and pleasure is powerful, but she must balance that against the consequences of disrupting a marriage. One could argue that "all is fair in love and war," but maintaining the inviolability of marriage and family is a social good. So, the young woman's personal interests, when balanced against the harm to the wife and to society, dictate the morally appropriate course of action, which is to pull away.

The moral picture, of course, gets more complex if there are extenuating circumstances that would support reasons why the husband "should" be separated from his wife. For example, the wife might be a bigamist; or perhaps she is having affairs with colleagues of her husband. Or, unbeknownst to her husband, she is a member of a radical feminist group, a type of Weatherwoman, who advocates the violent overthrow of the existing social order that the husband clearly supports. Now the balancing test becomes more complicated, mainly because the socially desirable consequences become somewhat attenuated. But the basic principle remains: A moral dilemma involves the weighing of competing interests for an outcome that takes into consideration personal interests while minimizing harm to third parties, which may include the social order or cohesiveness.

In reviewing the moral dilemma just described, most of us would readily acknowledge that the brain has something to do with our thinking about such issues. But how many of us would accept the idea that our personal choices in life are influenced, even determined, by brain biology? We resist this notion even if we've known older people, perhaps in our own families, who have suffered stroke or a serious disease such as Alzheimer's, and we've seen how such physical brain injuries can affect not only their ability to move but their ability to think rationally.[18]

Brain lesions or injuries related to deficits of thinking, memory, or behavioral problems inform us about discrete sections of the brain, how they function and their connections to other important centers. In addition, studies of brain pathology in neurological and psychiatric patients have enlightened us about where emotions and affect reside in the brain. New and sophisticated imaging technologies are adding to these data by providing images of the brain that allow us to correlate cognitive deficits with injured sections of it.[19] Through these methods, we have learned which clusters of neurons in the brain are necessary for specific mental functions. But information obtained from these technologies has not yet gone so far as to show that the physical brain might play an important role not only in the *way* we make decisions, but also in the very *content* of these decisions. Such a claim would seem absurd – most of us are personally convinced that our choices reflect what is in our mind, that is, are our own true, rational choices.

Let's look at a few of the myriad decisions we make during the course of a day. We get up in the morning; one of our first decisions is what to wear. Our motivations for the selection may be varied and not always consistent. On a given day we might be drawn to a dark color or an Italian-style suit. Aesthetics or physical comfort – the choice of warm clothing on a very cold wintry day – might direct our choice to one outfit over another. At times our choices might seem irrational, but once we've made them, we still view them as personal. "I made the choice because this is what I want to wear."

It seems the more complex the choice, the more we are fortified in our conviction of ownership, autonomy, and self-determination. We go into an ice cream parlor and choose chocolate over vanilla. It is a seemingly simple choice, and we claim that our taste preference has dictated it. Yet choices are never that simple. The choice of chocolate ice cream is influenced not only by taste but also by color, texture, presentation – and more than likely by early pleasant memories associated with the flavor.

Nonetheless, the decision about ice cream is simple compared to decisions regarding which strategy to select to solve a complex mathematical problem, or to personal choices like whether to leave one's job for one that pays less but might provide more opportunity for advancement – or, alternatively, for one that is more personally fulfilling though it might pay less and offer little chance of advancement. Choices of any complexity always involve layers of multifaceted mental activity, and often many interrelated decisions. Opting for a job in one particular location, such as the Northeast, over another is one such complex decision; preferring a small company to a large megacorporation is another; and so on. The sub-issues that lead to the choice of a job force us to engage our thinking and our feelings more intensely than we do when we make a "simple" decision. Wrestling with the issues binds us tightly to the ultimate decision, so that it would seem anathema to suggest that something other than our mind, our conscious will, influenced and perhaps determined the final choice. Even when the information on which we rely to arrive at a decision is sketchy, we insist that the choice we made was ours alone.

But neuroscience is forcing us to rethink the extent of our personal control over our choices, and the implications of limits on personal control over our choices are nothing short of mind-boggling. Imagine that *free will*, long regarded as a hallmark of the human condition, may not be an untrammeled quality. Imagine that we are not quite as "free" as we would wish – and that biological forces produced by genes and by the environment may be more powerful than anyone ever believed possible in influencing an individual's decisions. Suppose, further, that these decisions extend beyond choices of emotional preference to include moral decisions that are concerned with actions deemed right or wrong by society.

That moral choices may also be biologically driven is a revolutionary concept, one that flies in the face of religious and societal traditions defining human beings as free agents responsible for their thoughts and actions. This is not to say that free will is merely a device serving the needs of society, through law, to attribute blame. But it is to say that free will may not always be a true reflection of what actually happens in an individual's brain when thoughts and feelings are converted to action.

The traumatic effects of Ricky Green's dysfunctional family on his childhood and development stood out starkly, but underlying Ricky's family history and his experiences are genes and biology as well as environmental influences. All these factors left an imprint on Ricky's brain and ultimately played key roles in forming his identity and behavior. We must, therefore, conclude that brain biology affects both personality and the full panoply of intellectual features that shape our thinking.

The brain affects choice in many different ways. Its communications among its internal parts and with the outside world inform our thoughts and feelings, which lead to actions. Before we can have a well-conceived and articulated idea about something, an unformed image – perhaps linked to feeling – surfaces in the brain, and this neural activity conjures a particular thought or feeling that gives form to the image.[20]

Take, for example, a decision to send out for pizza. We suddenly feel hungry, and the thought of pizza surfaces in our conscious mind. This is because hunger – a bodily sensation – has stimulated our memory centers, which then associate the sensation with something tangible and real: in this case, pizza. So sensations create desire for a reward.

The combination of bodily sensation (memory of food, personal desires, and other interests) is an antecedent to action, and action flows from these promptings to secure reward.[21] Other strong emotions may also be put into play by the brain – feelings such as fear, guilt, empathy, sadness, disgust, and well-being[22] – to complicate the decision to act: These feelings often reflect other values or personal preferences, which may be in opposition to meeting the body's need for a particular reward. For example, I have only one ticket for a baseball game that I desperately want to attend, but my brother, who is visiting from out of town, also wants to attend the game. My degree of empathy, and possibly guilt, about him will affect whether I resolve the conflict in favor of him or myself.

The theory of how we reason about personal and social decisions, in particular, is called the *somatic marker hypothesis*.[23] This hypothesis addresses the way in which specific feelings (somatic, i.e., bodily ones), no doubt associated with past experiences and stored in our memory, act as a signal, a type of marker that informs us and guides our reasoning about a situation and our decision to act in a certain way. Simply stated: When we meet someone for the first time we get a gut feeling about the person. It's a type of chemistry that affects how we decide to deal with him (or her) – if he is applying for a job, whether we would feel he is appropriate; or if we want to get to know the person more and begin to forge a friendship. Gut feelings also affect us when we are asked to make more complicated, presumably cold analytical decisions. The feelings set the framework within which we use our rational capacities to decide a course of action.

Are Specific Moral Rules Innate?

The good news is that moral choice may be a lot easier than we think. Some recent findings indicate that a moral sense is innate – hardwired in the brain – and we begin to display signs of it at a very young age. Children as young as three begin to use language like, "That's not fair!" if one child takes advantage of another by stealing an object, or is treated better in a family or group by being given more.[24] This awareness of rules becomes striking when children participate in competitive games and frequently identify cheating behavior in the group.

Studies among preschool children have shown that this sensitivity to fairness is somewhat refined. When asked questions about competing "rights" among children – for example, between a child who is first in line at a movie and one who comes later but is seriously handicapped from an injury and can't physically endure waiting for a long time – many children come out in favor of allowing the child with the greater need to get ahead in line.[25]

Norbert and Elinore Herschkowitz, in their book, *A Good Start in Life,*[26] note that children begin to develop a conscience at some point between three and six years of age. This is evident from their early understanding, perhaps on a simple level, of concepts of honesty, loyalty, and caring toward others. Of course the ethical and moral standards of these children are in the formative phase, and will undergo greater development over the ensuing years; but it has been suggested that the preschool years are particularly important in setting down habits that will affect a child's values, choice of friendships, and selection of role models – those whose behavior they will want to emulate.[27]

But when it comes to handling complex social decisions, recent research in brain development is opening up new areas for debate on moral development.[28] MRI studies of adolescents are showing that both the white and gray matter of the brain continue to change structurally well past puberty, perhaps up to twenty-five years of age.[29] The areas of the brain that are last to develop affect some of man's highest mental functions, those involving judgment, such as deciding among competing interests and assessing consequences. Dr. Jay Giedd and his colleagues at the National Institutes of Health are showing that there is a phase of neuronal change, which occurs in the teen years, that appears to have its greatest impact on altering the number of synapses among the neurons. This is in contrast to the explosive period of brain growth during the latter part of gestation, characterized by neural growth and pruning. Giedd points out that by the age of five a child's brain is nearly 95% of its adult size.[30] Between the ages of three and eighteen or older there is growth in parts of the brain like the *corpus callosum* – the plate of nerve fibers connecting the right and left cerebral hemispheres – which adds another 1.8%. The corpus collosum, which integrates the two hemispheres, is thought to be involved with increasing the ability for higher-order cognitive functioning.

Another reason for believing that a moral sense is innate comes from studies of infants who have sustained injuries to their prefrontal cortex, particularly the orbitofrontal cortex. Two adult patients who had been injured before the age of sixteen months were subjects of a study of the long-term effects of early prefrontal cortex injuries.[31] The first patient, a woman twenty years old at the time of the study, had been injured at the age of fifteen months by being run over by a motor vehicle. The second was a male of twenty-three who had undergone surgery to remove a frontal tumor at the age of three months. The families of both of these patients were of the educated middle-class and had no psychiatric histories.

Though the siblings of both patients turned out to be socially well-adapted, the patients themselves demonstrated severe impairment of social behavior involving antisocial acts such as violence, irresponsible and reckless sexual behavior, and stealing. Furthermore they showed little or no guilt or remorse for their behavior and no evidence of empathy for others.

Unlike those who experienced similar prefrontal injuries while adults, the two patients injured as infants showed that they were unable to reason in a social and moral context. They lacked the factual basis and emotional capacity for understanding the morality of their behavior. It was as though the cortical control for reward and punishment had been severely compromised, as they were not able to acquire or retrieve the knowledge that depends on the presence of reward and punishment determinations for moral reasoning. Therefore, although they exhibited some of the same disruptive behavior as those afflicted with prefrontal lobe injuries during adulthood – such as insensitivity to others, unresponsiveness to behavioral interventions, and inability to follow through with plans – they were more seriously affected, as evidenced by their inability to shape a moral issue.

Consistent with Antisocial Personality Disorder, such as seen in Ricky Green, these subjects exhibited pervasive disregard for moral rules and standards, utter irresponsibility, and a complete lack of remorse for their behavior.[32] If they did something society would consider blatantly wrong, like driving off with someone's car without permission, they showed no guilt or contrition. Essentially, they had not acquired the knowledge necessary for socialization, such as the rules for getting along with others, and most particularly they were devoid of knowledge about reward and punishment for one's behavior. Furthermore, efforts to educate them about morality and changes in behavior were unsuccessful. This suggested that whatever capacity the subjects may have possessed before birth had been wiped out irreparably by their injuries. On psychological tests these subjects evinced Kohlberg's early "preconventional" Level 1 of moral reasoning (see Chapter 2), which is manifested primarily by an egocentric perspective involving the avoidance of punishment.

Another interesting gauge of the innateness of a moral sense comes from recent discoveries about primates. We have known since the 1990s that chimpanzees possess reciprocal altruism (generosity with food and sharing, for example) that is essential for achieving social status. Along with this they have also been shown to have a sense of righteousness and justice, abilities that are thought increasingly to be precursors of human morality.[33] But recently researchers at the Yerkes National Primate Center in Atlanta looked at "fairness" based on aversion to inequity and concluded that a critical feature of human cooperation involves comparing one's own efforts and rewards (payoffs) with others.[34] This, they presume, is a human universal. However, other animals are cooperative; therefore, inequity aversion is most likely *not* limited to humans.

The researchers studied how brown capuchin monkeys (five males and five females) respond to unequal rewards when compared with others in their group. In this experiment these monkeys were given tokens to be exchanged with an experimenter for a reward. When monkeys exchanged tokens for a slice of cucumber, which is an acceptable reward, there were no problems. However, if one monkey received a cucumber for a token and another a grape – which has been shown to be a preferred treat at least 90% of the time by these monkeys[35] – the response was different.

The researchers noted that the males, for no clearly discernible reason, showed little or no difference in response when a favored food item was given to one of them, whereas the females, observing another receiving the desired food item for equal effort, reacted by rejecting the offer. They were more tuned into issues of fairness. This rejection took the form of failing to surrender the token and pay for the food, or of accepting the slice of cucumber but refusing to eat it. If one of the female monkeys was given the grape for *no* effort, the others would react even more hostilely. Based on their findings the researchers concluded that these monkeys have an innate sense of equality and fairness,[36] and that this capacity, which is essential for cooperation, may have evolved in social primates before it did in humans.[37]

Morality: Selection and Instruction

Morality may be an innate attribute of the brain, but that doesn't mean that we are born fully capable of making moral choices. The current theory held by most evolutionary biologists is that, through a slow process of mutation over millions of years, the capacity for moral thinking – essential for survival because it provides the bases for human cooperation – became hardwired.[38] The mechanism operating through the centuries that resulted in the hardwiring of human traits is referred to as *selection* (similar to the "nature" aspect of the nature–nurture conundrum). The hardwiring of moral ability in our brain, according to selection, is genetically determined. Throughout our lives we discover, through personal moral challenges, what has already been built into our brains.[39]

Selection is another way of saying that nature has the dominant role in explaining the range and variability of the mind. The alternative theory, *instruction* (the "nurture" part of the equation), holds that morality is not innate and that individual variation is a result of environmental influences. The advocates of instruction see the brain as highly mutable and open to modification by external factors, such as learning. A good environment (parents, teachers, and playmates with "good" values) would support an individual's potential for "moral" thought, whereas a bad environment (a dysfunctional family, the "wrong" friends) causes frustration, thereby impeding the individual and preventing moral thinking from developing.[40]

Advances in neuroscience and cell biology, however, strongly back the selection theory, which holds that our brains possess all the built-in options for mental capacity and development.[41] The environment, through instruction, merely selects, but does not alter, options already built into the brain. An environmental challenge, or signal, at an appropriate time triggers the brain's capacity to engage in moral thinking.[42]

In many ways moral development is similar to language development. Since Paul Broca's discovery that language production (motor control of mouth, lips, jaw, and vocal apparatus) is centered in the posterior part of the left frontal lobe[43] and Carl Wernicke's identification of the site of language comprehension in the left superior temporal gyrus (i.e., above and behind the left ear),[44] many linguists believe that language is grounded in biology.[45]

Noam Chomsky, who conceived of transformational grammar (see Chapter 3) in the late 1950s,[46] was a particularly strong champion of the biological basis of language. He insisted that languages have many similar characteristics, such as a universal grammar.[47] Chomsky was also convinced that there was a special organ built into the brain for language, an innate brain circuitry for syntax.[48] He did not, however, accept the evolutionary view that language came from previous animal communication systems. He was convinced that this biological capacity in humankind sprang into being spontaneously, possibly as a mutation.[49]

Recognizing the importance of Darwinian evolution, Stephen Pinker and other linguists have held that selection is a far more plausible explanation for the development of human language than is spontaneous mutation.[50] The study of languages has shown that timing is a very important factor in a child's acquisition of language. Word sounds have to be acquired early in a child's training in order to achieve fluency in the language. (In Japanese some sounds have to be acquired very early in infancy. However, generally to avoid an accent, a language must be learned before twelve or thirteen years of age.) This fact is consistent with the relationship between selection and instruction, whereby the capacity for language is in the brain, but the timing of the signal (instruction) is important for the neuronal development.[51]

In the same way, moral development awaits activation by experience. As discussed above, by the time a child has started school she (or he) has a general sense of justice and is able to care about the rights of others, at least on a simple level. During these early formative years a child develops an "inner voice," or set of moral standards, that helps her discriminate between right and wrong[52] – unless, that is, something interferes with or prevents the activation of the moral capacity (as in those cases of infants suffering brain damage within the first several days of life, or of children experiencing serious abuse at an early age). As a child proceeds through adolescence and into early adulthood, the simple life lessons learned from parents and teachers grow more subtle and complex. So, it would seem, does the brain's capacity to handle more complicated moral judgments as the organ continues to develop into the late teens.

Like linguistic development, moral thinking and action depend on neural systems implicated in other cognitive and emotional processes,[53] specifically two systems in the brain: the emotional circuitry (the limbic structures), which processes our feelings, such as fear, empathy, reward, and disgust; and the so-called executive center (the prefrontal lobes), which we use to describe, analyze, and plan.

7

Sex and the Single Moral Code

At one point or another in an individual's life, questions about love and sex arise: Are we "normal"? What is "normal"? Are we capable of bonding, or achieving long-term relationships? Are we capable of being sexually moral? How can we determine our true sexual makeup – and how much control have we over this overwhelmingly important aspect of life? Do our desires shape us, or do we shape them?

In this chapter and the next we explore, through one case history of a young couple encountering difficulties in forming an enduring, worthwhile relationship, precisely these questions and how modern science has brought us closer to answers – though far from solutions. We'll explore universally intriguing subjects: sex, love, pleasure, and bonding – in humans and in animals. And we'll learn about the physiological, chemical, and biological role the brain plays in what may be life's most enduring mysterious issue.

Jodi and Art found themselves in what many would consider to be a disastrous relationship. They had been dating off and on for over a year. At twenty-eight, she was ten years his junior. Their families had been friends for some time; both families were affluent, and respected in their community. Jodi had attended Andover Academy in Massachusetts, and then Smith College, where she graduated with honors in English literature. Since graduation she had been working as an editor at a major New York publishing house.

Art had graduated from Yale University with a degree in biology and economics, and from Columbia Law School. He worked for a few years in the Manhattan District Attorney's office, became dis-illusioned with a career in law, and shifted his interests to invest-ment banking. With a friend's help he got an entry-level position at a noted European bank in New York, where he soon became an investment banker specializing in start-up biotech companies.

After more than a year of dating, Art and Jodi got engaged. He wanted her to move in with him after the engagement. She hesi-tated, fearing it might damage their relationship, because Art had never lived with another person, except for roommates in college. Jodi thought it would be better to enter into his private space slow-ly by keeping her apartment and spending increased amounts of time in his. However, Art was persistent, so Jodi finally gave in and moved into his Upper East Side apartment. A week later she com-mented to her best friend that she thought it would work fine be-cause they both seemed to respect each other's need for privacy and space. She would frequently take her work home in the evening and, after a brief dinner, when they would chat about their day, she would sit in the living room and read manuscripts. He would work at his desk, catching up on his reading of financial reports.

At first their sex life together was good. In the beginning Art couldn't get enough of Jodi, and she felt his intensity and desire for her. Within a few months, however, Jodi began to feel differently. Art seemed increasingly distant when they were making love. She would caress him and he would show little response. To Jodi, their lovemaking felt increasingly like a mechanical process which just happened to lead to an orgasm. She was becoming less and less sat-isfied, and would feel at times alone and alienated when they were through making love. Art would get up and go off to the living room to read the *Economist*. Although Jodi tried several times to discuss her feelings with him, Art seemed unable to understand the prob-lem and was not warm or supportive to her. In fact, she felt at times that he was utterly indifferent to her feelings. This was a distinct change from what she had perceived him to be when they were dat-ing and first living together.

While a student at Smith, Jodi had suffered a brief period of de-pression over a broken relationship. She had discussed her problems with her academic counselor, who had recommended that she see a therapist. After a few months of talking through her feelings and problems relating to separations, she felt she had improved and chose to stop treatment. However, she appreciated the benefits she had drawn from the process and decided that Art and she might be helped by a brief period of couple's therapy. She recognized she was having difficulties telling him about how and what she felt, and that a trained third person might be able to help them effectively bridge this communication gap.

The Male and Female Brain

Many books have been written in recent years detailing the difference between the ways in which men and women think. In *Men Are from Mars, Women Are from Venus,*[1] these differences were graphically highlighted by the supposition that men and women come from two entirely different planets, a metaphor for different psychological worlds. With this in mind, why should they think the same way?

In recent years many studies have focused on the neurobiological differences between women and men.[2] Gender-related differences have been attributed to a wide variety of functions: emotional processing, working memory, language processing, and facial processing. Anatomical differences in the brain have also been demonstrated. These differences include the size and shape of major fiber tracts that cross between the right and the left hemispheres of the brain, such as the corpus callosum and the anterior commissure (which connects the temporal lobes), as well as regions of the brain including the prefrontal cortex.[3] Some studies have shown that women have a larger corpus callosum – particularly the posterior portion – and anterior commissure than heterosexual men.

A far more interesting scientific approach to the differences between men and women can be found in the work of Simon Baron-Cohen. In his book *The Essential Difference: The Truth about the Male and Female Brain,*[4] he summarizes much of his neuropsychological research about men and women and makes a critical distinction between the female brain, which he sees as constructed to be primarily *empathetic,* and the male brain, which he perceives as more characteristically *systemizing.* By "empathetic" he means having the capacity to comprehend, to feel the other person's position, or in other words, to put oneself in another's shoes and identify with how another might feel and think in a particular situation.

Empathizing includes a cognitive element: the ability to understand how other people feel from their perspective of a given situation. To achieve this empathy, an individual must be flexible enough in his (or her) own personality to be able to step outside of his own state of mind and reconstruct for himself the state of mind or perspective of the other person, given the other's unique situation. This requires knowledge acquired through experience with people and with the imagination.

For example, let us suppose that I learn that my friend David has just been passed over for a promotion that he sorely wanted because it would have enhanced his future career opportunities within the company where he works. With the cognitive component of empathy I should be able to infer from his situation, and from what I know about David, what he is likely to be thinking and feeling about this disappointment. There is a predictive element in this dimension of empathy, in that it allows an individual the ability to step into the mind-set of another person and thereby anticipate the other's thoughts and behavior. The cognitive element of empathy may be combined with an affective component; but it may also stand alone, so that an individual would be able to comprehend intellectually. but not feel emotionally, the other person's situation.

The affective component, on the other hand, deals with the observer's emotional response to another's situation. Hence, the affective component allows one to "feel" the other person's situation and to experience through "sympathy" the desire to help another out of his or her plight. To illustrate: Suppose that while walking down the street one comes across an older woman who has just been mugged and is sprawled out on the pavement. An empathetic individual with a heightened affective element would feel the victim's pain and distress and want to assist her to improve her condition.[5]

In contrast, systemizing involves focus on systems – understanding how these work and how to construct them. A system is a broad notion, defined by Baron-Cohen as anything constructed and operative based on rules or principles that govern "input–operation–output relationships."[6] Systemizing occupies nearly every effort or action that we carry out in order to be productive in society. Systemizing requires observation of cause-and-effect relationships that are necessary to achieve specific outcomes, analyzing the components of these relationships, and applying the lessons learned in order to repeat the process. For example, a coach attending a football game involving a rival team would observe the actions of the players under a variety of circumstances, analyze their winning strategies, and use this knowledge to construct a countermaneuver.

Systemizing, therefore, is a carefully thought-out method for achieving specific goals. It runs the gamut of the dynamic structures in human endeavors, from technology (airplanes, rockets, and computers), to nature (chemistry, biology, and geology), to abstractions (mathematics, software programs and music). and to social systems such as law, religion. and politics.

Empathy is not seen as a primary trait in every female; nor is systemizing a dominant trait in every male. There is at best a cluster effect whereby women are generally more likely to be empathetic and men more likely to be systemizing. On the other hand, in any given individual the distribution may be very different. There are many women who have a "male" type brain, which means that they are not primarily empathetic but are more likely to be concerned about systems. Conversely, there are males who have "female" type brains. The dichotomy is simply a useful way of examining some basic thematic differences between the sexes. Furthermore, the presence or absence of empathy and systemizing is not an all-or-nothing situation in men and women. To some degree we all have both capacities. Baron-Cohen has devised a framework for the presence of the primary personality characteristics of empathy and systemizing as they may serve to explain the differences between women and men.[7]

Of course changes in gender roles may bring about alterations in the prevalence of traits of empathy in women. As women get more into the workplace in supervisory and higher levels of functioning that require greater systemizing, this distinction between men and women is unlikely to hold up. The environmental changes brought about by changing roles for women will inevitably affect the biology of their brain over time.

However, there are biological reasons for these differences at the present time. In fact, behavior in other primates demonstrates similar characteristics. Young males of various species from monkeys to chimpanzees to baboons engage in rough play or play-fighting, whereas young females are nurturing, particularly to the infants of their species.[8] Some researchers have suggested that this interest in their babies shown by young females is an indicator of the females' heightened sensitivity to others.[9] Male primates, on the other hand, are far more likely to develop strategies to achieve specific goals.[10] A young male baboon will occasionally join forces with another young male and plan an attack on a senior baboon to steal the senior's female companion. The younger baboons will frequently succeed, and one of them will benefit from the outcome, acquiring a sexual mate. This planning requires understanding the "system" of the older baboon in order to defeat him at his power game.[11] The second baboon joining the fray has his own vested interest, for he might well succeed himself in winning the female baboon. It is not believed that he acts out of altruism.[12]

A more powerful explanation for the differences between female and male brains has to do with testosterone. This hormone is produced primarily by the testes, but some is also secreted by the adrenal glands. Females have testosterone circulating in their bloodstream from the adrenal gland,[13] but overall they have much less of the hormone than males. Testosterone and other male hormones are the primary stimulators of sexual desire in men as well as in women. Increased testosterone levels in both men and women result in more preoccupation with sex and in more frequent sexual encounters.

Three developmental periods seem particularly relevant to the effects of testosterone on the male brain.[14] During each of these times, the testosterone level in the male increases to activate dramatically the brain, which is sensitive to the hormone. The first, the prenatal period, occurs from eight to twenty-four weeks from the date of conception.[15]

Evidence is strong that during this first period fetal steroids affect the developing brain. Some evidence for this has been obtained by studying humans who have been inadvertently exposed to a large amount of hormones. One blatant example occurred when women were given diesthylstilbestrol (DES), a synthetic hormone, for the purpose of diminishing the possibility of miscarriages. Male children born to these women frequently showed typical female behavior, such as caring for dolls.[16]

Several aspects of human behavior – particularly gender identity and sexual orientation, but also physical aggression, toy preferences, rough play in juveniles, and mathematical, visuospatial, and verbal abilities – demonstrate sex-based differences.[17] Studies of girls with congenital adrenal hyperplasia, a disorder brought about by an enzymatic defect that produces large amounts of androgens and other adrenal steroids, have shown that the subjects were exposed to these hormones during the gestation period. Females with this defect are recognized as girls, though there may be genital virilization. They frequently demonstrate many male traits, preferring toys like trucks, and objects that can be constructed;[18] they are prone to rough behavior; as grown women they tend to experience bisexual desires or even have homosexual desires.[19]

Other conditions as well illustrate the impact of hormones on human psychosexual development. One rare condition involves deficiencies of other enzymes [5 (alpha)-reductase deficiency, and 17 (beta)-hydroxysteroid dehydrogenase deficiency].[20] Males afflicted with these rare conditions do not produce specific androgens that are important for normal masculinization of the genitalia during the prenatal period. In such individuals, however, it appears that fetal and postnatal androgens are produced that masculinize the brain. Children with these disorders may be misidentified and raised as females until puberty, when the testes secrete increased amounts of testosterone and the external genitalia become identifiable as distinctly male. Moreover, at puberty these children develop male sexual behavior and gender identity. This is thought to be due to the fact that the brain had been masculinized, causing these children to think and act like males despite their social rearing as females.

It is also believed that during the prenatal period the testosterone in the fetus affects the rate of the brain's growth, particularly its two hemispheres. Some have speculated that testosterone enhances the growth of the right hemisphere, thus increasing the size of this hemisphere, whereas in females the left hemisphere is larger.[21] The specialization of the two hemispheres – the right involved with systemizing and spatial ability, and the left with empathy and language skills[22] – creates a *laterality effect,* a differential of abilities between the two sides, which explains the cluster of abilities that are predominantly found in the male brain and those in the female brain.[23] However, although large amounts of testosterone will enhance the right hemisphere and the abilities associated with that hemisphere, there are limits to the effects that can be achieved. Beyond a certain limit, increased testosterone will provide no added benefit. Conversely, it will not bring about a diminishment of left-hemisphere capacities below a certain amount. A male with huge amounts of testosterone during this period of activation will not ultimately lack empathy completely.

The second period when testosterone is released into the body in larger than usual amounts occurs at around five months after birth. The third and final period occurs at puberty. During both these periods testosterone has effects on the brain. Male animals, such as rats, that are castrated at birth do not show the depth of cortex that would otherwise be conspicuous on the right hemisphere. Furthermore, they show less capacity for spatial ability and systemizing. Additionally, testosterone is necessary for aggressive behavior. If there is no testosterone, because of early castration, for example, aggression is minimized. If the testosterone is increased, the aggression also increases, but at a certain point it reaches a plateau and remains at that level. Within a range of between roughly 20% of normal testosterone to as high as twice the normal percentage, no discernible difference in aggression behavior has been noted.[24]

What does all this tell us about Jodi's instincts regarding her fiancé? Well, Jodi's perceptions about Art were correct. He did not, in fact, have her sensitivity or her capacity for empathy; and her attempts to bring about changes in their relationship on her own were unsuccessful. Art could not understand her objections to his behavior. To him the issue was simple: Her constant presence and availability left him sexually indifferent. From Art's perspective, however, this did not mean that the prospects for marriage were dim. Since his early teens Art had been incapable of sustaining a steady relationship for long. His capacity for thrills and excitement included discovering new territory – by which he meant discovering new women.

Before Jodi entered his life, he would sometimes date two and three women during the same evening. He expected sex on the first date; if he didn't succeed in having sex on the first date, he would rarely ask the woman out for a second. When he was successful, he might date the woman at the most four times, but would lose interest as soon as she became too interested or he felt that he was in control. He rationalized his dating habits in chats with his male friends, some of whom would describe similar behavior. This convinced Art that he was just a normally sexual single male with a lot of sexual energy navigating through a sea of available women.

However, Art's job, his family, and the fact that he was getting older pressured him to come to the conclusion that he had to settle down, marry, and raise a family soon. Jodi had all the qualities desirable in a wife and mother and would be an asset to him. Furthermore, Art realized that he would have to make some adjustments in his life. He would have to accept the fact that he would become bored shortly after initiating a steady relationship with Jodi (because such a fate would likely await him with any one person he saw on a continuing basis) and might have to consider other options, such as extramarital affairs.

After much insistence on Jodi's part, Art reluctantly agreed to see a therapist who worked with couples. At first the issue of "empathy" as described by Jodi made sense to the therapist. It was clear that Art didn't seem at all attuned to Jodi's feelings. However, it wasn't long before the therapist realized that something far more compelling was happening with Art. Although the therapist could not precisely define the problem, she strongly suspected that he was not being forthcoming with her during their sessions. For various unknown reasons he was not revealing his true thoughts about his needs, nor his feelings about Jodi and their relationship. As a result, the therapist referred Art to me for individual therapy.

Neurobiology of Social Awareness

As we've discussed above, even though the "male" brain may not be as empathetic as the female brain, men are nonetheless capable of some empathy – although empathy may be completely absent in cases of psychopathology, as in the case of Ricky Green. Certain brain conditions can result in a total absence of empathetic feelings, conditions that may be the result of genetic abnormalities or of injury to parts of the brain. Much has been written in recent years about the neurobiology of social awareness.[25] Recent studies are showing that specific structures in the brain are involved in social cognition. Most particularly, the temporal lobe is the center for perceiving relevant social stimuli. The amygdala[26] as well as the orbito-frontal cortex, the cingulate cortex (i.e., anterior and posterior), and the right somatosensory cortices (at the front of the parietal lobe) assist in linking the perception of stimuli to emotions – particularly motivation – and cognition.[27]

Besides these functions, there is increasing evidence that the frontal lobe, through its executive function plays a major role in what is called *theory of mind* capacity.[28] This refers to the ability of an individual to perceive and essentially to predict another person's behavior based on intuiting attributes of that person's mental state. Tests have shown that patients with frontal lobe deficits have significant difficulty in sensing another person's state of mind and behavior. In addition, the amygdala, which (as we saw in Chapter 6) is involved in linking emotional significance to stimuli, plays an important role in helping us evaluate the emotions of others.[29] The amygdala is closely connected to many other areas of the brain, most importantly, the prefrontal cortex – especially the orbitofrontal and left medial-frontal regions – which plays a critical role in empathizing. It is speculated that there is a specialized brain system that is adapted with theory of mind reasoning ability. Problems in this area of the brain create difficulties in social functioning often encountered in patients with frontal lobe damage.

Finally, there has been progress in investigating the parts of the brain that are involved with empathy and forgiveness. The ability to infer another person's mental states and particularly his or her intentions, which is in large part mediated by the medial prefrontal cortex, is only part of the picture.

With the use of functional MRI, researchers studying the ability of ten volunteers to read and evaluate social scenarios based on high-level social reasoning found that empathic evaluations, along with the capacity for forgiveness, activated specific parts of the brain.[30] These specific regions are the orbitofrontal gyrus (OFG), left superior frontal gyrus, and the precuneus (a region in the parietal lobe involved with memory-related imagery).[31] The impulse to forgive also resulted in activation of the posterior cingulate gyrus, whereas empathic impulses also activated both the left inferior frontal and the left anterior middle temporal gyri. In addition, cells in the superior temporal sulcus (STS), which are located in the temporal lobes and connect to the amygdala, are activated by the physical aspects (the "looks") of another person or animal.[32] This region of the brain picks up from the eyes the attitude and mood of the other – such as friendly, flirtatious, or aggressive. Functional MRI studies have shown that this region and the amygdala respond when an attempt is made to understand another person's mood, intentions, and mind.

Social cohesiveness is facilitated by the human capacities for forgiveness and empathy that result from activation of specific areas of the human brain. Abnormalities in the formation of these areas of the brain impact adversely on the capacities for empathy and forgiveness. Imaging studies of true psychopaths, who lack empathic abilities, are demonstrating structural and functional abnormalities in some of these key areas of the brain, particularly the prefrontal cortex and the limbic system.[33] An fMRI study of psychopaths demonstrated much less activity involving affect in the amygdala and hippocampal formation, as well as in the limbic structures such as the ventral striatum and cingulate gyri.[34]

Art's apparent lack of empathy seems reflective of the basic difference between the male and female brain, rather than of the presence of a genetic abnormality or structural defect. Moreover, during individual therapy other dimensions of his sexual thinking and behavior emerged. He admitted that in the past he had often been obsessed with sex. If he passed an attractive, stylishly dressed woman walking down Fifth Avenue, he would stare at her body and become sexually aroused. By the time he would arrive at work his mind would be nearly in a trance, completely occupied with sex. In a locked drawer of his desk he kept several magazines, like *Playboy* and *Penthouse*, with photos of nude women, which he would dwell on during the remainder of the day.

If by the time Art's workday ended he was unable to get his mind off sex and didn't have a date that evening, he would go to a massage parlor in the city. This occurred at least twice a month, though some times more often. At the massage parlor he could relax, have a few drinks, snort cocaine – which enhanced him sexually – and be physically stimulated to orgasm by attractive young Chinese or Thai women. He might stay at the parlor for hours, so that by the time he reached his apartment early the next morning, he would be exhausted – in large part from the cocaine. He would have to call in sick and might not return to work till a few days later.

In between visits to massage parlors, Art admitted that he would frequently log on to the Internet and visit chat rooms for sex. These rooms offered everything: women who offered oral sex, genital intercourse, threesomes, the whole works. He had a large menu of sexual choices and interests before him to choose from, including bisexuality. At first he would log onto the chat rooms and simply "eavesdrop" on the dialogue among the visitors. But in time Art began to contact women in the rooms and engage in sexual talk himself. When Jodi was staying with him, he would wait until she fell asleep, and then take his laptop into the living room to log onto the chat rooms. Frequently the content would stimulate him sexually to the point of masturbation and orgasm. On occasions he would get the woman's phone number and call her to engage in phone sex. One night Jodi was having difficulty sleeping and walked in on him as he was chatting on the Internet. He quickly shifted the screen to a financial page and acted as though he were researching European futures. Some days he was so sexually driven that he would lock the door to his office, go online, and experience sexual pleasure.

Art divulged that this was a secret part of his life. No one in his family or at work knew of his escapades into massage parlors. Nor did they suspect his somewhat promiscuous sexual behavior, or that he was preoccupied with sex. The image he presented to his family, friends, and colleagues was completely the opposite. They thought of him as a serious, achievement-oriented young man whose primary preoccupation was success and whose secondary interests lay in normal heterosexual socializing. In the counseling sessions Jodi had admitted that she was attracted to him because of his intelligence, intensity, and single-minded determination.

We will continue the story of Art and Jodi in Chapter 8.

8

Brain Biology and Sex

The stimuli that induce sexual arousal between men and women differ. Men are far more sexually aroused by visual erotic stimuli than are women. Functional MRI studies were conducted on twenty men and twenty women to compare their sexual arousal while they were viewing excerpts from neutral films and from erotic films.[1] The level of sexual arousal was much higher in the males during the viewing of the erotic films. In both males and females the erotic films induced increased activation of several parts of the brain, most particularly the anterior cingulate, medial prefrontal, insular, occipito-temporal and orbitofrontal cortices, along with the amygdala and ventral striatum.

But something additional happened in the male brains. Activation occurred in both the thalamus and the hypothalamus, but in the latter it was much more intense. The hypothalamus is known to have a critical role in sexual behavior and physiological arousal. The researchers found that in males the intensity of sexual arousal was positively correlated with the degree of activation of the hypothalamus.

This study was confirmed by other studies that showed that sexual arousal from erotic film excerpts was associated with increased activity in the right amygdala, right anterior temporal pole, and the hypothalamus. The right superior frontal gyrus and right anterior cingulate gyrus were activated by attempts to inhibit the sexual arousal from the erotic films. The researchers concluded that humans implement self-regulation through a neural circuit involving some prefrontal regions and limbic structures.[2] Studies have also shown the relationship between brain activation of specific areas and sexual response. One such study involved exposing healthy young heterosexual males to two sequences of video material.[3] This material consisted of segments involving sports, relaxation, and erotic images. These were presented in an unpredicted order. Functional MRI of brain activation and penile turgidity were tested. These showed that strong activation of regions of the brain – the claustrum, left putamen, and caudate; middle temporal and occipital gyri; right sensorimotor and premotor regions; and bilateral cingulate gyrus – were concomitant with penile turgidity during sexual arousal. Less activation occurred in the right hypothalamus.

Studies in male rats have shown that dopamine activity in parts of the brain such as the medial preoptic area (near the front of the hypothalamus), which influences motivation for sexual behavior, plays a critical role in sexuality.[4] The researchers determined that during precopulatory exposure of a male to a female in estrous, the dopamine levels increased in the medial preoptic area, as did sexual motivation and copulatory proficiency. This increase did not occur with exposure to another male. Studies of animals with lesions of the medial preoptic area, which has widespread connections with the limbic system, have shown major impairment in male copulatory behavior.[5] This occurs primarily because the afflicted male is unable to recognize the sexual partner.

What seems clear from these studies is that there is a complex interplay between steroid hormone actions that impact on specific regions of the brain.[6] This impact induces sexual arousability, as do expectations from past experiences that have led to sexual reward. Therefore, the hormone actions essentially set the stage through inducing sexual excitement and arousal for sexual activity. However, each animal's or human's history of sexual behavior and reward outcome shapes the power of sexual incentives in any one situation.

There are unusual syndromes that reveal the importance of regions of the brain for normal sexual behavior. One such syndrome is called Klüver–Bucy syndrome.[7] This has been described in adults and recently in young children suffering from acute herpes simplex encephalitis. In adults this condition might occur as a result of a stroke, or of bilateral removal of temporal lobes due to accident or tumor resection.[8] The syndrome has also been seen in patients who have undergone frontal lobotomies.[9] The syndrome is characterized by symptoms ranging from altered emotional behavior to hyperorality and hypersexuality, to indifference or minimal social attachment to close relatives.

The striking feature of hypersexuality may relate to damage that occurs in the limbic system, particularly to the amygdala. Studies show that the medial amygdala plays a major role in controlling a male's sexual motivation.[10] Patients suffering from hypersexuality exhibit a very high sexual drive. This drive is not selective; it may be directed to anything around the afflicted person, even in some situations to inanimate objects.[11] In children, this hypersexuality may be manifested by intermittent thrusting of the pelvis, holding of one's genitals, or rubbing the genitals in a masturbatory movement on the bed.

During Art's one-on-one therapy session, he came to recognize that he had become obsessed with sex. However, much of his obsession seemed to be limited to desiring sexual novelty and experiencing arousal. He was not as interested in orgasm per se, though he admitted that he frequently ended his cocaine and chat sessions with an orgasm.

I asked him if he had developed relationships with any of the women he chatted with online. He said that was not in the cards. He had once been tempted to meet one woman with whom he had communicated several times online and on the phone, but he'd done nothing about it. Art insisted that his sexual interest in these women was limited to the time they spent online together. He had no desire to know them, or to integrate them into his life in any way. The massage parlors and Internet were only mechanisms for relieving his intense sexual tensions and desires. "Purely mechanical," he said.

Jodi was different. He claimed he really wanted to love her and feel bonded to her. The sex was good at times; at others not so good. But that was not what she was about in his life. She represented something potentially stable, permanent, a perfect person to marry for long-term companionship and to be the mother of his children.

Art felt that sexual pleasure was not the same as love. He could become sexually aroused by, and perhaps reach orgasm with, many women (he even wondered at times if the same would happen for him with men), but he could love only one. He felt he was hyper-sexed and that he had little control over this aspect of his emotions. At times his mind would be filled with only sexual images; he would then crave fulfillment through physical pleasure. When this was feasible, he would have little option but to pursue this pleasure. Overcome by lust, it would be nearly impossible for him to shift his thoughts to nonsexual matters.

Lust, Attraction, Love: The Path to Sexual Reward

Lust is a primitive human feeling, a strong craving for pleasure,[12] sexual pleasure for the most part. As we've already seen, men are different from women in this regard. Men are quickly aroused by erotic images,[13] which excite the amygdala – that part of the brain located on the brain reward circuit. The amygdala is involved in the anticipation of positive feelings.[14] Two factors translate this an-ticipation of positive feelings into a powerful force for sexual pleas-ure and make the amygdala the primary site for anticipating sex (or we might say that, given its critical connections to the prefrontal cortex, the amygdala becomes the base for motivation toward sex-ual reward).[15] In humans and some primates, the whole brain, in-cluding decision-making regions, is involved in sex,[16] and particu-larly in the selection of a mate.

However, on the level of emotional inducements, structures in the limbic system serve an essential purpose.[17] First, the amygdala, particularly the medial section of the amygdala, is known to be rich in testosterone receptor cells.[18] Studies have shown that the various nuclei of the medial amygdala are much larger in males than in fe-males. Therefore, if you castrate a male rat, in a short time its me-dial amygdala will shrink in size to roughly that of a female rat.

In rats and humans, as pointed out by Baron-Cohen, injury to the amygdala will bring about pronounced social aberrancies.[19]

Second, the amygdala has intricate connections with the visual system in the brain. We've seen earlier that sexually provocative images enhance male excitement. The impact of these images is most likely mediated through activation of the amygdala.

But a recent study of activation of the brain during male ejaculation in humans adds a wrinkle to the knowledge we have gained from animals and some research on humans about the activation of brain regions (particularly the amygdala and hypothalamus) and sexual excitement.[20] In this study eleven right-handed, heterosexual men were scanned during sexual excitement and ejaculation with the use of positron emission tomography (PET). The researchers discovered that the ventral tegmental area (VTA; see Chapter 4's illustrations), along with other areas of the mesodiencephalic transition zone (subparafascicular nucleus, lateral central tegmental field, and medial ventral thalamus), were among the strongest activated.[21] The VTA is particularly important because it plays a pivotal role in many reward behaviors. Increased activation of this region occurs during heroin and cocaine rushes.[22] In fact, there is evidence that heroin addicts experience something similar to orgasmic pleasure when taking the drug.[23] This mechanism common to drug addiction might also explain the biochemical basis for sexual addiction.

In the study mentioned above, parts of the cerebellum, which is involved in emotional processing, were also strongly activated. Less strongly activated were parts of the striatum (lateral putamen, claustrum, and insula) and parts of the right prefrontal cortex (likely involved with the timing and place of ejaculation), the right parietal lobe (which probably relates to focus on body surfaces), and the precuneus, a region in the parietal lobe associated with visual imagery.[24]

A surprising outcome of the study was that the amygdala and medial preoptic (hypothalamus) areas, which in rats appear to play an important role in arousal and ejaculation, were not activated during these periods in the human subjects.[25] One interpretation of the difference between the rat studies and this study might be that the amygdala and medial preoptic areas of the human brain help to create the conditions for sexual behavior, but don't participate as much in the actual reward. The amygdala, as we've discussed above, appears to be important for anticipating positive feelings, and thus shapes the motivation for achieving those rewards.

Studies have confirmed that strong positive correlations exist among appetite, aversive stimuli, and amygdalar activity.[26] In this regard, men and women show similar increased activation from sexual arousal, men differing in their heightened amygdalar activation to visual stimuli. The evidence is strong, therefore, that the amygdala processes biologically salient (or prominent) stimuli, whether appetitive or aversive,[27] and induces rapid responses by activation of other areas of the brain, most particularly the hypothalamus.[28] The amygdala is not alone in its role as a motivator for obtaining a reward. Recent studies are showing that a very old part of the brain, the caudate nucleus, also participates in assessing possible rewards, deciding on a particular reward, and providing motivation and strategy for acquiring that desired experience.[29]

The study of brain activation during ejaculation shows that activation of the medial temporal lobe, which includes the amygdala, has an inverse relationship with sexual arousal and penile tumescence. This part of the brain becomes deactivated as arousal reaches orgasm. Deactivation of the amygdala also occurs in a cocaine rush, which seems to suggest a relationship between this deactivation and the experiencing of euphoric states, such as that experienced during orgasm. One interpretation of this finding, which would reconcile the seeming inconsistency of other findings on the amygdala's role in processing biologically salient appetitive stimuli, might be that from the moment of sexual arousal to ejaculation, the amygdala's deactivation may be a necessary component for achieving a euphoric condition.[30] The deactivation at a particular key moment – that just before orgasm – lengthens the distance to the euphoric pleasurable state, thereby augmenting the intensity of the pleasurable experience.

Frequently one hears a woman or man say, after a blind date, that "there was no chemistry" with the other person, no "sparks," nothing that excited them about the date. In truth, attraction between people is actually a chemical phenomenon that takes place in the brain. Studies are pointing to particular neurotransmitters like dopamine, and perhaps less so norepinephrine, as largely responsible for mediating "chemistry" or attraction between people.[31] This need for "chemistry" is not unique to humans. It has also been shown to be true in the animal world, particularly among mammals. One particular animal that has been studied extensively and that illustrates this "chemistry" is the prairie vole (a species of rodent that lives in the Midwest).[32] This small animal forms a bond with a partner for raising their young. Studies have shown that following coitus between a female vole in estrous and a male vole, the dopamine level increases dramatically in the nucleus accumbens (where the caudate nucleus meets the putamen; see Chapter 4's illustrations). This part of the limbic system is known to be associated with pleasure, craving, and addiction in humans.[33]

A study of humans involving fMRI scans of eight males and eight females supports the key role that dopamine plays in human attraction.[34] In this study the subjects were directed to look at colored images of forty different faces. The eyes of these images were focused in different directions, some directly at the viewer and others away from the viewer. Following the viewing of the images and the fMRI scanning of the brain, the participants were asked to rate the faces they looked at in terms of attractiveness. The researchers discovered that facial attractiveness per se did not result in any particular brain activation. However, they discovered that when the gaze of the image was directed at the participants, there was a direct positive correlation between attractiveness and activation of the ventral striatum and other dopaminergic regions, which are strongly linked to the prediction of reward.[35]

The study suggests that the ventral striatum is involved with evaluating stimuli related to social interactions. Furthermore, the firings of the dopaminergic neurons that project to the ventral striatum predict error in future rewards. These neurons increase firing when an unexpected reward occurs, and decrease when an anticipated reward fails to occur. In other words, a returned gaze from an attractive face leads to an enhanced neuronal response. In contrast, both the failure to make eye contact with an attractive face and the achievement of actual eye contact with an unattractive face produce disappointing outcomes, manifested by decreased activation in the dopaminergic system.[36]

According to the anthropologist Helen Fisher, who has completed an fMRI study of seventeen people who had fallen in love, romantic love is separate from the sex drive.[37] She claims romantic love is motivated by the need for attachment, the drive to choose and prefer a specific mate with the overall objective of minimizing the energy and time devoted to mating and thus enabling individuals to fulfill "species-specific parental duties."[38] Fisher's study, conducted with researchers at two medical schools in the New York City area, identified a brain circuitry that involved activation of the dopamine pathways associated with motivation and reward. She claims that the regions of activation changed over time as the basic relationship continued.

As part of the research, the subjects were scanned with fMRI first to establish a baseline. They were then scanned again while viewing pictures of their partners with whom they had fallen in love. This was followed by looking at neutral images – random pictures – in large number on a screen.[39] The process was repeated six times, allowing for many scans of brain regions during the viewings.

Fisher focused primarily on the caudate nucleus as a major activating center when people experience passionate love. The power of this center is augmented by the ventral tegmental area, a part of the reward circuitry that is rich in dopamine as well as norepinephrine.[40] Fisher found that couples who remain in love for an extended period showed changes in the brain centers that were activated. After a few years the major activity occurs in the anterior cingulate cortex (center for interaction of emotions, attention, and working memory) and the insular cortex, an oval region within the cerebral cortex where information about bodily sensations is gathered.[41] The reasons for this shift are not understood, though they may reflect the consolidating of memories of the emotions associated with the love relationship.[42]

Before Fisher's research was published, Bartels and Zeki conducted fMRI studies of the brains of seventeen subjects who were in love.[43] As in the Fisher study, the scanning occurred while the subjects viewed pictures of their partners. This scanning contrasted with scans of brain activity while these same subjects viewed the pictures of friends of comparable sex, age, and length of friendship. The researchers found that when subjects viewed their love partners there was activation in the anterior cingulate cortex, the insular cortex, and in subcortical nucleii like the caudate and putamen.[44] At the same time that these centers were activated, there was corresponding deactivation of the posterior cingulate gyrus and the amygdala.

The authors pointed out that the sites for activation during romantic love appear to be different from those activated while experiencing other emotions such as lust, in which the amygdala and cingulate gyrus have an important role. They speculated that the affective state of "romantic love" involves a unique neural network. Through fMRI studies comparing maternal love with romantic love, they discovered that both of these states have their own unique regions that are activated, though they overlap by activating receptors in regions of the brain's reward system that are rich in attachment-mediating hormones, most particularly oxytocin and vasopressin.[45] The authors asserted that the deactivating of circuits (such as those involving the amygdala, insula, and cingulate cortex) associated with negative emotions and perhaps with critical social assessment enhances the bonding effect from the reward circuitry that they discovered. Fisher's study, however, shows that over time some of those more critical areas (the cingulate and insular cortices) are activated in a positive way to maintain the relationship.

The neurochemicals of social bonding are different from those associated with pleasure and the sex drive. Oxytocin and vasopressin are both produced in the gonads and in the hypothalamus, and both these hormones have been shown to be involved in selective social bonding, most particularly pair bonding and infant–caregiver attachment.[46] Receptor sites for both oxytocin and vasopressin are found throughout the limbic system, and also in the brain stem and other areas associated with emotion and reproductive and social behavior.

Sexual arousal and orgasm cause dramatic increases of these neuropeptide hormones in both men and women.[47] At orgasm men show striking increases, especially of vasopressin; whereas women show a significant rise in oxytocin.[48] Studies of the prairie vole support the notion that these hormones are essential for attachment. During orgasm male prairie voles show an increased level of vasopressin in their brains. Furthermore, when administered vasopressin the male prairie vole becomes more territorial: more attached and possessive of any female vole introduced into his space. Vasopressin in these animals seems to serve both the spousal and parental instincts.[49]

Though there are basic differences in the reward circuitries of lust and social bonding, the neurohormones involved in both these emotional conditions affect each other.[50] Increases in testosterone, which is important for sex drive, lust, and sexual pleasure, can under certain conditions increase both vasopressin and oxytocin levels, thus ensuring that sexual pleasure enriches the possibilities of attachment. Conversely, increases in oxytocin and vasopressin can result in greater amounts of circulating testosterone, ensuring that attachment can bring about lust. When this happens, feelings of attachment and romance will trigger sexual desires.

On the other hand, if the level of testosterone exceeds a certain limit, it may create a paradoxical effect, causing noticeable decreases in vasopressin and oxytocin and, similarly, a reduction of social bonding. Hence some sexual excitement helps the process of attachment, but too much can bring about the opposite effect. What's more, too much vasopressin can result in a decrease of testosterone, and thereby a diminution of sexual pleasure. It seems to be a complex dose-related problem.[51] We've all known men and women who are voracious about sexual intimacy. One of my married patients was consumed by sexual thoughts and was so needy for physical sex that she would sell her sexual services. She didn't need the money; she needed the sex. But in such cases there is little attachment with the object of that physical affection.[52]

The therapy with Art moved very slowly. He understood on an intellectual level that he needed to change, but his emotional needs were too compelling. Through the couples therapy Jodi held on to the relationship, though Art felt she was much less committed to the idea that they would end up together. Art, on the other hand, remained committed, waiting to see if the relationship would make it to the next step, although he acknowledged that he was unlikely to change much of his sexual behavior.

Early in the therapy it seemed he was making some good progress. He had stopped the cocaine massage sessions and was spending more time with Jodi. However, he couldn't sustain this for very long. During one of the sessions he admitted that he had recently had a homosexual fling with someone he met in a chat room. He didn't feel psychologically connected to the man, who wanted more from the relationship, so he found a female sex partner, a prostitute, whom he saw several times to meet his sexual needs without expecting more.

Things didn't seem to be changing for the better. One evening Jodi, who was feeling increasingly disconnected from Art, became suspicious about how he was spending his time away from her. She found several hundred dollars in cash in one of the pockets of his pants that she was preparing to bring to the dry cleaner. She asked him what the money was for and confronted him about his activities outside of their time together. Art stumbled during the conversation, and Jodi picked up his ambivalence. She asked him a direct question: Was he having sex with another woman? He was caught off guard and admitted to her that he occasionally had sex with a prostitute, but was not in any way psychologically involved with her.

Jodi reacted hostilely to his confession, and decided that was the last straw. She broke off the relationship, which traumatized him. They terminated therapy together, but he wanted to remain in individual therapy to help him through the loss.

Who Pleases Whom

Sexual preferences refer to an individual's choice or preference on how to achieve orgasm.[53] These preferences can vary from the conventional attraction for the opposite sex, which ensures the survival of the species, to preferences for same sex, for children, for other species, or for various kinds of behavior that are irrelevant to the reproduction of the species. From a Darwinian perspective, sexual acts that cannot result in reproduction are anomalous.[54]

Although the biology of sexual preference has been researched extensively, it is not fully understood. However, certain findings have informed our knowledge of this aspect of human relationships. To begin with, the evidence is strong that people do not choose their sexual interests; rather, they discover their general preferences, or sexual orientation, during the onset of puberty. Sexual orientation seems to be the result of hormonal events occurring during gestation that affect the organization of neural circuitry. We have discussed in Chapter 7 how genetic and other factors such as immunology can impact on the effects of androgens (testosterone in particular) on the fetus and the resultant consequences for gender identification and sexual preference.[55]

Heterosexual men have certain preferences that seem biological. They generally prefer young females endowed with physical attributes indicative of health and fertility.[56] On the other hand, heterosexual men seem to be inclined toward many sexual partners, and desire sexual novelty. This may include bisexual experiences, which are common among men, though such experiences rarely translate into bisexual preferences. Art, who was highly sexed, experimented with homosexuality but did not choose to bond to a same-sex individual, nor had he any desire to adopt that style of sexual behavior.[57] Alternatively, some men become attached to other men without desiring or experiencing same-gender sex.[58] We've seen in the discussions of lust and social bonding that these two types of relating involve different hormones and neural circuitries, though they may affect each other.

Homosexuality has long been thought to be a behavior limited to humans, with the implication that it was a lifestyle choice, not a biologically determined condition. Recent studies of animals have debunked that viewpoint. Homosexuality among animals has been found in nearly all species, from monkeys, bonobos, and chimpanzees to birds (such as western gulls) and even dolphins. A recent article in the Arts & Ideas section of the *New York Times* told of two male chinstrap penguins, Roy and Silo, in the Central Park Zoo that exhibit "ecstatic behavior" (entwine their necks, vocalize to each other, have sex).[59] When an egg was introduced into their nest, they both sat on it in turn, incubating it until a chick was born. They then raised the chick together.

Homosexuality, which seems to be caused by differences in neuro-humeral activity during the prenatal phase, also appears to be heritable in part,[60] with some indication that the genetic transmission is through the maternal side.[61] We've seen that abnormalities that limit testosterone during the prenatal period can affect gender as well as increase the likelihood that a male will become homosexual. Some biological similarities seem to exist between women and homosexual men: the anterior commissure, which has been shown to be larger in women than men, also seems to be larger in homosexual men than it is in heterosexual males.[62] On cognitive tests, it appears that homosexual men's scores are more similar to women's scores than to those of heterosexual men; that is, they evidence better verbal scores than spatial capacities.

Some years ago, researchers examining the effects of prenatal levels of testosterone and estrogen on sexual orientation had made some unusual correlations. One study involving a small group of homosexuals showed apparent differences in the length of fingers when compared with heterosexuals. They found that the ratio of the length of the second and fourth digits is positively related to prenatal estrogen and negatively to prenatal testosterone.[63] The 2D:4D digits ratio was lower in eighty-eight homosexual men tested versus eighty-eight controls. Other studies have shown that homosexual men have a 50% greater probability of being left-handed than do heterosexual men.[64] Recently Swedish researchers reported a biological difference in the responses of heterosexual and homosexual men to sexually arousing odors (pheromones).[65] Focusing on smell-related areas of the brain, most particularly the hypothalamus (medial preoptic and anterior area), with positron emission tomography, the researchers discovered that homosexual men (similar to heterosexual women) displayed maximal activation of that part of the brain in response to a testosterone derivative detected in male sweat. In contrast, heterosexual males responded to pheromones of an estrogen derivative found in women's urine.

Sexual interest in children, or pedophilia, appears from retrospective reports of offenders to develop before puberty.[66] Studies have shown that many pedophiles reported that, when children themselves, they were curious to see other children in the nude, and that this curiosity continued into adulthood. Furthermore, most sex offenders deny experiencing any sexual contact with adults when they themselves were children. Basically the evidence that early sexual experiences are responsible for this condition is weak. Most likely the development of pedophilia, like the development of homosexuality, has more to do with biological malfunction occurring during the prenatal phase of development in the masculinization of the brain.[67]

Pedophilia would be classified as a *paraphilia,* that is, one of the socially deviant sexual behaviors, exhibited primarily by males, that are characteristically compelling, repetitive, harmful to others, and personally distressing – and that manifest serious psychosocial impairment.[68] These disorders seem to involve a serious dysfunction of sexual appetite in the afflicted person. There is a persistent increase in sexual appetitive behavior, an enhancement of the desire phase of sex involving increased sexual arousal and sexual motivation.

Evidence is strong that these disorders are reflective of *monoaminergic dysregulation,* which means an imbalance of the monoamine neurotransmitters (dopamine, norepinephrine, and serotonin).[69] Higher levels of catecholamine metabolites – dopamine and norepinephrine – have been shown in compulsive paraphiliacs.[70] Dopamine and norepinephrine increase sexual desire, whereas serotonin results in a decrease in sexual arousal and functioning. Patients taking antidepressant medication such as selective serotonin reuptake inhibitors (SSRIs), which increase the concentration of serotonin at the synapses, frequently complain of sexual dysfunction while on the medication. As might be expected, treatment with SSRIs has shown benefits in minimizing sexual arousal and motivation.[71] Serotonin is also essential for modulating many neurobiological functions.[72] Decrease in serotonergic neurotransmission, which may be due to a decrease in the level of serotonin or in the sensitivity of serotonin receptors, leads to behavior disinhibition.

As discussed above, testosterone is the most important hormone for enhancing sexual desires. Animal studies have shown that testosterone impacts on the monoamine neurotransmitters by affecting the sensitivity of neurotransmitter receptors in the hypothalamus (medial preoptic and lateral hypothalamic nuclei).[73] Testosterone increases the sensitivity of dopamine receptors, and reduces the sensitivity of serotonin receptors, in the hypothalamus. High levels of testosterone, therefore, exacerbate the effects of the type of monoaminergic dysregulation (increased production of dopamine and norepinephrine, and decreased production of serotonin) that is seen in the paraphilias.

The Morality of Sexual Behavior

What we have learned from this discussion is that hormones and neurotransmitters have the basic role in determining sexual behavior and social bonding. During prenatal development the androgens, particularly testosterone, have a decisive effect on gender and sexual orientation. Testosterone is also a major factor in sexual arousal in both men and women, though when present in men in high concentrations it can induce serious dysfunctional behavior, like sexual addiction and the paraphilias, through its capacity to enhance or diminish effects on monoamine receptor sites.

The ventral tegmental area has been shown to be activated during sexual excitement. This area of the brain, along with other parts of the limbic system – particularly the nucleus accumbens – is strongly activated in drug addicts when they use cocaine or heroin. From a biological perspective the activation of the amygdala and hypothalamus during sexual arousal, and then sudden deactivation at the height of sexual excitement and ejaculation, may explain the euphoria that is experienced at orgasm. Both this mechanism and the activation of the VTA produce the "rush" characteristic of a "high" from drugs, which also occurs during sexual excitement.

As we discussed in Chapter 4, the emotional parts of the brain impact on the frontal lobe, which is the center for decision making and conscious control of behavior. The feeling states created by the limbic system, in particular, shape an individual's decision making. These feelings, according to Damasio's somatic marker hypothesis – the notion (encountered briefly in Chapter 6) that emotions have a pivotal role in the reasoning process – inform the brain for reward acquisition. Furthermore, in an exploration of the biology of social bonding we learned that the neurochemicals associated with attachment (oxytocin and vasopressin) are different from those involved with lust (testosterone-induced dopamine and norepinephrine).

The neurochemicals involved with these circuits affect one other. An increase in testosterone and dopamine, which is important for sexual drive, can result in an increase in vasopressin and oxytocin; increases in these neurochemicals responsible for social bonding can result in greater circulating levels of the neurochemicals of lust. However, if the neurochemicals of lust reach excessive levels, they will dampen the circulating levels of the neurochemicals of social bonding. The converse is also true. Therefore, some individuals with elevated levels of testosterone or dopamine will be unable to experience social bonding. They will seek out sexual contact, but never allow attachment to occur. Hormones and their influence on the brain may render an individual incapable of controlling sexual impulses.

On an intellectual level, Art wanted a long-term relationship with Jodi. However, his sexual desires, mediated by the neurochemicals of lust, were compelling and determined much of his behavior. The biochemical effects of imbalances in the neurochemicals in Art's brain further reduced his capacity for empathy.

To some extent this lessened capacity is basic to the male brain. In some men the empathy is further reduced by structural and functional abnormalities of key areas of the brain (the orbitofrontal gyrus, left superior frontal gyrus, posterior cingulate gyrus, and superior temporal sulcus) shown to be important centers for empathy and forgiveness.

Empathy, or the ability to intuit another person's attitude and mood, is an essential component for developing a moral sense. It allows one to understand, on both an emotional and cognitive level, the mind of another person and the ways in which one's behavior will impact on another. Empathy, therefore, is a critical factor in social cohesiveness. When it is at a reduced level, the results are destructive – certainly in terms of achieving a worthwhile relationship. The combination of imbalances in Art's neurochemicals of lust and social bonding, along with his inability to empathize, resulted in an inability to control his behavior in order to achieve successful bonding with Jodi. Art was not a psychopath, who basically lacks the capacity for empathy and therefore is destructive to society. The bottom line, however, is that his behavior was biologically compelled and this compulsion shaped his decisions and affected his ability to initiate controls.

On the other hand, after his breakup with Jodi and several months of individual therapy, Art found another relationship with a woman ten years older than he who had been through a divorce. He admitted that he still got the urge on occasions to get involved with other women, including prostitutes, but this time around he could admit that he had these feelings and discuss them with the therapist. He knew it would be a long and at times rocky road to having a truly successful relationship, but he was now committed to make this happen.

Like Art, each of us holds our own position on the spectrum of being influenced by neurochemicals and brain changes from the prenatal phase of our development. We may not be able to control gender or sexual preferences, as these appear to be shaped prenatally and during the early years of development, but most of us can exert some control over our behavior. Nonetheless, the *degree* of that control is largely determined by biological forces. Thus, so is the morality of our choices for sexual behavior.

The biological issues of sexual behavior inevitably raise many serious questions. Perhaps the two most important are these:

What can be done about this sexual behavior, particularly when it affects others? and

What are the moral implications of altering brain biology to modify sexual behavior?

9

Deception

Among the factors that most undermine human relationships is "lying," and particularly as it involves betrayal. We have all been taught that since early childhood. Most of us have also been told we will be punished if we are caught in a lie. Yet children lie frequently. They often exaggerate what happens to them or hide the facts to make them look better in the eyes of their parents. They may make up stories – some fanciful, others with a semblance of what would seem to be a reasonable pattern of facts. Or, they may twist the truth to their advantage, or just plain deny their involvement in some disallowed activity.

What is fascinating about children lying is that they don't need to be taught how to do it, nor do they need to be encouraged by others. Lying seems to come about naturally, as if something innate in a child enables him or her to deny what is even obvious or construct complicated stories to avoid an unpleasant or punishing reaction from parents, teachers, or friends. To a large extent lying is both self-protecting and exciting. It is similar to the thrill we experience from getting a bargain at a sale. Similarly, lying offers the excitement of manipulating a situation to our benefit and getting away with it. For the most part, young children lie about actions – something they have or have not done. They are not sophisticated enough to lie about how they feel until they get older – at least nine or ten years of age. Many experts in child development, as far back as Piaget, believe that children need to achieve a certain level of intellectual development and insight to lie. Piaget thought that children don't begin to deceive others intentionally until around seven years of age.[1]

The reasons children lie have always been thought to center on self-protection.[2] A child may be afraid that he or she will be punished for disobeying a parent or authority figure. In some cases, children will overreact by expecting a stronger parental response than their behavior would warrant. A second reason children lie is that they imitate others who lie. Children learn to lie by observing their parents, other adults, or their schoolmates deal with the uncomfortable dilemma of whether or not to admit that they have done something wrong. The child quickly picks up that lying offers an opportunity to get away with forbidden actions or infractions of a moral code. In this sense, they recognize that lying can be an effective "punishment-avoidant" technique.

For some, lying may become a habit, in which case the child may lie compulsively, even without a real reason to lie. Compulsive lying is not the usual lying behavior of most children; it is often associated with more serious behavioral problems, such as cheating on tests, violence, truancy, and impulsivity.[3]

Psychologists and behaviorists believe – Ana Freud was probably the first to propose this – that children learn to lie because they fear being punished when they are disobedient. However, this may not be the whole story. Some studies have shown that the instinct to tell a falsehood, even in a three-year-old child, seems unrelated to whether the child thought he or she would be punished.[4] It may be associated with simply not wanting to be caught, even if the only outcome is that the child feels embarrassed.

Children are not alone in this penchant for lying. Recent research on lying has shown rather staggering findings about the incidence and prevalence of deception.[5] Almost everyone at one time or another has told a lie. Furthermore up to 60 or more percent of people lie regularly.[6] The average number of lies told by an individual has been estimated to be as high as twenty-five during the course of a day. Adults are believed to lie to avoid trouble from others, to present themselves in the best light, or to prevent others from experiencing discomfort.

A long line of studies have shown that males lie nearly two to three times more often than females and that their primary objective in lying is to promote themselves. Men, these studies have said, lie not only in the workplace to achieve advantage by distorting their accomplishments, but also in the social world of dating and networking.

Women, on the other hand, lie primarily for self-protection. They may lie about a variety of things, such as how they spent their day, how they feel about their partners, medical reasons for not having sex, or that they have thoughts about another man or have become involved in a romantic affair.[7] But this finding of a difference between men and women might well be obsolete. By virtue of women becoming more involved in public affairs and corporate ambitions, one has to assume that their interests in lying are tending more in the direction of self-promotion, just like men.

Most people are not aware of how often they conceal the truth; one doesn't become aware of twisting the truth unless something major depends on the response. For example, most of us tell "white lies" – minor deceptions with little chance of harm to others – all the time, and feel no compunction in doing so. Some studies have shown that people "shade" the truth in their favor one to six times per hour during interactions with others.[8] Studies by researchers at the University of Virginia on the demographics of lying have corroborated the high frequency of lying[9] and shown that people lie particularly to those to whom they don't feel emotionally close. College students lie to their parents more than 50% of the time. In addition, studies of romantic relationships have shown that as many as one out of three interactions between lovers involves lies. People who are particularly manipulative are more inclined to lie, to feel comfortable about their lying, and to cheat and manipulate others for their personal gain.[10]

Is Lying Always Immoral?

What is a lie? A lie is not mere deception. For example, a zebra while running, because of its many stripes, affects the visual acuity of its enemies, thereby confusing them about where it is at any one moment and making itself difficult to capture and kill. This is clearly a deception; it is not, however, a lie because a lie requires an intention to deceive or mislead others about the truth. When it comes to intentionally communicating a falsehood likely to lead another person to think or act erroneously, most people have little doubt that lying is wrong. Moral philosophers from Saints Augustine and Thomas Aquinas[11] to Immanuel Kant[12] have seen lying as immoral mainly because it weakens the fabric of social relationships. Contemporary thinkers, like Sissela Bok, also view lying as destructive because trust in others is a necessary element for order and the healthy structure of society.[13]

But even though lying is universally condemned, it is prevalent – and not merely because of people's instinct for self-preservation. Because not all lying is equally damaging, we have to evaluate a spectrum of deception to determine the seriousness of a lie. "White lies" are usually innocuous, and the motive is often to make the listener feel good. A "white lie" might include the omission of information when that information would hurt an individual's feelings.

An innocuous "white lie" might be, for example, telling a woman at a cocktail party that she looks attractive in her new outfit, when in fact she may look quite unappealing. Another example is false flattery, such as complimenting a hostess for her dinner despite the fact that the guest found the food bland and tasteless.

White lies are generally so acceptable and so pervasive in social discourse that everyone expects them. Such lies have become part of the basic language of social intercourse.

Another rather innocuous type of "lying" is pretending,[14] which can be serious if the truth of the feigned role is concealed from others. Many years ago, when I was in medical school in Philadelphia, a man walked into a city hospital and passed himself off successfully as a surgeon. He had participated in several operations – sometimes as the principal surgeon – with a surgical text in hand before anyone realized that he was not part of the surgical staff and had never attended medical school, let alone received instruction in surgical techniques as a resident. Despite all that, no one was seriously injured, but the potential for major, if not fatal, injuries was very high. In addition, the patients as well as the staff were utterly deceived; all had put their trust into the hands of an imposter.

Serious lies motivated by self-interest are also prevalent. These lies may involve claims about one's abilities to handle a job, about the investment of money, about the level of one's loyalty or commitment to another person – the range is infinite. They take the form of overt falsehood, or language that is sufficiently equivocal to give a false impression.

"All's fair in love and war" is an old adage, but it is only partly true. During war the argument that anything goes is very strong. Deception is expected by all parties, since the objective is to win the battle. Either one does what one can, including deception, to gain the advantage over the adversary, or the alternative is to be defeated. We saw this play out during World War II through elaborate intelligence operations in which spies working for the English and American foreign services risked their lives to infiltrate the German military. Deception was not only acceptable in this context, but necessary for victory.

In matters of love, however, deception does not seem equally warranted or excusable. Human relationships are difficult under the best of circumstances. They become nearly impossible when a spouse or partner lies about involvements with others, makes claims of passionate love, and causes another to accept seriously the notion that their relationship is one of love and fidelity.

Perhaps the most outrageous deception in love I have seen personally was in a case on which I consulted about five years ago. This involved a man married for twenty years to the same woman, the mother of his two teenaged children. It turned out he also had a second family living eight miles away in a northern New Jersey suburban community. With his second wife he had a son who was fourteen. Neither family knew about the other. He was able to pull this off without any discovery for years. Neither wife would have ever learned about the existence of the other had it not been for a downturn in the man's financial situation. He had been working at two jobs, but one of the companies went bankrupt, which strained his finances considerably.

When it came time to help his eighteen-year-old son pay the tuition for a year at Rutgers, he was unable to come up with the money. His wife couldn't understand why he was having financial problems. She thought they lived well within their means. But then checks began to bounce, and she received telephone calls from creditors. He was unable to give a reasonable explanation for his financial problems. So she hired a detective, who learned of the existence of the second family.

When his first wife confronted him, he developed severe anxiety and panic and sought psychiatric help. During the session all the unusual facts of his life surfaced. Since childhood he had been unable to confront others or to say "no," which would disappoint them. During a rough spot in his marriage he had an affair with his second wife. She got pregnant, and he couldn't tell her about his marital status.

When his second wife learned that he was still married to his first wife, she sued for divorce and brought a civil suit against him for severe emotional distress. His first wife stood by him while he was in the midst of legal proceedings and the possibility of a criminal action against him for bigamy. Unfortunately, he lasted about six months in therapy, then suddenly dropped out.

Is Lying Hardwired in the Brain?

We can be sure that lying evolved from the process of natural selection. Clearly individual benefits from skillful lying and its payoffs have given humans an advantage in evolution. These benefits include self-protection and self-promotion, both of which work well enough to make the capacity to lie an evolutionary advantage. The fact that lying is exciting also points to natural selection. Since lying may have some desirable effects on social interactions, it would seem reasonable that natural selection would make lying a pleasurable experience.[15]

In addition to the process of natural selection, three other pieces of evidence seem to support the idea that lying is hardwired in the brain.

First, lying is not only a human behavior. Studies of primates and even lower animals have shown that lying is pervasive in the animal kingdom. Of course the key question is whether the animal is able to perceive the mind of another animal or human when the deceiver tries to manipulate a situation. In his book *Good Natured: The Origins of Right and Wrong in Humans and Other Animals*, Frans de Waal, a leading specialist in primate behavior, profiles the case of a gorilla who feigned that her arms were trapped by the bars of her cage.[16] The zookeeper rushed in to relieve the gorilla, which hid behind the door and ultimately trapped the keeper. It is difficult in such a case to insist that the gorilla was incapable of understanding the likely reaction of the keeper, and getting into the keeper's mind to manipulate the situation to the gorilla's advantage.

De Waal points out that chimpanzees are capable of projecting a false image of intention or knowledge to their own advantage. They are able, he claims, to discern how their behavior is interpreted by the outside world.[17] He points out that chimpanzees will often take a mouthful of water, appear to be doing other things in their cage, then spit it out at a stranger approaching them. People also have reported deception by dogs who will feign injury to secure food.

Much has been written about Koko and Michael, two gorillas that had been taught sign language. Penny Patterson, an expert in teaching sign language to apes, claimed that Koko intentionally lied under various situations to avoid punishment. During one such episode Koko reportedly dropped and broke a dish. When Patterson asked the ape what happened, Koko signaled that Michael was responsible.[18]

Second, the studies of children as young as three years of age who are capable of lying, even when punishment is not likely, strongly imply something innate in the brain. To children lying seems natural and is often pleasurable, particularly when the child is successful in manipulation.

Third, and finally, neuroscience is unlocking the mystery of where lying occurs in the brain. With imaging technologies such as functional MRI, researchers in the laboratory of Daniel Langleben at the University of Pennsylvania have discovered that a structure involved in decisions and error recognition, the anterior cingulate gyrus, and

parts that handle planning, working memory, and organization –
the prefrontal and premotor cortex – are activated during lying.
These areas of the brain are also concerned with focusing, paying
attention, and controlling as well as monitoring errors. When people lie, these brain areas are far busier than when they are telling
the truth.[19] The fact that the brain biologically accommodates for
lying argues strongly for genetic and biological hardwiring of the
system.

The Neuroscience of Detecting Lies

Research on the biology of lying has opened the door to the development of sophisticated neuroscience-based technologies for detecting when a lie occurs. Lie detection has been of fascination since
ancient times. Devices for detecting lies from the Middle Ages until
recently have been crude.[20] Tests for truthfulness included tying a
person up and throwing him or her into a lake or river. Those who
sank were seen as having told the truth. Another device was putting a hot iron on the tongue of the accused: If it burned, it established guilt.

During the past century, because of our understanding of the
human body's reactions to lying, detection devices, such as the traditional lie detector, were constructed to pick up physiological
changes in blood pressure, pulse, respiration, and perspiration. Humans can't lie without some alarm going off. The traditional lie detector, the polygraph, has been relatively effective at determining
if an individual is deceptive, but it is not always so accurate – there
are ways to get around the detection of a lie – as to be readily admissible in court to prove truth telling. Thermal imaging, particularly of blood flow around the eyes, though still in the experimental
stage, has been considered by some to have more potential as a
physiological marker of lying.

With the growing interest in lie detection of government institutions like the FBI and the CIA, as well as concern about the need
for surveillance fueled in large part by the terrorist activities of 9/11,
newer devices have entered the field that capitalize more directly

on the advances of neuroscience. Tests include the infrared brain scans that detect small changes in the prefrontal cortex, which is the center of decision making – including the decision to deceive.

So-called *brain fingerprinting* – the most advanced of the newer technologies – is done with the use of a helmet of electrodes placed on the subject that is attached to an electroencephalograph (EEG) machine.[21] While the subject is asked questions or presented pictures, the EEG records his (or her) brain waves. If he lies in response to a question to which only the offender would know the answer, a specific brain wave, called the P300 pattern, is produced. The presence of this wave reveals at a high level of accuracy that the person lied. Brain fingerprinting has been admissible in at least one legal case involving a capital crime, and will surely be used more in the future.[22]

Functional MRI for lie detection offers an exciting future for a test that focuses directly on the brain structures that have been shown to deal with decisions and error recognition – the anterior cingulate gyrus and the prefrontal cortex – during the telling of a lie.[23] Although still in the experimental stages of development, fMRI has revealed that during lying these specific areas of the brain are activated, creating a distinctive brain "print." This does not occur when the subject tells the truth. On the other hand there are confounding factors, such as the possibilities of activating these parts of the brain merely by having a thought that induces an anxiety-evoking event, unrelated to the problem that is being addressed by the examiner. However, more research is likely to improve the precision of fMRI for lie detection by identifying brain patterns that are highly specific.

With the refinement of lie-detecting techniques, it is likely that they will be used extensively not only by law enforcement agencies, but possibly even schools and the health care system. Though MRI machines are now very large and expensive, it will not be long before smaller units will be available that will serve the purposes of these social institutions. When this occurs, the issues will center on the moral questions of how these technologies are used. Most particularly, there will be concerns for the privacy rights of individuals, and regarding the opportunities for abuse and discrimination.

Take, for example, schools using a portable fMRI machine to determine if students are cheating during an examination. Or an example that would likely affect all of us who use airplanes regularly: being examined by an fMRI detector through the security process at an airport, when questions may be asked and brain structures studied. Such developments will bring us from the presumption that people are not guilty of lying unless something clearly suggests otherwise, to the possibility that people may well be lying unless the test shows they are not. Such a reversal of position is a potential serious wedge into our individual rights in this society.

10

The Biology of Money

Let's assume you've just had a windfall and inherited a million dollars from a distant relative. The local real estate market has just undergone a major run-up, reaching higher levels than ever. Interest rates are very low; stocks have declined at least 42% from their high a few years ago, but all the indicators suggest they may rally in the near future. You are facing a very difficult decision: Should you keep the money in interest-bearing notes at a low 3%, invest in some solid Dow Jones stocks, put some of the money in high-risk securities, or consider buying a condominium?

Ask your brain: At least three areas of the brain affect monetary decisions – the amygdala and hippocampus; the frontal lobe, especially the prefrontal cortex; and the anterior cingulate cortex (along with the dorsolateral [top–side] area of the prefrontal cortex).

The amygdala is the brain's hot spot for emotions. Through its linkages with the sensory cortex and the frontal lobes, the amygdala quickly inspects and looks for dangers and attractions in the outside world.[1] Once it has characterized the environment, it attaches an emotional importance to the stimulus, and then notifies the mind to act upon our emotions for our survival.[2]

Fear and anger are two of the most powerful emotions generated by the amygdala, which plays a major role in *conditioned fear,* that is, fear derived from exposure to a fear-inducing or frightening object or situation. Confronting a frightening event, the amygdala will induce the secretion of adrenaline – which intensifies panic and is capable of causing the event to be embedded in memory. The amygdala seems to be both the repository of learned information on conditioned fear and the mechanism for expression of fear once learning has occurred.[3]

We've long known that physical danger is threatening to the amygdala, which will direct the mind to either attack or escape, but lately we are discovering that the amygdala also responds to winning and losing. Changes in the magnitude of positive (reward) or negative reinforcement (no reward, or perhaps even punishment) bring about differential responses in the amygdala: The left side is activated during winning, the right during losing.[4] Economic dangers are especially threatening.

According to fMRI studies, losses have a profound activating effect on the amygdala.[5] It revs up, creating apprehension, anxiety, and fear, and these in turn cause the hypothalamus to accelerate, resulting in a full range of parasympathetic bodily symptoms – increased breathing, racing pulse, and profuse sweating. The amygdala is preparing for "fight or flight," much like our primitive ancestors when confronting a predatory animal. The expectation of loss also triggers the amygdala, creating that unpleasant feeling of anxiety in the pit of the stomach that we associate with uncertainty and a fear of losing something valuable. Gains also activate the amygdala, but not to the same extent.[6]

If we have had an earlier experience of a similar fearful event, such as a loss, the hippocampus, which frequently works in tandem with the amygdala, becomes activated.[7] Although the hippocampus does not generate emotions directly, it does have the power to affect arousal and quiescent reactions[8] by linking specific memories with emotions, thereby influencing the amygdala and the hypothalamus. For example, suddenly finding yourself alone in a dark alley might jog memories of an earlier experience of being mugged in an alley. The hippocampus would dredge up this linkage between the image of a dark alley and the fear of assault and create a fear response in the amygdala, which stores the emotion-conditioned memory, while firing off signals to the hypothalamus to generate an autonomic response such as increased pulse, sweating, and the sick sensation in the stomach.

A pattern of loss would elicit similar autonomic reactions. During the stock market downturn of the late 1990s, the pattern of loss continued over a protracted time. The hippocampus of every loser almost certainly registered this perduring loss, programming the memory of fear and anxiety of that period into long-term memory to be stored in the cerebral cortex.[9] Once reactivated, the hippocampus will uncover this history, which then affects the amygdala, creating more anxiety and fear. Thus, for some interested in investing in stocks now, the fear and anxiety experienced during the 1990s downturn may stop them from taking subsequent risks on otherwise rational investments.

Let's say your sudden good luck is to now inherit a commercial office building along with the million dollars from your distant relative. Your amygdala could be activated by several factors. Rising real estate prices would activate it positively if you didn't need the commercial real estate and were interested in selling as close to the high as possible. If, however, you were also experiencing pressure to purchase a home (because you need more space, for example), the increasing cost of real estate might represent the threat of potential loss of too much of your million-dollar windfall.

But these are not the only developments that might trigger the amygdala. Here are two possible scenarios. In the first, a prospective buyer who has recently sold a home at a profit perceives the rising cost of real estate as a potential loss of profits should he or she invest in another home. In the second, a buyer who has paid top dollar for a new property fears a sudden market collapse; the amygdala might produce a series of scary images associated with loss, and cause fear and apprehension.

Deciding to put your million bucks in stocks could also induce an amygdalar reaction. Given the decline of 42% over a period of years, the hippocampus could dredge up memories of fear and anxiety experienced during a past episode of financial loss. Keeping the money in a 3% interest-bearing note would offer stability without the prospect of winning or losing (since it is about the same rate as inflation); however, if the real estate or stock market improved, your amygdala might react to the potential loss of opportunity with your investment in fixed income-bearing notes.

It is, however, important to bear in mind that people do not have uniform amygdalar responses. Genetics and brain biology play an important role in how an individual's amygdala will react in given situations and the degree of that response. A recent study conducted at the National Institutes of Mental Health revealed one such genetic abnormality that affects the amygdala – a single gene that affects the brain's response to emotionally charged stimuli.[10] This gene is responsible for producing a protein that transports serotonin from the synapse back into the nerve cell after it has been released into the synapse. Some people are born with an abnormal gene that produces less of this "transport protein," thus allowing serotonin to accumulate and to overactivate the brain; this causes abnormal levels of fear, and may lead to withdrawal or disruptive aggressive behaviors.

Because of the amygdala's function in conditioned fear, the researchers did fMRI scans to observe the amygdala in individuals possessing either the normal or the variant gene, who were scanned both before and during the viewing of scary, angry faces. Those with the abnormal gene demonstrated considerable activation of the amygdala during the test, and reported experiencing greater fear. This biological range of response would apply to money matters as well. Those with lower production of the transport protein are more likely to react with excess of fear when confronted with a risky financial decision.

The second main area of the brain that influences financial decisions is the frontal lobe – most particularly the prefrontal cortex, "the brain's command post."[11] This cortex is essentially the chief executive officer of the brain because it is responsible for capacities such as purposefulness, intentionality, and complex decision making.[12] It plays a major role in human cognition.[13] As the "attention association area" of the brain, the prefrontal cortex orchestrates the necessary skills and behaviors to accomplish goals successfully. An illustration of this would be the integration of an intellectual skill, such as reading music, with motor skills in the hands for playing an instrument. This cortex organizes purposeful control and concentration of thinking to achieve well-defined objectives. It has the power to manage every phase of behavioral planning,[14] from the accumulation and synthesis of data, including mental images,[15] to learning associations, guiding decision making, and finally controlling reward-based behavior.[16]

The prefrontal cortex also has the ability to retain relevant information in working memory and to exclude irrelevant information that might interfere with rational decision making. Neurologists describe this process of sifting out unnecessary sensory input and ideas for furtherance of a specific goal as "redundancy."[17] The prefrontal lobe intentionally eliminates superfluous information so as to focus and concentrate the mind on important defined tasks. But at the same time, it has been demonstrated that the prefrontal lobe pays attention to, or even makes up, novel information in order to accomplish the important tasks at hand.[18]

Virtually every operating system of the brain has direct communication with the prefrontal cortex (see Chapter 4). This includes the premotor cortex, the association cortices, the basal ganglia, and the cerebellum. The prefrontal cortex is also connected to the major limbic structures, most particularly the amygdala, the hippocampus, and the hypothalamus, as well as the thalamus. As a result, the prefrontal cortex is able not only to send, receive, and analyze data from memory and current events, but also to draw conclusions and mitigate the emotions generated by a heated amygdala to arrive at a balanced judgment about sensory input and an appropriate course of conduct. When the limbic structures overreact to fear, the prefrontal cortex is often able to intervene and put reactions into perspective through careful evaluation of the data at hand.

By the same token, the prefrontal cortex and frontal lobes in general depend on the limbic structures for guidance in making "rational" decisions. Patients with early childhood injuries of the prefrontal cortex, especially the orbitofrontal cortex (the ventromedial section of the prefrontal cortex), show striking thought abnormalities resulting from an inability to benefit from information sent by limbic structures such as the amygdala.[19] Patients with damaged amygdalae also show abnormalities in their decision-making abilities because the prefrontal cortex is getting faulty signals from the amygdala.[20]

Much of our understanding of the importance of what the prefrontal lobe does has come from studying people with injuries that diminish the quality of their decision making. A particular "gambling" test has revealed a specific pattern in individuals with injured prefrontal cortices or damaged amygdalae.[21] Injured subjects are given four decks of cards containing varying schedules of reward and punishment unknown to them at the outset. The player-subjects not only do not know when a penalty may arise, but they receive no clue about how to estimate with any precision the net gains or losses from each deck. Nor do they know the total number of cards used in the game. They are asked to select cards from the decks. When the cards of decks A and B are turned over, the possible immediate reward is high. In contrast, for decks C and D the reward is low.

Decks A and B may also contain cards that have a high penalty. Subjects are allowed to switch their choices among the decks, but the system is constructed so that subjects choosing mainly from decks A and B will, on balance, experience a loss. Those choosing from C and D will experience an overall gain.

The testers compare the injured subjects to normal participants, using skin conductance responses (SCRs) to measure their physiological responses while they ponder their choices.[22] Injured subjects show no anticipatory SCRs and choose disadvantageously even when they can correctly describe the good and bad decks available for them to choose from for their own advantage. Normal participants, on the other hand, express a sense or "hunch" that decks A and B are riskier shortly after selecting from those decks. They also develop anticipatory SCRs, and before long, their behavior changes and they begin selecting from decks C and D.

This test points to the importance of hunches (sometimes called "covert biases") that help shape reasoning based upon available facts. Normal participants in this gambling task develop hunches; the injured subjects do not. The latter never learn to avoid selecting cards from the riskier decks.

Hunches are part of a complex process for nonconscious signaling, a capability informed by previous experiences that creates the emotional content for expectation of reward or punishment. In our card-playing experiment, damage to the amygdala prevents the triggering of a sensation of discomfort that the normal players experienced toward the riskier decks. In contrast, damage to the prefrontal cortex, especially the orbitofrontal cortex, prevents transfer of information about related past experiences from the amygdala and other limbic structures.[23] When either of these injuries is present, players cannot make "advantageous" choices, though they may be able to think about what they are doing. Paradoxically, however, such thought often has little effect, and the players continue the disadvantageous behavior.

Some patients with frontal lobe damage have difficulty making decisions, as is the case with amygdala-injured patients. But the frontal damage may have impaired their ability to use information from limbic structures advantageously. Researchers found that when presented with a financial decision-making task, patients with frontal lobe injuries were inconsistent in their use of advice provided by advisors and were poor at forecasting an economic outcome. Both these functions – heeding advice and forecasting outcome – relate to planning and working memory performance.[24]

This is not the whole story of how areas of the brain impact on how we would manage a windfall. The dorsolateral prefrontal cortex (i.e., its top and sides) and the anterior cingulate cortex, two areas of the brain that respond separately – or at times reinforce each other – to stimuli that occur in patterns of repetition, constitute the third major area of the brain that influences decisions involving money.[25] The prefrontal cortex accommodates to patterns of events or occurrences in the environment.[26] Events may be purely chance occurrences, but the prefrontal cortex, along with other interconnected parts of the brain, is always working to make sense of things and looking for patterns. Often for the prefrontal cortex, only two repetitions of a stimulus will create anticipation for the third; with an alternating pattern, six or more repeats may be necessary.[27]

When repetitive or alternating events violate expectations, the prefrontal lobe springs into action – how excitedly depends on how long the pattern has been in place.[28] For example, if I go to a casino every day and win at the slot machines, a loss will likely activate my prefrontal cortex. The longer the winning streak, the greater the activation of the prefrontal cortex when the streak stops, which can be emotionally upsetting by causing anxiety, depression, and even violent reactions such as kicking the slot machine. When the pattern is finally broken, neurons in the more primitive parts of the brain – the caudate, putamen, and insula – become more active. These areas of the brain respond by creating fear and apprehension, much as the amygdala does.[29] A possible consequence of these responses might favor more conservative, relatively safe behavior, such as preserving one's money by not participating in the casino activities even though that might mean no chance of winning big on the machines.

The anterior cingulate cortex is very active in complex problem solving,[30] and in recognizing error,[31] which includes recognizing inconsistencies that might reflect changes in the rhythm or repetition of a pattern. This latter ability is compatible with the ability of the prefrontal cortex to figure out the rhythm of patterns, react to disruptions or inconsistencies in repetition, and finally to forecast based on the patterns.

Studies of monkeys have shown that the closer the animal gets to achieving a reward, the greater its expectancy of motivation and reward. The neurons in the anterior cingulate cortex become progressively stronger when reward is expected. Studies have shown that the ACC plays an important role in judging the value of a reward; it also assesses the value of an action directed at achieving a specific outcome.[32] When the certainty of reward no longer exists, the progressive modulation in strength of activation disappears.[33]

The anterior cingulate cortex is strongly activated when something goes amiss between expectations (or plans) and the anticipated reward. Suppose that you invest in a stock and, based upon financial indicators, are led to expect an increase in its value. If the indicators actually switch in their significance – so that instead you get a loss in the value of the stock – the prefrontal cortex (especially the orbitofrontal cortex) and ACC are activated. The activations create a visceral response, or warning – such as that awful feeling in the pit of your stomach – that things are not right. Hence, the anterior cingulate cortex participates in identifying an error and creating a response,[34] and it is particularly activated during uncertainty.[35]

Recent studies are suggesting that the *posterior* cingulate cortex (PCC) serves to update the expectations of a reward in the light of changes in circumstances.[36] If some of the individual indicators of a stock rise continue to change prior to the movement of the stock, the posterior cingulate cortex registers these changes over time and continues to signal the diminishing likelihood of an increase in the stock's value.

In short you will give a major workout to your frontal lobe, particularly the prefrontal cortex, and to the anterior cingulate cortex in deciding what to do with your windfall. The hunches or biases created by the amygdala and other limbic structures will help guide the cognitive part of your brain toward a reasoned decision about what to do with the money. On the other hand, in an uncertain market the hot emotions of fear and anxiety generated by the amygdala could get out of control and induce an impetuous "fight or flight" reaction.

This is where the CEO capacity of the prefrontal lobe comes in to counteract the "fight or flight" reaction. This part of the brain will take control and move toward a balanced judgment about the money by evaluating the wisdom of "fight" versus "flight." Along with the anterior cingulate cortex, the prefrontal lobe will closely survey and perceive patterns in the investment environment. The trend of escalating cost of real estate would likely cause you to forecast that real estate would be the appropriate investment. On the other hand, the ACC, which is tuned into uncertainty and error detection, would consider conflicts in the indicators. A turnaround of the interest rates and the stabilization of stocks after a 42% fall might cause the ACC to nudge the prefrontal cortex to hold tight and do nothing, or to invest in stocks and other instruments.

The final decision may rest less on the capacities of the amygdala, the prefrontal cortex, and the anterior cingulate cortex and more on what makes people happy – which brings us to the neurotransmitter dopamine.

Dopamine: The Allure of Monetary Reward

We do not just consist of a bunch of gears whirring like a machine when our brain makes decisions concerning money. We also naturally approach the handling of money with a lot of emotional input, and that input is distinctly biased toward reward. It is at this focus on reward where we are likely to see morality issues surface.

The more rudimentary machinery – amygdala, anterior cingulate cortex, frontal lobe, and prefrontal cortex – is in communication with the brain's reward circuitry. The brain at its most basic is designed to obtain rewards and avoid punishment.[37] Appetite behaviors necessary for survival – sleep, eating, drinking, and sex – are reward-directed behaviors.[38] Motivated behaviors, such as remembering and learning, and the cognitive and emotional tasks of processing reward-directed behaviors all do their work primarily through the *dopamine system*.[39] This is very simply all the connecting cells that use the neurotransmitter dopamine to send and receive signals – that is, to communicate with each other.

The brain's reward circuitry consists of the frontal lobes and limbic structures, working together as a highly integrated network to produce feelings and behaviors.[40] The system is full of subtleties enabled by the participation of several distinct areas. One in particular, the nucleus accumbens (see Chapter 4's illustrations), has the job of figuring out if a potential reward is new or not. This part of the brain has been shown to be activated by the anticipation of rewards especially if the outcome is unpredictable.[41] Unexpected rewards are far more pleasurable than those that are predictable. The human brain loves risks. But, there are degrees of risk: A less predictable reward will activate more dopamine neurons to fire, thereby flooding the brain with dopamine, causing excitement, euphoria, and the desire to take additional risks.

Similar to cocaine's effects on neurons, money is reinforcing as a reward to humans because we have given it this capacity to stimulate.[42] Money seems to act on more different pathways of the reward system than do natural rewards, such as food and water. Being more predictable, natural rewards activate primary reward circuits.

Certain regions of the brain – particularly the orbitofrontal cortex[43] – have a central role in determining the "saliency" or importance of an event and experience, including money.[44] Stimulation of the dopamine receptors in these regions signals that an experience or event is deserving of attention and should be relegated to memory for future reference.[45] These brain regions also work together with the anterior cingulate cortex to prevent potentially harmful decisions. When an action or cue no longer predicts a reward, an individual stops the preceding action. If, however, these brain regions are damaged, the injured person is no longer able to determine that the reinforcer has lost its saliency.[46]

This process also applies to the relationship of a cue to a gain. Similar to the classic Pavlovian experiments of conditioning, the brain may react to a cue – perhaps something as simple as sitting down with the *Wall Street Journal* early in the morning – by producing dopamine, which creates a euphoric mood, a "high," even before one reads that an actual gain has been realized. In a sense there is a resemblance between the brain of someone predicting a financial gain and that of a drug abuser. A dopamine "buzz" is created by the cue, which prompts us to be more aggressive with our money.[47] When acting on the cue fails to produce a reward, the dopamine level still increases dramatically in expectation of a reward; but it can decrease just as dramatically, leaving us in a profound funk.

We've all known someone who seemed to care more about money than approval. Maybe it's true of most of us – at least one study suggests that it is. That study involved ten men between the ages of twenty-two and thirty-seven. The researchers gave them a "Go/No-go" task – instructions provided on a computer screen to press or not press the mouse within a specific time sequence – under two very different reinforcement circumstances. When the participants gave a correct response in accordance with the instructions, they were rewarded by one of two reinforcers: money or a simple "OK." Using positron emission tomography, the researchers found that behavior rewarded by money significantly activated dopamine centers. "OK" had a much weaker effect.[48]

So there you stand with your million-dollar windfall. The excitement comes from the prospect of acting in a manner that ensures an unpredictable reward. Let's say this would be investing in stocks. From the description of the economy at the time, stocks are the most uncertain choice, but a reward resulting from such a long shot would be very pleasurable. Your dopamine neurons become more active with risk. If the investment begins to go up, your brain will get excited over more investments in the same area. This will enhance the risk, surely, but also the likelihood of euphoria.

Let's assume that you went ahead and invested a large amount of money in company X, but that the stock's success was highly unpredictable. The unpredictability caused heightened stimulation of your dopamine receptors, thus adding to your anticipation and excitement that the stock would rise. That first week, you were a genius: The stock went up more than three dollars, and your dopamine level rose in much the same way. So you put more money into that company. But suddenly adding more money did not result in a greater increase of your holdings. The stock didn't move for months. The cue of adding money to this risk was strong enough that you became exhilarated by your belief in success, which of course is now just a pleasant memory.

But let's say the stock's value vacillated: It went up a few points, which reinforced the value of the cue to invest more money; but then it fell dramatically. While it was oscillating, adding more money made you feel good, but soon, realizing that the cue was no longer salient, you felt a wrenching sense of doom, akin to a dramatic shift from euphoria to severe depression. The result: You overreact and prematurely remove your money from the market. If enough people did that, the market would inevitably drop precipitously – which in fact it did in the late 1990s.

Greed Out of Control

The late 1990s and early 2000s witnessed many corporate scandals affecting some of the world's largest companies. Chief executives of these companies and their reputed illegal actions made headlines. Legal actions were taken against them, and several were convicted of crimes from obstruction of justice to conspiracy and securities, wire and bank fraud.[49] Executives at other levels were indicted for similar crimes, including insider trading and orchestrating accounting frauds.

The scandals implicated high-profile figures: Martha Stewart, a household name, was sentenced to five months in prison and an additional five months of house arrest for lying to the government regarding her actions on an inside tip to sell ImClone stock, which netted her a profit of $45,000. Kenneth Lay, the former Chairman of Enron, was charged for trades allegedly netting him a profit of at least $90 million and for falsely claiming that Enron was in fiscal good health, though its stock fell from $90 to $1 a share, wiping out the retirement money of more than well over 4,200 families.[50] L. Dennis Kozlowski, Tyco International's former chief executive, was recently convicted of fraud and insider trading, with conspicuous expenditures on parties and the "high" life adding sensational details to the allegations made against him.[51] But these are only the high-profile individuals accused of illegal activities involving money. The list goes on to include many other men and women in positions of power in industry and the financial world.

Although greed would seem to underlie these crimes, it is by no means the only explanation for money-related misbehavior. Something seems very different about the way these men and women perceive themselves and their moral obligations – as if because of their money and power they are not accountable for the consequences of their actions. There may be some truth to this assumption, in that their money does, to a limited extent, buy some immunity from social sanctions for criminal behavior. Money provides a means whereby assets can be hidden and, should an action ensue, the best attorneys can be hired to defend one's interests. From this perspective, the rich and powerful may, not surprisingly, see themselves as superior to the average individual and "above the law."

But even this explanation seems incomplete. Men and women who get involved in white-collar crimes are often highly intelligent and have seen some of their colleagues brought to accountability for their illegal actions. Yet their lifestyle and the power they wield create its own energy, its own momentum; these leaders of industry lose control and spin off wildly in aberrant ways. Under proper conditions, the same dynamics can result in creative activity, producing a drive that propels a person to greater heights in building a company or promoting a product. Such creativity may lead to the development of unusual ways of using money to make new products, enhance old ones, or to acquire property with an eye to greater profits. However, uncontrolled power, as we've seen in the eruption of prosecutions, can also be responsible for excesses or abuses in acquiring and spending money.

Nevertheless, the source may not be all in the character and intentions of the misguided executives alone, but also in the nature of money itself and especially in the way the human brain responds to it. The expectation of making money, or of obtaining any reward for that matter, leads to motivated behavior (greed), which can induce lying, fraud, embezzlement, and the sequestering and theft of assets.

We tend to think that motivated behavior is under our personal control, but this control may not be as firm as we think. In many circumstances abnormal brain biology can stimulate immoral and even criminal money-related behavior. At one end of the spectrum is the pathological gambler – an extreme condition: An individual's control over money is weakened considerably in the face of compelling desires and needs. Other brain abnormalities prompt the desires that are not so powerful, though they are enough to diminish an individual's self-control to the point that the desires win out. This raises an important socioethical issue: What are the moral implications of abnormal or antisocial behaviors (gambling among them) that are, indeed, biologically driven? And we mustn't forget that there was an evolutionary advantage for many of these behaviors, which we now see as criminal because of their disruptive potential to society. Being powerful and winning remains a strong biological drive that ensures survival.

Although we can speculate that many of those individuals motivated to commit criminal acts have abnormalities in their judgment and decision-making abilities, functions basic to the frontal lobes, there nonetheless seem to be three broad biological explanations that may reasonably underlie their illegal actions. The evidence for these conditions promoting bad decision making and illegal activity is not obvious as they have not been thoroughly studied in this context. Still, from my experience as a psychiatrist it seems reasonable to expect that something is seriously skewed in their intellectual and emotional functioning.

First, many may suffer from bipolar illness, which would cause them to take risks and become grandiose about their abilities, importance, and power. In the upswing of inflated feelings, bipolar individuals exhibit very poor judgment and are prone to make rash decisions, particularly with regard to money, and to bring about serious mistakes. Second, many of these corporate "criminals" have a basic obsessive–compulsive dimension to their personality that may cause them to ignore social norms and doggedly and impetuously engage in self-serving acts. Third, many of these people have a pathological fear of failure. They are high fliers in terms of their status in the community and corporate success, but underneath they have a basic fear of being found out as incompetent frauds. This motivates them to become even more acquisitive and more willing to take risks in order to accumulate money and status. Money, by virtue of its effect on various parts of the brain, strongly supports deviant behavior among those already compromised with a significantly mental condition.

Bipolar illness, obsessive–compulsive disorder, and fear of failure involve major parts of the brain, such as the prefrontal and temporal lobes and the amygdala. Hence money augments the impact of personality features of these disorders and brings about unlawful behavior in those suffering from abnormal brain processes.

Where Pathological Gambling Fits In

Gambling is fun. Taking a risk like buying tickets for the New York State Lottery or betting on a horse to win the Kentucky Derby is exhilarating. Even though most everyone who buys lottery tickets knows rationally that their chance of winning is minuscule, it is still exciting to buy the ticket; lurking in the back of the mind is the remote possibility that this might be one's lucky day.

Studies say an estimated 86% of the general adult population in the United States has gambled at some time in their lives.[52] If we consider any risk with money to be a form of gambling, then the number is just about 100% of us.

Roughly 10% of the adult population who engage in gambling develop a problem; that is, gambling becomes so compulsive or addictive it interferes with basic functioning.[53] Problem gamblers often have difficulties managing their finances, performing their job, and maintaining good personal relationships.

The clinical term for the most severe forms of disordered gambling is *pathological gambling,* and it is currently estimated to involve up to 3.4% of the adult population.[54] Historically, psychiatry viewed it as a disorder of impulse control;[55] but recently a second theory, that it is a "nonsubstance" addictive disorder, has begun to look like a better explanation.

Pathological gambling has been included as a disorder in the *Diagnostic and Statistical Manual of Mental Disorders* of the American Psychiatric Association since 1980;[56] this manual lists both impairment of impulse control and addictive behavior as part of the pathology. The impulsive and addictive features of gambling can be so strong that the afflicted person is virtually unable to control his or her behavior. This fact alone poses issues regarding the morality of that behavior.

The evidence is strong that there is a powerful biological basis to gambling, even affecting those who are not as pronounced in their behavior as pathological gamblers.[57] We know that males with pathological gambling are prone to sensation seeking, impulsiveness, and substance abuse.[58] These behaviors are consistent with the fact that pathological gamblers have abnormal serotonin function – low levels in many areas of the brain – which has been shown to be associated with poor impulse control.[59]

Structures like the anterior cingulate cortex – shown to be involved in drug cravings – are activated in the pathological gambler.[60] Furthermore, research has shown that gambling can bring about a stimulating effect resembling that induced by a psychostimulant drug, ensuring that the gambler becomes addicted to the behavior and loses the ability to control his or her desires and actions.[61]

Dopamine, which has played an important role in the rewarding and reinforcing of drug abuse, has also been shown to be involved in gambling. Marc Potenza points out that the amount of dopamine, which activates u-opioid receptors in the brain, has been demonstrated to be elevated in cerebrospinal fluid levels during certain types of gambling.[62] Consistent with this observation, medications like naltrexone, which is a u-opioid antagonist, have been shown to be effective (certainly in the short term) in dampening strong urges to gamble.[63]

Though it has not yet been shown in any research studies, the role of dopamine in gambling more than likely parallels its role in substance abuse. Neuroimaging studies conducted by Nora Volkow and her colleagues at Brookhaven National Laboratory have shown that dopamine D2 receptors in the brain are reduced in cocaine abusers as well as in those suffering from other addictions, such as alcoholism, methamphetamine, and heroin.[64]

The dynamic goes like this: The amount of dopamine liberated and therefore available to interact with the dopamine D2 receptors helps to determine saliency. But according to Volkow, the dopamine has only a very short period – at most 50 ms – to communicate to the receptors that an event or experience is important and should be set in memory for the future, after which the dopamine is removed from the synapse by the dopamine transporter. Therefore, because there are fewer D2 receptors, there is less dopamine signaling.

Volkow speculates that the decrease in signaling renders the person less responsive to daily events such as talking on the phone with friends, reading books, exercising, or going to the movies, all of which would act as natural reinforcers. Boredom sets in because the natural reinforcers are no longer motivating the brain. Drugs of abuse like cocaine and amphetamines block the dopamine transporter, thereby allowing dopamine to remain longer in the synapse to increase signaling in the presence of fewer D2 receptors. Therefore, although the natural reinforcers are no longer salient, drugs of abuse such as cocaine are salient, and therefore very reinforcing.[65]

More than likely, a similar mechanism occurs with pathological gambling: Dopamine is liberated in the presence of diminished numbers of D2 receptors, which preclude stimulation by natural reinforcers. Gambling in the pathological gambler likely induces excess dopamine, which increases signaling, thereby becoming strongly reinforcing and taking over the usual role of natural reinforcers.

Individual Variations in Response to Money

It is important to realize that brain responses are not uniform in people. Genetics and brain biology play a critical role in how individuals will react to money and risk. In some people the amygdala will respond strongly and hot emotions will dominate, maybe even enough to prevent the frontal lobe and anterior cingulate cortex from controlling a decision about money. Or perhaps the frontal lobe will be dominant over the emotional brain and make unfortunate decisions by muffling an informed hunch about the decision.

These valuations don't matter much when decisions involve minor amounts of money with minimal impact on anyone's life. But dysfunction in these brain areas may produce bad decisions concerning large amounts of money – decisions that may not always comport with what would be considered morally "right." The question is, given the biological dimensions of money and the brain, can an individual be held responsible for bad decisions?

The issue of responsibility is even more compelling when the question is about gambling. Some people are in complete control; they can take or leave the gambling experience. Toward the other end of the spectrum are the problem gamblers on the verge of addiction, with capacity for considerable risk taking but little control over their gambling. Then, finally, come the pathological gamblers, clearly addicted and impulsive. For both the problem gambler and the pathological one, control and power over one's behavior is a primary issue. The implications of the degrees of lack of control over monetary decisions and gambling as they impact on individual decisions are far reaching. They call into question the individual's ability to exert free will and self-determination, and therefore his or her responsibility for engaging in an immoral act. The evidence is strong that the way we treat money depends to a great extent on the nature and degree of our brain's hardwiring.

The Bad and the Mad

Only one letter distinguishes "bad" from "mad," but these notions have been considered to be at opposite ends of a spectrum of extreme and unacceptable social behaviors. Both of them reveal the power of abnormal human forces that affect personal controls. "Madness," we feel, means the afflicted person's behavior is beyond his or her control. When we think of "badness," we see the person as having free will and motivated by malevolent, self-serving interests.

But the perception of "madness" and "badness" are changing with the revolution in neuroscience. We are learning that many of the distinctions we are accustomed to making are not so clear; significant overlaps appear to exist. Understanding how parts of the brain work to affect our thinking and behavior may eventually transform our formerly sacrosanct beliefs about personal identity and free will.

Nevertheless, madness and badness will likely remain as two distinct entities – although much more closely linked than we once believed possible. The underlying factors, such as mental control over intentions and behavior, that have persuaded society to treat madness and badness differently may no longer stand up in the vast majority of circumstances. This is not to say that "bad" individuals who have personal control over their actions do not exist, but rather that those who have full control are likely to represent a very small percentage of those we now label as bad. Excellent illustrations of

143

changing notions of behaviors thought of as "bad," but increasingly seen as due to brain biology, are the conditions of addiction and alcoholism. They are no longer perceived as resulting from character defects.

What Is Madness?

Madness – that is, being disordered in mind, without reason and judgment, and given to frenzy or irrational behavior – has been seen differently at various times in history, based on our changing perceptions of human nature.[1] Ancient Greek society had a specific notion as to the nature of people and their function in the world. They saw humankind as essentially controlled by external factors.[2] Man was understood as being under the power of the "gods"; the later idea of internal identity was unknown. The "seat" of thinking and behavior was believed to be located somewhere between the gods and the individual.

In the *Iliad* you find no term for the "self." Homer viewed the *psyche,* considered external to oneself, as the center of reflection or of emotions, which was mythologized at the time as a woman, Psyche. Other writings of the ancient Greeks tell us that they did not believe that people were capable of thinking for themselves.[3] The individual was felt to be in a continuous fluid dialogue with other parts of himself, another person, or a god. In this view, forces in part outside of the control of the perpetrator directed an act such as murder, though he (or she) would still likely be held responsible.

Hence, good and evil did not emerge from the individual; nor, therefore, was the individual seen as responsible for his actions in the way in which personal responsibility is established in our culture. Because of humanity's fundamental lack of control, a person was seen as not only the perpetrator of evil, but the victim as well.

Similarly, madness was considered to be the result of forces outside the individual. What we now would view as madness was believed to be some form of inspiration or direction from the gods. Before we could write our thoughts, and thereby examine ideas – the process of objectifying knowledge – those who heard voices, like the oracles, were highly influential. They were thought to be receiving input from the gods, and their advice was considered necessary for dealing with unexpected contingencies. They helped society organize around the unknown.

This was an era of predominant right-hemisphere function, of the dominance of subjective experience.[4] Only through writing – and some claim particular significance to the emergence of the copular verb "to be" – was humankind able to systematize its thinking and begin to understand the relationships between the means and the ends of the way things happen in the real world.

Plato, who died in 374 B.C. and was believed to have lived at least five centuries after Homer – it was not certain when Homer lived; some claim 1200 B.C., others 900 B.C. – approached the issue of madness in a unique way. He viewed an abstract entity, the mind, as a battlefield on which warring "parties," shaped by external forces, struggle within the individual for control. When the impulsive, erratic part of the mind wins out, madness results.[5]

The psychodynamic understanding of the mind was ushered in at the turn of the twentieth century by Freud and other analytic thinkers in psychiatry. It too focused on the power of external factors on the development of the child, but these influences were not the "gods" or invisible forces. Rather, they were the child's early experiences encountering members of his or her immediate family – mother, father, and siblings – in addition to others in the community.[6]

Behavioral scientists looked at the mother–child relationship to discover the key to serious illnesses like schizophrenia, paranoia, and manic depression. Maternal bonding has been the subject of much study,[7] as it is often seen as the conveyance of mixed messages between parent and child. Gregory Bateson, in his "double bind" theory, incorporated the phenomenon of the "schizophrenogenic mother," who created conflicts and frustration ("no-win" situations) for her children, which induce serious mental illness.[8] Other thinkers, like Theodore Lidz with his theories regarding skewed and schismatic families, focused on sibling as well as parental relationships and basic family dynamics for clues to why a person becomes psychologically disturbed.[9]

Starting in the last two decades of the twentieth century, interest in the biology and genetics of mental illness, particularly schizophrenia and manic depression, provoked yet another shift in focus from external forces to internal ones arising from the biology of the afflicted person. This emphasis on biology in studies of mental illness actually has its roots in the early years of that century when Emil Kraepelin, a German psychiatrist, wrote about genetic subtypes of schizophrenia that he claimed "breed true" – that is, reappear through succeeding generations within some families.[10] His thinking resulted in observational studies in Germany of families in which schizophrenia was prominent.[11]

In the Danish Adoption Studies of Schizophrenia of the late 1960s, which dealt to a large extent with studies of adopted twins, Seymour Kety and his colleagues observed the extent of family associations that suggest schizophrenia is inheritable. They demonstrated, for example, that first-degree relatives of someone with schizophrenia have a nearly tenfold risk of developing the illness. These studies contributed to the controversy of whether genetics or environment was responsible for the family patterns. They showed that genetic factors were important in the origin of this disease. Kety's research was essentially responsible for rekindling the interest in the genetics of schizophrenia[12] that has persisted for the past fifty years.

In the past ten years we have gained further evidence of the importance of biology in madness through both neuroimaging and genetic studies. Studies using MRI, in particular, have investigated the shape and size of various parts of the brain of patients with schizophrenia and compared these with healthy individuals. This work has shown that schizophrenia is associated with structural brain abnormalities that likely reflect problems or aberrations in nervous system development that began as early as the embryo stage.[13] The range of abnormalities described in schizophrenia includes, among others, reduced folding of the cortex;[14] reduced gray-matter volume, especially in specific areas on both sides of the brain; and, in chronic schizophrenia, reduced volume of part of the cerebellum.[15]

Valuable new genetic studies have observed family patterns in schizophrenia and manic–depressive illness[16] by narrowing the gene search to particular stretches of DNA. This has enabled scientists to identify three or four regions of the genome that most likely contain susceptibility genes. For example, the 2002 Irish Study, which involved ninety Irish families with schizophrenia,[17] identified linkage of the disease to chromosome 6.[18] Other studies seem to home in on an association with a gene (referred to as the "dysbindin" gene) on that chromosome.[19] Although we are in the early stages of genetic research into schizophrenia, few in the field doubt that biological susceptibility will be established at the molecular level for this and other serious mental illnesses.

Are the Mentally Ill More Likely to Be Bad?

Reports of a seriously disturbed man or woman who loses control and becomes violent toward others appear frequently in the media. Many scientific studies have sought to determine whether the mentally ill are more likely to commit serious crimes, particularly acts of violence. During the 1980s such research appeared to find no association, but more recent work has altered that conclusion. Schizophrenia and affective illnesses do modestly increase violent crimes.[20] However, the diagnosis is not as important as active symptoms, such as agitation,[21] for determining if an individual may commit a violent crime.

An important community study, the Epidemiologic Catchment Area surveys of the relative prevalence of violence and mental disorder, was conducted in several communities in many states in the late 1980s. The surveys showed that 8–10% of people with schizophrenia reported that at some point during the prior twelve months they had been violent, though not necessarily seriously violent.[22] That incidence was notably greater than 2% reported in the general population. In that same study people suffering from affective disorder had a slightly higher rate of violence than the general population.

A study in Denmark that followed roughly 350,000 individuals born between 1944 and 1947 to the age of forty-four years found that those hospitalized for a major mental illness accounted for a disproportionate amount of the violence committed by persons in the birth cohort.[23] The primary diagnosis for violent men was organic psychoses, whereas women arrested for criminal violence were more often diagnosed as schizophrenic.

Pamela Taylor and John Gunn, two leading British criminologists, point out that the percentage of criminal acts performed by the mentally ill is really quite small – although perhaps above the national average in any particular country.[24] They observed that in their own regions, England and Wales, roughly 10% of people convicted of homicides have schizophrenia.[25] This involves at most forty to fifty cases annually.

People with schizophrenia and manic depression who commit homicides often suffer from delusions, or false beliefs, that motivate their behavior.[26] The delusion may be as simple as believing that a particular person is after them, and it might be triggered by anything: eye contact, an angry look, an innocent statement that is misunderstood - or an actual threat.

Delusions can also be very elaborate. I was confronted once at a city library in Manhattan by a woman who pulled me aside to tell me that she had been bound and gagged in Sweden, put on a plane to Kennedy Airport, and by luck managed to escape as she was going through U.S. Customs. She was also convinced that the CIA was after her because they saw her give directions to a passerby in London a week before she had been "kidnapped" in Sweden.

Seriously disturbed individuals may experience hallucinations, frequently hearing voices telling them to beware of a particular person. The voice may be that of a dead relative, a mythical figure, or one's next-door neighbor. Often, the person may "hear" many different voices expressing the same ideas. Patients often describe such voices as quite compelling – strong in tone and authoritative – and commanding voices can instruct the individual to do something, such as striking first before the "bad" person has a chance. At times, the voices can lead the person to commit blatantly self-destructive acts, including suicide.

Historically psychiatry has viewed psychotic symptoms, particularly delusions and hallucinations, as wholly subjective with the patient. Especially where hallucinations are concerned, corroborative evidence, such as a neuroimage or a blood test, has never been available to support the psychiatrist's interpretation of the symptoms patients report.

This, however, appears to be changing. Since the early 1990s many different types of study examining brain circuitry, anatomy, and function have found distinct biological differences in the schizophrenic brain. Some of these findings have been specific to the symptoms of hallucinations and delusions. For example, recent research in Switzerland points to abnormal alterations of certain fiber tracts as responsible for auditory hallucinations.[27]

Other research has also called into question the long-held notion that delusions are purely psychological. In these studies using MRI scans, researchers have found that, in psychotic patients who are delusional, a memory-associated brain area in the medial temporal lobe called the entorhinal cortex is slightly smaller than normal.[28] The entorhinal cortex has a role in autobiographical memory, novelty detection, episodic recognition, and associative learning.[29] The researchers made these measurements with patients having delusions of different severity and concluded that delusion formation likely requires near-normal – but nonetheless impaired – function of the entorhinal cortices.

Some cases within the past few years have involved especially heinous acts, such as the killing of children. One of the most notorious was that of Andrea Yates, a Texas woman in her midthirties who in 2001 drowned her five children in the bathtub.[30] She was brought to trial and, despite a strong history of mental illness and obvious psychotic thinking during her psychiatric examinations, was given forty years imprisonment without parole.

Andrea Yates was a classic case of a mentally ill woman who committed criminal acts while under the influence of a severely compromised mental state. She had had earlier hospitalizations for depression with psychotic features, including hearing voices and being under the delusion that others were out to get her. She had a history of postpartum depression, a condition that can be severe and life-threatening and frequently includes psychotic thinking. Yates's first depression had developed in 1999, after the birth of her fourth son; the fatal recurrence seemed triggered by the birth of her fifth.

On June 20, 2001, just five days after the killings, Andrea Yates underwent a psychiatric examination that revealed she not only heard voices but was also delusional. She insisted that Satan was living inside her and that both she and he had to be punished. She told the psychiatrists she had received instructions from various cartoon characters that Satan would be destroyed if she drowned her children. But, she insisted, she had been told that if she didn't kill her children, they would be tormented in hell forever. To her, protecting her children's souls from the devil meant that she would have to end their lives. The combination of hallucinations and delusions so affected Andrea Yates's judgment that she could no longer discern what was real from what was imaginary.

Even though most forensic psychiatrists (and I) would have found her not responsible for her crime, the prosecution argued that she still knew the difference between right and wrong. The expert psychiatric witness for the prosecution, forensic psychiatrist Dr. Park Dietz, concurred, though he acknowledged that she was seriously delusional. He insisted that her delusion that her thoughts were coming from Satan demonstrated that she must have known they were wrong. She recognized that it was wrong to kill, but the delusion was so compelling that she could not control herself. Texas law (in accord with the M'Naughten rule, discussed in the next section) was clear on the right–wrong issue: That was all the law required to convict – which the jury did.

However, a new trial has recently been granted in her case, based primarily on the fact that Dietz, the prosecuting psychiatric witness, had given flawed testimony. He had claimed that an episode of the television show *Law & Order,* involving a woman suffering postpartum depression who drowned her kids and was found insane, had aired shortly before Ms. Yates drowned her children. (In fact, the episode – on which Dietz had worked as a consultant – had not yet aired, and its storyline was not exactly as he'd recalled.)[31] In the trial the prosecution had suggested that Yates had patterned her actions after that show. This had likely influenced the jury because it indicated that she was capable of reasoning and developing a plan for the murders.

Several years earlier a mother named Susan Smith had strapped her two sons – one was three years old, the other fourteen months – in their car seats and rolled her Mazda into a lake near her home in South Carolina.[32] Smith went on national television to claim that her children had been kidnapped. Nine days after the crime her story that the car had been stolen with the children inside fell apart, and she was arrested. During the trial it came out that Smith, who was divorced, had fallen in love with a man who did not want to be hampered with stepchildren. In fact, her lover took the stand and read a letter he had written to her indicating his intentions to end their relationship because her children didn't "suit" him.

The prosecution portrayed Smith as a cold-blooded killer and sought the death penalty. The defense pointed out her troubled history: Her father had committed suicide; she'd been sexually molested by her stepfather and had made suicide attempts herself. This information was enough to spare her the death penalty, though she was sentenced to life in prison.

This case is an interesting contrast with that of Andrea Yates. Susan Smith was not blatantly mentally ill: She had no history of serious psychosis such as would be seen with delusions, hallucinations, or a "break" from reality. She had a troubled past, but she also had reasons, or incentives, for her behavior. She was motivated to kill the children for her own self-interest, to secure the affection of her lover. Because Smith had these motives, one would have to conclude that she fits more into the category of "bad" rather than "mad." This is not to deny that she was biologically pushed in the direction to be "bad"; but her condition was decidedly different than that of Andrea Yates.

The Mad and Bad: Is Brain Biology the Critical Link?

Research showing the powerful role of genetics in serious mental illness along with that linking brain biology to psychotic symptoms may be opening up Pandora's box on the similarities between the mad and the bad. If we determine that both psychosis and criminality arise from brain biology, what happens to our distinction between the two? Must we abandon it? Strongly favoring a distinction is that in the mad, the biological influences through delusions and hallucinations damage the very basis of the individual's rational capacities. With delusions, hallucinations, and distortions of thinking, madness prevents functioning that is advantageous to the individual, resulting in actions that may be even random in nature. Hence, the mentally ill person cannot exercise normal control over his or her thinking, behavior, or acts, and thus cannot be held to normal standards of responsibility.

Conversely, the "bad" or antisocial individual who commits immoral, violent, or criminal acts is usually engaging in behaviors that have been reinforced to accrue to his (or her) advantage. In such actions the "bad" person frequently lacks empathy, as it is not advantageous to the achievement of his desired ends to be empathetic. The "bad" may also claim biological changes, as did the serial killer Ricky Green. These changes may not directly affect an individual's capacity to be rational, but their impact may nonetheless be so compelling that the afflicted person cannot truly rely on his "rational" abilities to control his behavior.

Increasingly, scientific information – especially that gathered from imaging technologies – has been introduced into the courtroom to establish a basis for exculpation. Imaging studies of offenders and psychopaths, using such technologies as PET and MRI, support the biosocial model of violence. This model involves both upbringing and the biology of the brain.

Adrian Raine, a researcher at the University of California–Irving, has done several studies investigating the brain biology of violent criminals. In one such study using PET, Raine and his colleagues examined forty-one alleged murderers who had pleaded not guilty by reason of insanity, comparing them to the same number of age- and sex-matched controls. They discovered that, compared to control subjects of the same age and gender, the murderers had reduced glucose metabolism in various parts of their brain, especially some areas important to reason and moral controls over behavior, including the prefrontal cortex.[33]

We know that damage to the prefrontal region can cause serious symptoms, such as impulsivity, immature behavior, aggression,[34] and an inability to modify one's behavior. In a subsequent study, Raine and his colleagues again looked at forty-one persons who had been charged with homicide and who had pleaded not guilty by reason of insanity.[35] This group was divided into those with or without a history of psychological and social deprivation. The researchers discovered that those alleged murderers who had a somewhat normal upbringing had lower prefrontal glucose metabolism when compared both to those with deprivation and to the control group. This would suggest that murderers are strongly affected by prefrontal deficits even without the "social push" from environment.

By the same token, a recent study of deprivation in rats suggests that if the animals are not licked and groomed for an extended period of time from birth, a glucocorticoid receptor gene promoter in the hippocampus doesn't get expressed or activated, which has the effect of rendering the animal unable to handle stress later on in life.[36] A similar dynamic, if operative in humans, would certainly explain one important reason why some have a difference in threshold of control against forces pushing toward "bad" actions.

In a 2003 study Raine and his team investigated fifteen psychopathic, antisocial prisoners, none of whom had previous criminal convictions.[37] Using structural MRI scans, Raine discovered that the subjects had an increase of connections between the right and left hemispheres. An earlier study by these researchers had found that a group with Antisocial Personality Disorder had about an 11% reduction in the volume of their prefrontal gray matter. This reduction, they speculate, may account for the subjects' lack of conscience, and for diminished physiological responses such as low arousal and inadequate fear conditioning,[38] which would prevent most of us from engaging in bad acts. This study was particularly important because it introduced the idea that people might be born with prefrontal brain damage rather than acquire it through an injury to that part of the brain.

Two other recent findings support the notion of inborn characteristics related to violence and other criminal behavior. The first, which we discussed in Chapter 5, is the discovery of abnormal alleles that produce less monoamine oxidase to degrade neurotransmitters, thereby leaving boys with this condition, if abused early in life, vulnerable to becoming violent during adolescence.[39] The second is a study recently conducted by University of Chicago researchers of boys between seven and twelve years of age who engaged in bad behavior and were found to have lower levels (than controls) of the stress hormone "cortisol." The researchers opined that the lower levels of cortisol suggest that the boys are less sensitive to stress and therefore significantly less troubled by what might happen if they behave badly.[40]

The Case of "The Durham Boy"

An unusual case that occurred in Durham, Maine, almost two centuries ago illustrates the ongoing struggle in society – and particularly in the law – as to how to handle the biological and deterministic aspects of badness. In this case, which took place in the mid-1830s, a nine-year-old boy named Major Mitchell assaulted and maimed eight-year-old David Crawford with seemingly no provocation.[41] Mitchell was arrested and imprisoned in Portland for five months while he awaited arraignment.

Mitchell claimed in his confession that his crime was justified. He said he went to school one morning not knowing that classes had been canceled, and met David and other students, who teased and made fun of him. He said David was particularly offensive, and they got into a fight. Another boy had to separate them. Mitchell then followed David and forced him into a wooded area where he tried to drown him in a pond.[42] Then, he stuffed leaves and mud into David's mouth, stripped him naked, tied him to a tree, and partially castrated him with a piece of tin. Mitchell claimed that, although he did try to drown the boy, he didn't kill him, because he feared repercussions from another child.

A lawyer who took an interest in the case suspected that Mitchell was intellectually deficient and investigated his background. He learned that, when Mitchell was one week old, he had fallen from a high chest, landing on the top of his head on the floor. The physician who treated him had thought the infant would never recover, or that if he did, he would never be the same. As the baby grew into childhood, according to reports, his behavior was often seen as "wild."

A physician who had studied the (later discredited) concept of phrenology examined Mitchell and appeared as a defense witness in his trial.[43] He testified that he had found a remarkably pronounced depression on the boy's skull. Phrenology, which was based on the idea that personality and behavior could be understood by mapping out the shape of a person's skull, was then gaining acceptance by many physicians and scientists as a "legitimate" science.[44] Thus, the information was admitted into evidence in the Mitchell trial, and the doctor went on to explain that the boy's right ear was lower than the left, and that the fall had caused a protuberance of his skull. The doctor speculated that this injury might have changed Mitchell's intellectual and moral character, enhancing feelings of destructiveness, irritability, and exasperation that the boy probably experienced. A phrenologist also examined Mitchell's mother and, based on her skull formation, concluded that she was of bilious temperament, with a faculty for destructiveness similar to her son's.

The defense attorney emphasized this information in his summation to the jury. The attorney general disputed the value of the medical and phrenological information, claiming that the only germane issue was whether Mitchell was capable of knowing right from wrong. The judge made an emotional charge to the jury, and Mitchell was found guilty and sentenced to nine years of hard labor in a state prison.

This case illustrates several legal issues regarding those who are "bad" and those who are "mad." To begin with, Mitchell would have had a better chance of being acquitted had it been possible to show that he was "mentally ill." The fact that he had protuberances on his skull and a history of a serious head injury (a report disputed by at least one member of his family) was not deemed sufficient to explain the reasons for his behavior. Had he instead been diagnosed as seriously mentally ill, the inference of incapacity would have been much stronger for the judge and the jury.

On the other hand, the case also introduces the importance of an examination to determine insanity for exculpatory purposes, based on the perpetrator's cognitive ability to distinguish "good" from "evil." The prosecution emphasized that Mitchell was cognitively capable of making this distinction. Not only is this test an important element in determining insanity, but it has become also an important test in the issue of moral culpability. About fifty years after the Mitchell case, the *M'Naughten rule* – the test of insanity based on whether a defendant could tell right from wrong – was adopted by many jurisdictions as the primary test for "insanity." Today nearly half the states still follow this rule.

M'Naughten is considered separately from the diagnosis of a mental illness. A defendant could be diagnosed by a psychiatrist as suffering from schizophrenia and still be convicted of a criminal act. The distinction rests much less on the mental condition of the offender and more on whether that condition compromised the individual's ability to recognize the wrongful nature of his or her act.

Had the Durham case occurred today, imaging technologies no doubt would be used to show the presence of a defect in Mitchell's brain functioning, which could then be linked to the boy's ability to make a moral judgment. In this respect, some individuals who would have been judged "bad" in the past would now come under the umbrella of a medical "diagnosis" for the purposes of establishing their inability to arrive at a moral judgment; the "badness" must be linked to something mental or some physical damage in the brain.

The same standard of requiring a biologically causative connection does not apply to mental illness. The psychiatrist's evaluation alone, without supportive tests, may serve to define an individual as schizophrenic, and this evaluation alone has often served as a sufficient basis for assessing the capacity of the afflicted person to distinguish right from wrong. Without a clear-cut diagnosis of mental illness, "badness" must prove that such a linkage exits before it is treated positively under an insanity plea.

The law does not see "badness" as biological unless a particular injury to the brain can be shown or unless a demonstrable dysfunction is established in the way the brain works with respect to criminal conduct. Nevertheless, the insanity plea requires that even individuals diagnosed with a mental illness must establish an inability to distinguish right from wrong – or, in the case of more recent tests of insanity, establish that they could not "appreciate" the difference between right and wrong and therefore could not conform to the law.[45] Thus the fundamental result of any test for insanity is in reality to test "moral accountability": the ability to understand society's bedrock rules

But what about people who are "mad" or "bad," or both, and can distinguish right from wrong when put to the test, yet are still unable to conform to the rules of social behavior? Such individuals have the cognitive ability to understand social sanctions. When someone who knows the rules can't follow them, the question is one of personal control. To get to the bottom of that, we have to know whether biology or morality is guiding that person's judgment.

Personal and Impersonal Judgments: A Biological and Moral Distinction

Moral judgments fit into two broad types. One type is judgments that are "personal," which means they are influenced primarily by our own social and emotional senses. Such judgments are responses to interactions in our social lives and are guided by intense feelings such as anger, empathy, jealousy, love, and fairness. When violations of a personal nature evoke powerful emotions, these emotions can cloud our judgment and, in the extreme situation, result in bodily harm directed at a specific person or groups.[46] For example, a married couple squabbles over money and, in the course of the argument, the wife picks up a knife, hurls it at her husband, and it lodges in his shoulder.

Judgments that do not have personal consequences for us fall into the second class of moral judgments, or impersonal judgments that are driven by "cognitive" processes. For the classic example: One is confronted with the dilemma of deciding whether to allow a trolley that is out of control to continue on a course where it is likely to kill seven people, or to detour it by hitting a switch so that it follows a different track, where only one person would be killed. This decision is impersonal, since the decision maker knows none of the parties involved and is merely deciding to hit a switch.[47]

However, involve the decision maker more personally and the morality likewise becomes more personal: Have the decision maker stand beside a man on a platform a short distance from the seven people who would be killed. Now the moral dilemma has to do with the decision maker choosing between pushing the man onto the track to stop the trolley, or letting it pass and kill a larger number of people.

With the use of fMRI, researchers have determined that personal moral judgments involve activity in the emotion-related regions of the brain. Impersonal moral judgments, by contrast, involve cognitive brain areas, those that focus on problem solving and abstract reasoning.

While asking subjects to make judgments on a range of cases – from difficult personal moral dilemmas to mainly impersonal problems – the researchers discovered that the moral dilemmas, even though personal in character, activated brain areas associated with abstract reasoning. In other words, when personal moral dilemmas become complicated, brain regions involved with purely abstract reasoning and other forms of cognition are recruited. Furthermore, they discovered that parts of the brain associated with abstract reasoning are also activated when utilitarian moral judgments – the acceptance of personal moral violations out of concern for the greater good (e.g., soldiers on a battlefield fighting for homeland security) – are required.[48]

This study is particularly interesting because very few decisions are made for purely impersonal reasons. The majority of the moral dilemmas we confront involve some sort of personal violation that brings emotional and cognitive factors into conflict. The most graphic example often cited is the crying baby scenario: You and several others from a besieged community are hiding from enemy soldiers and your child begins to cry. His crying will almost certainly alert the enemy to the hiding place.[49] Your only option is to smother the child. This is a complex dilemma involving a personal violation (the death of your own child) and the impersonal, utilitarian concern (saving more lives).

Thus what looks to the outside observer at first blush as a clear-cut matter of decision making may not be so clear-cut. Impersonal decisions often involve complex considerations of balancing many outcomes, as we've seen in the trolley and baby examples: It can be very difficult to recognize a "bad" act.

A biological reason may frequently underlie a "bad" behavioral response. Most research into the ways brain injury and genetic defects affect behavior strongly suggests that both can interfere with moral decision making. The impairment of moral competence appears to be associated with malfunctioning connections between the cognitive and the emotional parts of the brain.[50] For example, if the communication link is broken between the fear response and the behavioral restraint that results from having experienced many anxiety-producing events, a new fearful experience may produce an abnormal (or "bad") reaction.

As pointed out by Antonio Damasio, the University of Iowa neuroscientist who has done groundbreaking research in this area, the emotional part of the brain plays a critical role in making rational decisions because, over time, a response history has been created; this guides the cognitive part of the brain (the prefrontal lobes) in particularly desirable directions.[51]

If that guidance is absent or impaired, therefore, "badness," much like "madness," can be biologically driven. For example, in the scenario of the crying child we could speculate that less drastic alternatives might have been available – say, a safe exit from the hiding place – but were not considered by the parent. We learn that the parent has a history of impulsivity and violent acts. In the parent's heightened fear and lack of personal control, he or she suffocates the child.

"Badness" may not always be the result of biological abnormality – it may even have served evolutionary advantages in some circumstances – but given our understanding of how the brain works, it would be fair to recognize that "bad" acts may reflect a biological problem that inhibits or distorts the exercise of free will. In this sense mental illness and "badness" may both indicate some pathology in the brain. Often, people (especially psychopaths) who commit "bad" acts display impulsiveness, lack of objective reasoning, uncontrollable anger, and lack of empathy that may be manifestations of a biological condition beyond the control of an afflicted person.

If as a society, we are willing to assert that the presence of mental illness may indicate a lack of responsibility, why are we reluctant to apply the same argument mitigating responsibility to many who, not meeting the criteria for any mental illness, are categorized as "bad"?

The mere presence of mental illness does not excuse a person from killing another. However, when it can be shown that someone who kills is mentally ill and unable to differentiate good from evil or control his or her behavior, then the arguments are very strong for either morally excusing the act or, in a court of law, applying the insanity plea. The same should apply to those who are "bad" where it can be demonstrated that a biological condition is present and operating to prevent the individual from distinguishing "good" from "evil," asserting free will, or controlling his or her behavior.

I am proposing that "mad" and "bad" share similar characteristics, despite their distinct differences. This is not to suggest that the definition of "madness" should include those who are "bad." Rather, the relationship between "mad" and "bad" is growing ever closer, and both conditions relate to the assertion of power over one's own thinking and behavior *and how the exertion of such power may be impaired or inhibited*. Degrees of badness exist where it can be argued that biology controls behavior, just as there are degrees of madness where biology controls behavior.

The impressive advances in our knowledge of brain biology, as they apply to behavior, suggest that "madness" and "badness," despite involving different areas of the brain, should be subheadings including the seriously "mad" and the compellingly "bad" under one broad new category: *"aberrant actions directed by brain biology."* We know, for example, that delusions and hallucinations involve brain biology that also has been associated with violence or other criminal acts. Similarly, we know that abnormalities in the connections of cognition and emotion can result in criminal acts.

Surely behavior that can be shown to accompany biology abnormal enough to dominate thinking and behavior should qualify. Our objective should be to use neuroscientific information – including diagnostic measures such as imaging technologies – to address rationally the responsibility of those who commit "bad" or criminal acts.

12

Creating a Moral Brain

Sometime before the end of the twenty-first century, will neuroscientific discoveries and modern medical technology allow us to fulfill the utopian dream of a morally "perfect" society? Will the Seven Deadly Sins be banished from the human condition? Since many of those "sins" are already being understood as originating in biological differences, it's not much of a stretch to imagine a future focused on correcting the biology and thereby eliminating the prospects of these sins. So let's imagine (fast-forward, please). . . .

In the election of a century from now, legislative reformists promoting The New Society take over the government. They are convinced that the brain directs the mind, that it is hardwired, that genetics creates the foundation of this wiring, and that the tuning-up process involves a delicate exchange between environment and brain biology.

Imagine now that headway has been made in the many ways that biological mistakes can be corrected or counterbalanced so that the brain operates according to the biology now known to underlie "mainstream" morality.

But during their campaign, our future legislators are questioned hard about time-honored notions of free will, individual responsibility, and the ability of human beings to change their behavior just by learning and accepting basic precepts of social morality. The reformists face the fact that the public's supposedly sophisticated understanding of brain science did not discard the notion that our species basically has control over its thoughts and intentions and, therefore, should be held individually responsible for immoral and illegal actions.[1]

Despite that difficulty, the reformist candidates manage to convince most voters that they understand such concerns but are on top of the scientific knowledge about the brain. This superior knowledge persuades the voters that, at the very least, these candidates are the ideal ones for the job, knowing not only how to promote good moral values but also able to ensure that those values will prevail.

Upon taking office, the reformists introduce a stream of bills to put government support behind a wide array of treatments, technologies, and procedures that have been developed to change brains. In advocating these measures, the reform legislators argue with that, over the course of the twenty-first century, neuroscience research has demonstrated the role of multigenes working in concert to produce thinking and behavior. They also claim that basic human emotions have come to be understood in terms of genetics and brain biology. The way these emotions specifically affect moral and intellectual development, they insist, has been "worked out," including individual differences. They recognize that people have varying thresholds of control over being pushed to act in abnormal ways. Such thresholds, they acknowledge, are shaped by differences in genetics and circumstances – for example, sleep deprivation and the memory of a bad incident at a particular location. Furthermore, imaging studies, particularly functional MRI, had been done on people in group settings, revealing the difference in the brain when a person is scanned alone and when he or she engages in the dynamics of social interaction, or works within a group context.

Major evidence for their position is that the brain is plastic and, with knowledge of how brain biology works, society has the means to reshape individuals effectively to meet certain moral standards. These standards apply across the board to human interaction; they prohibit lying, psychological and physical abuse, violence, and other destructive acts. They also reflect what society considers acceptable expressions of sexual impulses and desires, how money is to be handled, and how society is to distinguish – and manage – the bad, as distinct from the mad.

As it did in the campaign, the question of "free will" continues to come up, but the reformists argue that the biology of unconscious processes, particularly repression and denial, has been studied and that, fundamentally, "free will" is a bogus concept. At most, they concede, it has a small if not insignificant role in human decisions. Hence, they propose that "free will" is a conceit that impedes social efforts to homogenize American society into a strong country of consistent morality.

They point out that they have carefully crafted their proposals to match the body of neuroscience information available to them. So if we, their constituents, are to buy their plan for a moral America, we ought to examine their claims.

Genes, Biology, and the Brain

It was widely expected that by the end of the twentieth-first century the relationship of various genes, working alone and together, to behavior would be completely understood. The illustration of the defective gene for the production of MAO-A and its relationship to violent behavior[2] in 2002 would be only one of many correlations made between gene defects and a full panoply of undesirable behaviors – such as murder, suicide, sexual aberrations, theft, and white-collar crime. In addition – and even more to be desired – the genetic foundation for traits such as empathy, trust, generosity, caring for others, intelligence, and sensitivity would have come to light.

By the year 2100, the reformists point out, this genetic information has been linked to discoveries of the brain's specific mechanisms for the production of human feelings. The various limbic structures – amygdala, hippocampus, hypothalamus, and the anterior cingulate gyrus – were now thoroughly understood in terms of how they interact to create and inhibit emotions, which impact on the prefrontal lobe and condition individuals over time to react in specific ways to their environment. The reformist legislators also insist that neural pathways for these feelings, as well as those for imitation and understanding of patterns of behavior through the mirror-neuron system, and the specific ways they influence the cognitive functions of the prefrontal lobe, have been successfully tracked and mapped out. The neuroscientist of 2100 understands how the mechanisms behind the brain's reactions to the environment operate.

The frontal lobe linkage to deep emotional responses in the limbic areas such as fear, guilt, shame, regret, grief, disgust, and trust, which is generated mostly in the caudate nucleus, gives rise to an individual's actions and serves as the foundation for the creation of "moral" behavior.[3] This linkage, they point out, is consistent with Damasio's somatic marker theory, whereby emotions created over time, through specific experiences, serve as "informative feelings" essential for good decision making. In keeping with this, moral development has to home in on that linkage to foster good behavior and prevent bad behavior.

Biology of Moral Development

A century after Ritalin became standard fare, according to the reformists, the Piaget–Kohlberg staging of intellectual and moral development is far better understood on a biological level. The child's emotional capacity for control – especially guilt and shame – derive from stimulation of limbic structures at each stage of moral development.

At first, the reformists state, restraint for fear of punishment motivates elementary moral decisions, decisions that fall within the secondary, "conventional" level of adherence to social rules and expectations. Over time, with learning and emotional maturity, the fear of punishment is not necessary for achieving higher levels of moral understanding. For the most morally capable, this understanding culminates in the "postconventional" level. It is at this level where social rules are critiqued in the background of higher-order rights, such as human rights. Essentially, they insist, we now have enough knowledge about how feelings are generated to control instinctual desires.

The reformists further point out that the correlation of genes, brain biology, and variations in human behavior have been facilitated considerably by the computer. The complex tracking of external stimulation on the sensory cortex, through the limbic structures, to the prefrontal lobe and the production of a decision to act are easily predicted by computer modeling. Highly accurate modeling has been achieved for all conceivable environmental stimulations of the brain. It is now possible to map, in any individual, the passage of sensations to the prefrontal lobe and their effect on decision making and behavior.

The Unconscious and Free Will

Free will, according to the reformists, has been debunked, not only by virtue of the biology of emotions and decision making, but in many other ways as well. Their examples range from the impact of hormones such as testosterone on sexual behavior to imaging studies linking abnormalities of the temporal lobe to uncontrollable violence and crimes.

They get specific. Citing a man, shown by PET scans to suffer from abnormal metabolism of limbic structures, who randomly stabs shoppers in a department store, they argue that this case represents the tip of an iceberg. Most others who become violent have some abnormality of brain structures, and therefore are not operating wholly out of volition.

In addition, they point to the pathologies that involve complex, goal-directed actions outside of the control of the individual. As far back as 2005, such pathologies came to light, though they were confirmed in just a few unusual "motor release phenomena," such as the "anarchic hand syndrome." But during the past 95–100 years some not-so-obvious conditions were found to have features similar to these seemingly unconscious "goal-directed acts," including many serious crimes or immoral acts that are at least in part beyond the full control of the actor.

To clinch their case for uncontrollable acts, they cite decades of confirming studies built on the Nobel Prize–winning research of

Libet, and that by Platt and Glimcher.[4] These researchers demonstrated that some part of the human brain takes action toward a decision, such as to move a part of the body, long before the actor is even aware that this is about to happen. Therefore, the reformists emphasize that voluntary movements are not really voluntary; they are preceded by activity in the motor area of the brain, and the individual, they claim, has only the power to "veto" the movement before it occurs, not actually to initiate the action.[5] They further emphasize that the brain's initiation of action frequently overpowers the effectiveness of the individual's veto. This research was capped by a long line of studies that prove that the "unconscious," as described by Freud, is in fact the brain acting independently of the mind.

In conclusion, the new legislators argue, free will, if it exists at all, has a minor role in behavior. All the factors discussed above – working alone or, more powerfully, together – are largely responsible for a person's behavior. In other words, neither morality nor immorality is the product of conscious intent. Morality is the result of proper shaping of the individual brain, conditioning it to deliver socially acceptable outcomes.

Creating the Moral Brain

The legislation for The New Society embodies the reformists' certainty that it is now possible to "create" the moral brain. Having mesmerized their legislative colleagues by itemizing the salient features of the brain involved in moral decisions, they now turn to intervention and the possibilities, during various stages of child development, of ensuring formation of a "moral" brain.

Their bill calls for genetic studies on umbilical cord blood for all babies born – as a matter of routine. These genetic tests will be used to profile children's future potential not only for developing certain conditions that may impact on thinking and behavior, but also for identifying the range of behavioral manifestations they will likely experience. Along with genetic studies, they recommend using fMRI for early assessment of how each child's brain is working.

These images and tests would earmark certain genetic abnormalities known to be associated with violence proneness and inability to abide by social regulations. Children who manifest such abnormalities would be observed closely during their development. When they begin to depart from normal moral development, remedial measures would be employed to return them to the moral mainstream.[6]

The reformists' goals are buttressed by evidence that the brain is much more plastic than it was believed to be in 2005. Now it is possible, they claim, to contour the brain through various techniques and to assess the effectiveness of these measures. Genetic engineering has taken huge leaps forward in the past ninety-five years; genetic defects directly related to functional problems in the brain, including immoral decision making, are now routinely detected. When these defects are present, normal DNA can be introduced into the damaged cells and substituted for the abnormal form, returning the cells to normal functioning, and correcting the defect.

If the DNA is so damaged that genetic therapy is too complex and not therapeutic, stem cells can effectively restore function. These cells, our new leaders are quick to add, can be induced to replicate in the child's own body through chemical stimulation, or they can be obtained from embryo sources and inserted into damaged areas of the brain. With their unique ability to adapt to the environment in which they are placed, stem cells will produce the needed enzymes and proteins to bring about the normal state.

Of course, less drastic measures such as creative learning techniques, which have been shown to bring about plastic changes in the brain, will be required before invasive therapy. However, the reformists caution that such techniques generally are not effective where serious brain biology is the underlying cause of the disability. The exception might be when these techniques are administered alongside other measures, such as transcranial magnetic simulation (TMS). When TMS is applied with a rapid pulse, it has been shown to stimulate the brain, bringing about enhancement of select capacities, such as the capacity to make reasoned, "right-minded" decisions.[7]

Three measures are affected by the bill soon to be ratified by the House of Representatives to augment or replace areas of the brain that do not work properly for moral decision making. These measures include brain implants, the transplantation of tissue, and the "downloading" of information to be "straightened out" and uploaded back into the brain. Many of these techniques are brand-new, but they have been in development for most of the twenty-first century and deserve to be converted from their experimental status for routine use under the National Health System.

Brain implants, such as neurosilicon hybrids, as well as computer chips, have been shown to substitute for injured neurons or to act as sites for stimulation of the brain.[8] Individuals, for example, with impairment of parts of an amygdala can have that region "cured" with implants. This can restore emotional responses, such as fear and enthusiasm, that have been diminished or eliminated by brain injury.

Transplantation of parts of the brain, which was in development as early as the 1990s, has advanced to even highly specialized structures such as the hippocampus, and such complex capacities as memory have been successfully repaired. Memory, as the new legislators point out, is an essential ability for both moral development and the sustaining of moral "mindedness" in humans. Transplantation has by now been perfected for regions of the brain, such as the anterior cingulate cortex, which is essential for using experience to create emotional and cognitive ways of handling new situations and for conflict resolution. Parts of the prefrontal lobe – essential for reasoning and executive functioning – have been transplanted with success.

The impending practicability of these techniques gives a sharp boost to technologies that have been growing steadily since the early years of twentieth-first century experimentation. The bill supports more technical development of the sophisticated decoding of higher-level signals in the brain to position cursors on a computer screen. This research, initially done on monkeys, allowed for information from these animals' brains to be used to instruct the operation of computers, vehicles, and robots.[9] The reformists show that this ability to distinguish when the brain of an animal intends to pick up a specific object, and to translate that signal into something that is operational, opened the door for downloading information to a computer. It wasn't until a major breakthrough of converting signals to language, which the reformists indicate occurred around 2050, that downloading was actually possible on a large scale.

Removing the constraints on this technology is important to the reformists because the downloading reveals the basic structure of thinking embedded in the person's memory. It is not only a critical window into an individual's moral structure, but also fundamental to altering features that are incompatible with the social morality of the majority. Use of many of the techniques enabled by the legislation (genetic therapy, stem cells, implants, and transplantation) – as well as reversing the downloading process of information flow from outside into the brain of an individual through "uploading" – will allow major changes to be induced in almost anyone's morality whether the disability is mild or severe. This is the pivotal issue in The New Society's political program: assessing an individual's capacity for moral responses and making alterations that will strengthen areas to meet an overall societal system of morality.

To convince skeptical colleagues, one of the newly elected legislators arranges to have in the gallery the mother of a child who is a living example of the success of these techniques. (A news clipping of her story forms a hologram image visible to the representatives during the session.) While pointing to her in the gallery, he tells the members of the House that the young mother had approached him with concerns she was having about her seven-year-old boy, who had a serious conduct disorder. She claimed that ever since he had begun to walk, her son had frequently gotten into trouble. At school, he had taken things from the cloakroom lockers of other students and been caught with watches and minicomputers stashed in his locker. During the past year she had also caught her son in many lies, including lying about attending classes when he was out playing instead.

The reformist had referred the mother and child to a neurologist, who had reviewed the genetic studies done on the child at birth. He'd found ambiguous changes in some of the boy's behavioral genes, but those changes had not been sufficient to predict a conduct disorder or antisocial personality traits. However, an fMRI the neurologist then ordered showed abnormal changes in the child's prefrontal lobe and anterior cingulate cortex – areas of the brain involved with decision making and conflict resolution, which could be consistent with the development of antisocial personality traits.

The neurologist, who was a specialist in "moral" brain development, had recommended a program of behavioral conditioning augmented by frequent TMS treatments to discourage the dissocial conduct. Three months later a follow-up fMRI had revealed only slight improvement in those areas of the brain. The next step he had proposed was the insertion of neurosilicon chips along the two areas of the brain. These chips were to stimulate the neurons in the prefrontal lobe and ACC to improve their functioning. They would be effective for a long time and could be easily reactivated by external generating devices.

The reformist concludes his recital, pointing again to the mother in the gallery and pacing the floor of the House.

"The neurosilicon hybrids work! The child is able to understand the immoral nature of his acts and to control his behavior. But even if more drastic measures – brain transplantation and uploading of rudimentary 'moral principles' into his memory centers – had been necessary to correct the disorder, they could have been tried on an experimental basis, with minimal physical invasion to the child."

The Perils of Streamlined Morality

The powerful case the reformists present for The New Society stuns the chamber, but not to silence. Opponents have been watching the same advances the reformists found so exciting, and these minority leaders are prepared to fight. They denounce what they call "a masquerade posing as a public good." By streamlining a system of morality that diminishes the rough edges of aberrancy and that will be applicable to everyone, proponents of The New Society are essentially trying to create a world devoid of "evil." Though the reformists have certainly demonstrated that science would allow for the early detection and correction of aberrant moral thinking, their goals, however laudable they may think them, could have devastating consequences for individuality, creativity, and social evolution.

One after another, opposition speakers rise to expose the weaknesses in the proposed New Society. How would we determine what elements are essential in the structuring of a moral community? To achieve this fairly, it would be necessary to glean the viewpoints of the diverse groups that now constitute society. People's viewpoints on moral issues may be similar regarding serious acts, but they differ widely about less serious behaviors. Many people are more tolerant of certain marginal behaviors, particularly victimless "crimes," than others. To work effectively a moral framework for eliminating "evil" would have to incorporate all dominant views into a system of regulation and control.

The opponents are not objecting to the biological capacities for altering feelings and thinking of people to create an effective system of internal controls over behavior. Sufferers of many mental illnesses were indeed benefiting from the new technologies. If stem cells, transplanted to parts of the brain, or even neurosilicon hybrids, can improve the functioning of parts of the brain, resulting in mainstream behavior, then more power to the doctors and patients between whom these cures were being crafted. But, some egalitarians suggest, is the game here to unburden the rich of the cost of external controls, such as police, courts, and the criminal legal system? And for that should we sacrifice the concept of agency or personal responsibility?

After weeks of debate – one of the longest in the history of the House of Representatives – the bill for The New Society is narrowly defeated. The reformists, though temporarily disheartened, remained committed to the idea and promised to return again.

Rewind – back to the present. . . .

The objections of the opposition are not hard to envision because we are having this very discussion today. With the wide array of available medications – stimulants like Ritalin and Adderall, drugs for depression, anxiety, and even the management of sexual desires – the control of behavior has become an important issue in the schools and other institutions. The objections to social control through manipulation of brain biology go far beyond those discussed in the dystopian scenario we just imagined.

For the sake of eradicating "evil," other important qualities of human thinking and expression are indeed likely to be sacrificed. The most important of these would be personal identity, or what may be referred to as the "autonomous" self. Those regions of the brain involved in moral decisions, as we've seen with serious criminal offenses, sexual misconduct, manipulations with money and lying, to name a few, are also the brain parts that create our personality. Regions like the prefrontal lobe and the limbic system figure dominantly in our cognitive capacities, our ability to reason, and, perhaps most important, our ability to recognize and handle novel ideas. These areas of the brain come together to form the "self"; they create that which is unique about each of us.

The idea of streamlining people is not new. In his book *Great and Desperate Cures,* the sociologist Elliot Valenstein discussed psychosurgery, which was performed on thousands of mentally ill patients – primarily those suffering from schizophrenia or severe obsessive–compulsive disease – between 1945 and 1955.[10] The procedure referred to as a *frontal lobotomy* was conducted through insertions of metal rods in an opening above the eye (the supraorbital fissure). This procedure would often result in lacerations of blood vessels causing strokes, permanent disability, and even death. At the very least, many of those undergoing the treatment ended up in very serious physical condition.[11] Most of these patients had major alterations in their personalities. They were without enthusiasm, the ability to get excited about ideas or art, or to experience pleasure.

Then in 1973 an important legal case surfaced that involved the use of behavioral modification and psychosurgery.[12] This was an experimental psychosurgery program to treat sexual psychopaths by performing cingulotomies (destroying the cingulate gyrus in the brain) on them. The experiment was never conducted because it was argued that the prisoners were in a vulnerable position, the treatments were not proven to be effective, and the side effects were not thoroughly understood. In fact, one of the serious concerns was that the afflicted person's personality would be significantly altered.

The merits of creating a moral, if not monolithic society, have to be balanced against the possibilities of altering basic elements of an individual's personality and the benefits of diversity – even deviancy – to further the creative interests of a society.[13] Groups like Blooms-bury, which fostered immense creativity with major figures in literature, economic theory, and art like Virginia Woolf, John Maynard Keynes, and Clive Bell, succeeded because they were composed of free-thinking idealists who, in rejecting socially imposed rules and restrictions, created their own moral structure.[14]

The dangers inherent in neuroscience capabilities for creating a morally streamlined society can not be underestimated. Though our 2100 scenario may seem fanciful, it should not be taken lightly. Preventive medicine has a long history of its applications in Western civilization. We have long been applying preventive measures like ensuring clean water, proper disposal of wastes, vaccinations, and control of venereal diseases to prevent the spread of physical diseases in communities. Extending this process to controlling aberrant moral or mental behavior is not a huge step.

Understanding the biological basis of moral thinking is important so that when very serious problems surface, we have the ability to alter *specific* elements of an individual so that he or she can function in society. For example, a sexual psychopath with highly elevated testosterone and diminished ability for conditioned fear because of damage to the amygdala would benefit by being treated through neuroscientific techniques.

Therefore, most of us would support the *voluntary* treatment of individuals who have experienced damage to a part of their brain or suffer from abnormal metabolism that induces destructive behavior. But the objective should not be to create a homogenized group of people with the same internal controls over their thinking and behavior.

This set of issues of how neuroscience is to be used will come up over and over again as we advance in our technological capabilities to detect and "treat" abnormalities in the brain that affect behavior. Many policy makers with utopian interests and somewhat rigid notions of how society should be structured will be unrelenting in their efforts to create a "moral" society. Over the next thirty to fifty years the prospects for major discoveries in understanding and altering the brain are remarkable. Unfortunately, so are the possibilities of misuse of this information for seemingly well-meaning but ultimately destructive ends. The marvels of neuroscience must be used for the good of people and humanity, not as an instrument for control.

In some respects, we've "been there, done that" with regard to creating an "ideal" society. The Human Genome Project and the promises of genetics have created a continuing debate about issues that address eugenics. But eugenics is not a new notion. The Nazis during the 1930s–1940s advocated eugenics, which justified their extermination of "defective" members of their society. Even earlier, during the late nineteenth century, a eugenics movement – social Darwinism – emerged after Darwin's discovery of the natural selection of the fittest.

The human desire to create a society of people with mainstream morality has been with us a long time. The Old Testament, containing the fundamentals of the Seven Deadly Sins, was intended to teach moral principles that would lead to a morally harmonious society. We have not achieved that goal. Yet, whether through religion or through science, it is a goal that humankind will inevitably pursue with zeal, especially with the extraordinary findings of research in genetics and neuroscience.

It is to be hoped that this goal will be pursued with intelligence and caution.

Notes

1. Neuroscience and Morality

1. *Catholic Encyclopedia* (1913): The Encyclopedia Press, Inc. See also the electronic version by New Advent Inc. (1997) at www.newadvent.org/cathen/.
2. "De institutes coenobiorum et de octo principalium vitiorum remedies libri XII (or Institutes of monastic life in common), and "Collationes XXIV" (the "collations" or Conferences).
3. *Catholic Encyclopedia,* on "Pope St. Gregory I (The Great)."
4. Ardrey R (1966): *The Territorial Imperative,* Atheneum, New York.
5. Wright R (1994): *The Moral Animal: Why We Are the Way We Are,* Vintage Books, New York, 242 ff.
6. Ibid., 1–15.
7. For a detailed examination of the evolution of morality, see Broom DM (2003): *The Evolution of Morality and Religion,* Cambridge University Press, Cambridge, UK.
8. Darwin C (1982 [1871]): *The Descent of Man, and Selection in Relation to Sex,* Princeton University Press, Princeton, NJ, 71.
9. Huxley TH (1980 [1904]): *Evolution and Ethics,* Princeton University Press, Princeton, NJ.
10. Dawkins R (1976): *The Selfish Gene,* Oxford University Press, Oxford.
11. Flack JC, de Waal FBM (2000): Any animal whatever: Darwinian building blocks of morality in monkeys and apes, *Journal of Consciousness Studies* 7: 1–29; republished in book form as Katz, LD, ed., *Evolutionary Origins of Morality: Cross-Disciplinary Perspectives,* Imprint Academic, Thorverton, UK, 1–29.
12. For a good discussion of cooperation, see Sachs JL, et al. (2004): The evolution of cooperation, *Quarterly Review of Biology* 79: 135–60.

13. De Waal FBM (1996): *Good Natured: The Origins of Right and Wrong in Humans and Other Animals,* Harvard University Press, Cambridge, MA.
14. Sachs et al. (2004): The evolution of cooperation, 135–7.
15. See also Dugatkin LA (1997): The evolution of cooperation, *Bioscience* 47: 355–62.
16. Trivers RL (1971): The evolution of reciprocal altruism, *Quarterly Review of Biology* 46: 35–57.
17. For a full discussion of the capabilities of primates for cognition and concomitant emotions, see Byrne R (1995): *The Thinking Ape: Evolutionary Origins of Intelligence,* Oxford University Press, Oxford.
18. Flack & de Waal (2000): Any animal whatever, 2, 3.
19. Wang GJ, et al. (2004): Exposure to appetitive food stimuli markedly activates the human brain, *NeuroImage* 21: 1790–7.

2. Morality and the Mind

1. Wilson JQ (1993): *The Moral Sense,* Free Press, New York, 240 ff.
2. Brandt R (1979): *A Theory of the Good and the Right*, Clarendon Press, Oxford; see 327 ff, "Is It Always Rational to Act Morally?"
3. Insanity as an issue for criminal responsibility goes back to the Greco-Roman period, when the idea prevailed that an individual must have free choice to be held morally and legally responsible for his or her actions. For a discussion of the insanity defense, see Goldstein AS (1967): *The Insanity Defense,* Yale University Press, New Haven.
4. Freud S (1961): *The Ego and the Id,* trans. Rivière J, W. W. Norton, New York (originally published 1923).
5. Though instincts and unconscious factors influence behavior, Freud was committed to the power of in-depth understanding as a way to bring about personal change, growth, and freedom.
6. Piaget J (1965 [1932]): *The Moral Judgment of the Child,* trans. Gabim M, Free Press, Glencoe, IL. Piaget's four major stages of development are as follows: *sensorimotor stage* (birth to 2 years), children learn through sensory observation; *preoperational thought* (2–7 years), children use symbols and language more; *concrete operations* (7–11), children operate and act on concrete world of events and objects; *formal operations* (11 through end of adolescence), their thinking operates in formal and highly logical processes, including the ability to think abstractly and to reason deductively.
7. Piaget saw intelligence as an extension of biological adaptation.
8. Kohlberg L (1964): Development of moral character and ideology; in Hoffman, ML, ed., *Review of Child Development Research*, vol. 1, Russell Sage Foundation, New York.

9. Kohlberg L (1976): Moral stages and moralization: The cognitive-developmental approach; in Lickona T, ed., *Moral Development and Behavior: Theory Research and Social Issues,* Holt, Rinehart & Winston, New York, 31–53.

10. Note that each of these three levels comprise two stages of moral reasoning and unique social perspectives.

11. Jennings WS, Kilkenny R, Kohlberg L (1983): Moral-development theory and practice for youthful and adult offenders; in Laufer WS, Day JM, eds., *Personality Theory: Moral Development and Criminal Behavior,* Lexington Books, Lexington, MA, 281–355.

12. Ibid., 286.

13. See Gilligan C (1982): *In a Different Voice,* Harvard University Press, Cambridge, MA. See also Gilligan C, Ward JV, Taylor JM (1988): *Mapping the Moral Domain,* Harvard University Press, Cambridge, MA.

14. Bowlby J (1980): *Attachment and Loss,* 3 vols., Basic Books, New York.

15. Bowlby J (1958): The nature of the child's tie to his mother, *International Journal of Psychoanalysis* 39: 350–73, at 350.

16. Wilson (1993): *The Moral Sense,* 126.

17. Ibid., 128.

18. Romanucci-Ross L (1985): *Mead's Other Manus: Phenomenology of the Encounter,* Bergin & Garvey, South Hadley, MA. Note that kuru, a degenerating brain disease believed to be induced by a prion transmitted through cannibalization of the brain, where the infectious agent resides, was discovered in New Guinea.

19. Chess S (1990): Studies in temperament: A paradigm in psychosocial research, *Yale Journal of Biology & Medicine* 63: 313–24.

20. Aristotle (1984): *Eudemian Ethics,* trans. Solomon J; in Barnes J, ed., *The Complete Works of Aristotle,* Princeton University Press, Princeton, NJ, vol. 2, 1922–81.

21. Aquinas, St. T (1997): *Summa Theologica,* New York, Christian Classics; see also Elders L (1994): *Philosophy of Nature of St. Thomas Aquinas: Nature, The Universe, Man,* Peter Lang, New York.

22. A. Smith (1976 [1759]): *The Theory of Moral Sentiments,* Raphael DD, Macfie AL, eds., Clarendon Press, Oxford.

23. For a discussion on the origins of natural law in law as well as morality see Grady MF, McGuire MT (1997): A theory of the origin of natural law, *Journal of Comparative Legal Issues* 8: 87–129.

24. Marx K, Engels F (1959 [1848]): *Communist Manifesto;* in Feuer LS, ed., *Marx and Engels: Basic Writings on Politics and Philosophy,* Doubleday/Anchor Books, New York, 1–41.

25. Ayer AJ (1946 [1936]): *Language, Truth and Logic,* Dover Books, New York.

26. Sartre JP (1948): *Existentialism and Humanism,* trans. Mairet P, Methuen, London.
27. Freud S (1961 [1923]): *Civilization and Its Discontents,* trans. Strachey J, W. W. Norton, New York. Freud posited that people shape a conscience out of a profound fear of losing their parents' love. He resorts to the critical role of attachment and fear of loss as the predicate for the development of a conscience, a Superego.
28. Cohen D (1979): *J. B. Watson: The Founder of Behaviorism,* Routledge, London. Also, Glynn I (1999): *An Anatomy of Thought: The Origin and Machinery of the Mind,* Oxford University Press, Oxford, 369–70.
29. Skinner BF (1953): *Science and Human Behavior,* Macmillan, New York.
30. Wilson EO (1975): *Sociobiology,* Harvard University Press, Cambridge, MA. See also Wilson EO (1994): *Naturalist,* Island Press, Washington, DC.
31. Hamilton WD (1964): The genetical evolution of social behaviour, *Journal of Theoretical Biology* 7: 1–52. Hamilton speculated that the social behavior of ants and bees was due to their "haplodiploid" genetics, which made their sisters closer genetically than their daughters. See also Ridley M (2003): *Nature via Nurture: Genes, Experience, and What Makes Us Human,* HarperCollins, New York, 242–5.
32. On the issue of Wilson's influence over Dawkins versus Dawkins over Wilson (since both *Sociobiology* and the first edition of *The Selfish Gene* were published within a year of each other), see Dawkins R (1990): *The Selfish Gene,* rev. ed., Oxford University Press, Oxford.
33. Quartz SR, Sejnowski TJ (2002): *Liars, Lovers, and Heroes: What the New Brain Science Reveals about How We Become Who We Are*, William Morrow, New York, 9.
34. Ibid., 20.

3. Beyond the Mind Zone

1. Libet B (1993): The neural time factor in conscious and unconscious events, *Ciba Foundation Symposium,* 174: 123–37. Also, Libet B (1999): How does conscious experience arise? The neural time factor, *Brain Research Bulletin* 50: 339–40.
2. Libet B, et al. (1983): Time of conscious intention to act in relation to onset of cerebral activity (readiness-potential): The unconscious initiation of a freely voluntary act, *Brain* 106(3): 623–42.
3. Ibid., 640–2.
4. Platt ML, Glimcher PW (1999): Neural correlates of decision variables in parietal cortex, *Nature* 400: 233–8.
5. Gazzaniga MS, Steven MS (2004): Free will in the twenty-first century: A discussion of neuroscience and the law; in Garland B, ed., *Neuro-*

science and the Law: Brain, Mind, and the Scales of Justice, Dana Press, Washington, DC, 51–70.

6. Platt & Glimcher (1999): Neural correlates, 237–8.

7. For a discussion of this see Gazzinaga & Steven (2004): Free will in the twenty-first century, 57–60.

8. Platt ML (2002): Neural correlates of decisions, *Current Opinion in Neurobiology* 12: 141–8. See also Platt ML, Glimcher PW (1997): Responses of intraparietal neurons to saccadic targets and visual distractors, *Journal of Neurophysiology* 78: 1574–89.

9. Bekoff M (2002): *Minding Animals: Awareness, Emotions and Heart,* Oxford University Press, Oxford; also Griffin D (2001): *Animal Minds: Beyond Cognition to Consciousness,* University of Chicago Press, Chicago. Also note Compassion in World Farming Trust's recent International Conference, "From Darwin to Dawkins: The science and implications of animal sentience," Queen Elizabeth II Conference Centre, London, March 17–18, 2005.

10. Platt & Glimcher (1999): Neural correlates, 233–5.

11. For an interesting examination of the impact of culture on brain, what has been termed "cultural biology," see Quartz SR, Sejnowski TJ (2002): *Liars, Lovers, and Heroes: What the New Brain Science Reveals about How We Become Who We Are,* William Morrow, New York.

12. Alternatively, imagine a quintessential scene from Piranesi's portfolio of Roman prisons.

13. Chomsky N (1957): *Syntactic Structures,* Morton de Gruyter, The Hague.

14. Calvin WH, Bickerton D (2000): *Lingua ex Machina: Reconciling Darwin and Chomsky with the Human Brain,* MIT Press, Cambridge, MA.

15. King-Casas B, et al. (2005): Getting to know you: Reputation and trust in a two-person economic exchange, *Science* 308: 78–83. Also see Fountain H (2005): Study of social interactions starts with a test of trust, *New York Times,* April 1: A20. Note that this recent research by King-Casas et al. strongly points to feelings of trust as beginning in the caudate nucleus, a C-shaped structure on each side of the brain, toward the center. Williams syndrome may involve this area, but it may also be simply the fact that these children lack approach inhibition. For an interesting discussion of the findings of researchers such as Dr. Helen Fisher on the role of the caudate nucleus in affecting the brain during a new romance, see Carey B (2005): Watching new love as it sears the brain, *New York Times,* sec. Science Times, May 31: F1, F6.

16. Herschkowitz FN, Herschkowitz EC (2002): *A Good Start in Life: Understanding Your Child's Brain and Behavior from Birth to Age 6,* Dana Press, New York, 268–71.

17. Davidson RJ (2000): Affective style, psychopathology and resilience: Brain mechanisms and plasticity, *American Psychologist* 55: 1196–214.

18. The assumptions made, however, about the findings of imaging technologies in *individual* cases may be open to question. These technologies are being used increasingly in civil and criminal cases. Nevertheless, their use for researching the brain, as a method for understanding brain function, is recognized by the scientific community – they are used on large numbers of people, and subject to reconfirmation from other studies.

19. Caspi A, et al. (2002): Role of genotype in the cycle of violence in maltreated children, *Science* 227: 851–4.

4. The Moral Brain

1. For a thorough discussion of the "emotional" brain see Le Doux J (1996): *The Emotional Brain: The Mysterious Underpinnings of Emotional Life,* Touchstone (Simon & Schuster), New York.

2. Schwartz JM, Begley S (2002): *The Mind and the Brain: Neuroplasticity and the Power of Mental Force,* HarperCollins, New York, 68–9; see also Niehoff D (1999): *The Biology of Violence,* Free Press, New York, 86–94; and also Newberg A, D'Aquili E, Rause V (2001): *Why God Won't Go Away,* Ballantine Books, New York, 43.

3. David M, Whalen PJ (2001): The amygdala: Vigilance and emotion, *Molecular Psychiatry* 6: 13–34. See also Goosens KA, Hobin JA, Maren S (2003): Auditory-evoked spike firing in the lateral amygdala and Pavlovian fear conditioning: Mnemonic code or fear bias? *Neuron* 40: 1013–22. Goosens et al.'s article points out that associative activity in the lateral amygdala encodes fear memory and contributes to the expression of learned fear behaviors. Note that studies conducted using imaging technologies have verified that the amygdala has a central role in a subject's response to emotionally charged stimuli: In one study, adults and children were scanned with fMRI while viewing a series of faces. When the subjects looked at scary faces, researchers detected increased activation in their left amygdala, as well as in an adjacent part of the brain, the substantia innominata. When the faces were neutral, activation of the left amygdala decreased considerably. See Thomas KM et al. (2001): Amygdala response to facial expressions in children and adults, *Biological Psychiatry* 49: 309–16.

4. Ninan PT (1999): The functional anatomy, neurochemistry, and pharmacology of anxiety, *Journal of Clinical Psychiatry* 60 [Suppl. 22]: 12–27.

5. Goldberg E (2001): *The Executive Brain: Frontal Lobes and the Civilized Mind,* Oxford University Press, New York, 31.

6. Newberg et al. (2001): *Why God Won't Go Away,* 45–6.

7. Manns JR, et al. (2003): Recognition memory and the human hippocampus, *Neuron* 37: 171–80.

8. Ferbinteanu J, Shapiro ML (2003): Recognition memory and the human hippocampus, *Neuron* 37: 1227–39. This study produced three new findings: Retrospective, current, and prospective coding were common and recorded in neural ensembles; recent memory could modulate neuronal activity more than spatial trajectory; and neuronal signals were shown to be important for task performance as seen from diminished retrospective and prospective coding. Information thus encoded in hippocampal neurons were about recent pasts, present, and imminent future, consistent with episodic memory. Nakazawa K, et al. (2003): Hippocampal CA3 NMDA receptors are crucial for memory acquisition of one-time experience, *Neuron* 38: 305–15. In this study, the context in or incident about which facts were learned includes learning about one-time, unique experiences.

9. Scoville WB, Milner B (2000 [1957]): Loss of recent memory after bilateral hippocampal lesions, *Journal of Neuropsychiatry & Clinical Neurosciences* 12: 103–13. For transformation of short- to long-term memory, see Cui Z, et al. (2004): Inducible and reversible NR1 knockout reveals crucial role of the NMDA receptor in preserving remote memories in the brain, *Neuron* 41: 781–93.

10. Allman JM, et al. (2001): The anterior cingulate cortex: The evolution of an interface between emotion and cognition, *Annals of the New York Academy of Sciences* 19: 107–17. See also Lane RD, et al. (1998): Neural correlates of levels of emotional awareness: Evidence of an interaction between emotion and attention in the anterior cingulate cortex, *Journal of Cognitive Neuroscience* 10: 525–35.

11. Carter CS, Botvinick MM, Cohen JD (1999): The contribution of the anterior cingulate cortex to executive processes in cognition, *Reviews in the Neurosciences* 10: 49–57.

12. Posner MI, Rothbart MK (1998): Attention, self-regulation and consciousness, *Philosophical Transactions of the Royal Society of London B Biological Sciences* 353(1377): 1915–27.

13. Goldberg (2001): *The Executive Brain,* 142 ff.

14. Matsumoto K, Tanaka K (2004): Conflict and cognitive control, *Science* 303: 969–70.

15. Ibid., 969. See also Schwartz & Begley (2002): *The Mind and the Brain,* 65.

16. Schwartz & Begley (2002): *The Mind and the Brain,* 64–7.

17. Researchers have shown that the ACC does respond during conflict by recruiting the assistance of the lateral prefrontal cortex. See Kearns JG, et al. (2004): Anterior cingulate conflict monitoring and adjustments in control, *Science* 303: 1023–6. The authors point out that although there seems to be a direct relationship between ACC activity on high conflict

and error trials and behavioral adjustments, nonetheless, the ACC does not seem to direct the manner or direction of the control to be exerted by the lateral prefrontal cortex. The prefrontal cortex is essentially responsible for execution of cognitive control. See also Matsumoto & Tanaka (2004): Conflict and cognitive control, 970: They propose that cognitive control that is recruited by the ACC may be "consequential" (based on conflicts between evoked plans of concrete actions), whereas control through the lateral prefrontal cortex may be "preemptive," which means more capable of preventing future conflicts of a similar nature.

18. Goldberg (2001): *The Executive Brain*, 31. Also see Newberg et al. (2001): *Why God Won't Go Away*, 88–9.

19. Allman JM, et al. (2001): The anterior cingulate cortex, 107–17. Note that large spindle-shaped cells are found in apes and humans, but are absent in other mammals. They are far more numerous in humans than in chimpanzees. These neurons are not present at birth; they do not appear in the ACC until about the fourth month. See Quartz SR, Sejnowski TJ (2002): *Liars, Lovers, and Heroes: What the New Brain Science Reveals about How We Become Who We Are*, William Morrow, New York, 31 ff. It has been suggested that the presence of spindle-shaped cells is affected by the impact of culture on brain plasticity and is directly linked to decision-making capacity, social competence, and the development of a framework for dealing with life's conflicts and survival.

20. Quartz & Sejnowski (2002): *Liars, Lovers, and Heroes*, 165–6.

21. Newberg et al. (2001): *Why God Won't Go Away*, 194; also see Cowley MA, Smith RG, Diano S (2003): The distribution and mechanism of action of ghrelin in the CNS demonstrates a novel hypothalamic circuit regulating energy homeostasis, *Neuron* 37: 646–61.

22. Goldberg (2001): *The Executive Brain*, 321–36.

23. Vogeley K, et al. (2000): Essential functions of the human self model are implemented in the prefrontal cortex, *Consciousness & Cognition: An International Journal* 8: 343–63.

24. Goldberg (2001): *The Executive Brain*, 2.

25. Ibid., 35.

26. Wagner AD, et al. (2001): Prefrontal contributions to executive control: fMRI evidence for functional distinctions within lateral prefrontal cortex, *NeuroImage* 14, 1337–47.

27. For a more detailed discussion of this topic, see Goldberg (2001): *The Executive Brain*, 35 ff.

28. Koechlin E, et al. (1999): The role of the anterior prefrontal cortex in human cognition, *Nature* 399: 148–61.

29. Rowe JB, et al. (2001): Imaging the mental components of a planning task, *Neuropsychologia* 39: 315–17.

30. Rogers RD, et al. (1999): Choosing between small, likely rewards and large, unlikely rewards activates inferior and orbital prefrontal cortex, *Journal of Neuroscience* 19: 9029–38.

31. Rizzolatti G, Craighero L (2004): The mirror-neuron system, *Annual Review of Neuroscience* 27: 169–92.

32. Ibid., 172–5. Mirror neurons are a class of visuomotor neuron. They exist in some primates as well as in humans. The mirror-neuron system in humans has elements not seen in monkeys: (1) mirror-neuron system activation occurs from intransitive meaningless movements; and (2) temporal characteristics of cortical excitability, during action observation, suggest that this system in humans codes also for the movements forming an action – not only for the action itself, as in monkey mirror neurons. See Wagner et al. (2001): Prefrontal contributions to executive control, 1337–40.

33. Buccino G, et al. (2001): Action observation activates premotor and parietal areas in a somatotopic manner: An fMRI study, *European Journal of Neuroscience* 13: 400–4.

34. Rizolatti G (2004): The mirror-neuron system and imitation; in Hurley S, ed., *Perspectives on Imitation: From Mirror Neurons to Memes*, MIT Press, Cambridge, MA.

35. Quartz & Sejnowski (2002): *Liars, Lovers, and Heroes,* 22–6; also see Schwartz & Begley (2002): *The Mind and the Brain*, 96–131.

36. Schwartz & Begley (2002): *The Mind and the Brain*, 15–16.

37. Taub E, Uswatte G, Pidikiti R (1999): Constraint-induced movement therapy: A new family of techniques with broad application to physical rehabilitation, *Journal of Rehabilitation Research & Development* 36: 237–51.

38. Martin SD, et al. (2001): Brain blood flow changes in depressed patients treated with interpersonal psychotherapy or venlafaxine hydrochloride, *Archives of General Psychiatry* 58: 641–8. See also Sackeim HA (2001): Functional brain circuits in major depression and remission, *Archives of General Psychiatry* 58: 649–50; and Thase ME (2001): Neuroimaging profiles and the differential therapies of depression, *Archives of General Psychiatry* 58: 651–3.

39. Goldapple K, et al. (2004): Modulation of cortical-limbic pathways in major depression: Treatment-specific effects of cognitive behavior therapy, *Archives of General Psychiatry* 61: 34–41.

40. Edeline JM (1999): Learning-induced physiological plasticity in the thalamocortical sensory systems: A critical evaluation of receptive field plasticity, map changes and their potential mechanisms, *Progress in Neurobiology* 57: 165–224.

5. Bad without Conscience

1. *Note:* The information in this chapter regarding Ricky Green came from two interviews I conducted on June 11 and August 3, 1990, at the Tarrant County Jail in Forth Worth, Texas. This information was supplemented by the following: (1) psychological evaluation by Dale W. Williams, Wise County Outreach Center; (2) report of psychological testing conducted by J. Randall Price; (3) memo to Suzie Johnson re: Jail Conference on July 13, 1990; (4) psychiatric evaluations by Richard E. Coons, M.D., P.S., Mark A. Kalish, M.D., M.P.H., and George Parker, M.D.; (5) undated letter to Ricky Green from Jim Dollar, Sharon's father; (6) worksheets from when Ricky Green was in the Care Unit; (7) newspaper clippings from: *Fort Worth Star–Telegram,* June 18, 1989; the *Dallas Morning News,* July 26, 1989; *Fort Worth Star–Telegram,* May 21, 1989; (8) autopsy reports of Jeffrey Lynn David (dated April 27, 1985), Betty Jo Monroe (dated October 14, 1985), Steven Fefferman (dated December 29, 1986), and Sandra Bailey (dated December 2, 1985); (9) sworn statements by Ricky Green to detectives R. N. SoRelle and D. F. LaRue on April 27 and 28, 1989; (10) copies of evaluations consisting of physical exam, psychiatric evaluation, and psychological evaluation done by the Texas Department of Mental Health and Mental Retardation to determine if Ricky Green was competent to stand trial; (11) memo from Suzie Johnson dated 4.14.90 re: notes on Sharon Green's trial; (12) memo from the Texas Resource Center dated March 22, 1990, concerning the recent legal developments in the *Penry* v. *Lynaugh* case; (13) report of neurological evaluation of Ricky Green conducted by Dr. Sheff D. Olinger; and (14) medical records from Dr. Byers, from Northeast Community Hospital, and from the Care Unit Hospital of Dallas–Fort Worth.

2. Kirwin BR (1997): *The Mad, the Bad, and the Innocent,* HarperCollins, New York, 86. See also Ressler RK, Schachtman T (1992): *Whoever Fights Monsters,* St. Martin's Press, New York.

3. American Psychiatric Association (2000): *Diagnostic and Statistical Manual of Mental Disorders,* 4th ed. (Text Revision), American Psychiatric Association, Washington, DC: "Antisocial Personality Disorder," DSM-IV-TR 301.7. This definition comprises four broad criteria and seven subsets:

   A. There is a pervasive pattern of disregard for and violation of the rights of others, occurring since age 15 years, as indicated by three (or more) of the following:
      1. Failure to conform to social norms with respect to lawful behaviors as indicated by repeatedly performing acts that are grounds for arrest.
      2. Deceitfulness, as indicated by repeated lying, use of aliases, or conning others for personal profit or pleasure.

3. Impulsivity or failure to plan ahead.
4. Irritability and aggressiveness, as indicated by repeated physical fights or assaults.
5. Reckless disregard for safety of self or others.
6. Consistent irresponsibility, as indicated by repeated failure to sustain consistent work behavior or honor financial obligations.
7. Lack of remorse as indicated by being indifferent to or rationalizing having hurt, mistreated, or stolen from another.

B. The individual is at least age 18.
C. There is evidence of Conduct Disorder with onset before age 15 years.
D. The occurrence of antisocial behavior is not exclusively during the course of Schizophrenia or a Manic Episode.

4. Stone MH (1998): The personalities of murderers: The importance of psychopathy and sadism; in Skodol AE, ed., *Psychopathology and Violent Crime*, American Psychiatric Press, Washington, DC, 29–52.

5. Cleckley H (1972): *The Mask of Sanity*, 5th ed., C. V. Mosby, St. Louis, MO.

6. Hare ED, et al. (1990): The Revised Psychopathy Checklist: Reliability and factor structure, *Psychological Assessment* 2: 338–41. See also Hare RD (1996): Psychopathy: A construct whose time has come, *Criminal Justice and Behavior* 23: 25–54.

7. For a discussion of this, see Harpur TJ, Hakstian R, Hare RD (1988): Factor structure of the Psychopathy Checklist, *Journal of Consulting and Clinical Psychology* 56: 741–7.

8. Finn PR, Ramsey SE, Earleywine M (2000): Frontal EEG response to threat, aggressive traits and a family history of alcoholism: A preliminary study, *Journal of Studies on Alcohol* 61: 38–45; Lau MA, Pihl RO, Peterson JB (1995): Provocation, acute alcohol intoxication, cognitive performance and aggression, *Journal of Abnormal Psychology* 104: 150–5.

9. Henderson M (1982): An empirical classification of convicted violent offenders, *British Journal of Criminology* 22: 1–20; also Henderson M (1983): Self-reported assertion and aggression among violent offenders with high or low levels of overcontrolled hostility, *Personality and Individual Differences* 1: 113–15.

10. Sher KJ, Trull TJ (1994): Personality and disinhibitory psychopathology: Alcoholism and antisocial personality disorder, *Journal of Abnormal Psychology* 103: 92–102.

11. Borrill JA, Rosen BK, Summerfield AB (1987): The influence of alcohol on judgment of facial expressions of emotion, *British Journal of Medical Psychology* 60: 71–7; Smith SS, Newman JP (1990): Alcohol and drug abuse–dependence disorders in psychopathic and nonpsychopathic criminal offenders, *Journal of Abnormal Psychology* 99: 430–9; O'Connor S, et al. (1994): Reduced P3 amplitudes are associated with both a family

history of alcoholism and antisocial personality disorder, *Progress in Neuropsychopharmacology & Biological Psychiatry* 18: 1307–21.

12. See Lewis DO (1992): From abuse to violence: Psychophysiological consequences of maltreatment, *Journal of the American Academy of Child & Adolescent Psychiatry* 31: 383–91.

13. Loeber R, Stouthamer-Loeber M (1986): Family factors as correlates and predictors of juvenile conduct problems and delinquency; in Tonry M, Morris N, eds. *Crime and Justice: An Annual Review of Research,* University of Chicago Press, Chicago, vol. 7, 29–149.

14. Eysenck HJ, Gudjonsson GH (1989): *The Causes and Cures of Criminality,* Plenum Press, New York. See also Pincus JH (2001): *Base Instincts: What Makes Killers Kill?* W. W. Norton, New York.

15. Farrington DP (1989): Early predictors of adolescent aggression and adult violence, *Violence Victims* 4: 79–100; Raine A (1993): *The Psychopathology of Crime: Criminal Behavior as a Clinical Disorder,* Academic Press, San Diego. Regarding correlation of violence, crime, academic problems, and behavioral problems, see also Raine A, et al. (1996): High rates of violence, crime, academic problems, and behavioral problems in males with both early neuromotor deficits and unstable family environments, *Archives of General Psychiatry* 53: 544–9.

16. See, for illustration of impact of "stress," Adams RB, et al. (2003): Effects of gaze on amygdala sensitivity to anger and fear faces, *Science* 300: 1536–7. Anger and fear have direct effects on the functioning of the amygdala. Depression, meanwhile, has been shown to bring about loss of brain tissue. See Sheline Y (2003): Untreated depression and hippocampal volume loss, *American Journal of Psychiatry* 160: 1516–18.

17. Texas Department of Criminal Justice, "Last Statement – Ricky Green," www.tdcj.state.tx.us/stat/greenrickylast.htm .

18. Rutter M, Giller H, Hagell A (2001): *Antisocial Behavior by Young People,* Cambridge University Press, Cambridge, UK.

19. Caspi A, et al. (2002): Role of genotype in the cycle of violence in maltreated children, *Science* 227: 851–4.

20. Morell V (1993): Evidence found for a possible "aggressive gene," *Science* 260: 1722–3.

21. Stokstad E (2002): Violent effects of abuse tied to gene, *Science* 297: 752.

22. For a detailed discussion of "selection" versus "instruction," see Gazzaniga MS (1992): *Nature's Mind: The Biological Roots of Thinking, Emotions, Sexuality, Language, and Intelligence,* Basic Books, New York.

23. Hariri AR, et al. (2002): Serotonin transporter genetic variation and the response of the human amygdala, *Science* 297: 400–5. See also Adams et al. (2003): Effects of gaze on amygdala sensitivity.

24. Schwartz CE, et al. (2003): Inhibited and uninhibited infants "grown": Adult amygdalar response to novelty, *Science* 300: 1952–3.

25. Blair RJR (2001): Neurocognitive models of aggression: The antisocial personality disorders and psychopathy, *Journal of Neurological & Neurosurgical Psychiatry* 71: 727–31.
26. Siegel A, et al. (1999): Neuropharmacology of brain-stimulation-evoked aggression, *Neuroscience & Biobehavioral Reviews* 23: 359–89.
27. Raine A, et al. (1998): Prefrontal glucose deficits in murderers lacking psychosocial deprivation, *Neuropsychology, Neuropsychiatry, & Behavioral Neurology* 11: 1–7.
28. Chretien RD, Persinger MD (2000): "Prefrontal deficits" discriminate young offenders from age-matched cohorts: Juvenile delinquency as an expected feature of normal distribution of prefrontal cerebral development, *Psychological Reports* 87: 1196–202.
29. Volkow ND, Tancredi L (1987): Neural substrates of violent behavior: A preliminary study with positron emission tomography, *British Journal of Psychiatry* 151: 668–73; also see Volkow ND, et al. (1995): Brain glucose metabolism in violent psychiatric patients: A preliminary study, *Psychiatry Research* 61: 243–53.
30. Raine A, Bucksbaum M, LaCasse L (1997): Brain abnormalities in murderers indicated by positron emission tomography, *Biological Psychiatry* 42: 495–508.
31. Anderson SW, et al. (1999): Impairment of social and moral behavior related to early damage in human prefrontal cortex, *Nature Neuroscience* 2: 1032–7.
32. For a detailed discussion of the Phineas Gage case, see Damasio AR (1994): *Descartes' Error: Emotion, Reason and the Human Brain*, Grosset/Putnam, New York, 1–19.
33. Kiel KA, et al. (2001): Limbic abnormalities in affective processing by criminal psychopaths as revealed by functional magnetic resonance imaging, *Biological Psychiatry* 50: 677–84.
34. For a detailed review of the role of the frontal lobe in criminal behavior, see Bower MC, Price BH (2001): Neuropsychiatry of frontal lobe dysfunction in violent and criminal behavior: A critical review, *Journal of Neurological & Neurosurgical Psychiatry* 71: 720–6.
35. Blair (2001): Neurocognitive models of aggression, 728.

6. The Biology of Choice

1. Kuhn T (1976): *The Structure of Scientific Revolutions*, 2d ed., University of Chicago Press, Chicago. Kuhn first articulated the importance of the process of thought itself in the mechanisms of knowing, and of the *paradigm shift* as being the development that advances science into new creative areas. The scientist's personal view of reality is shaped by categories, relationships, and decisive examples. When the paradigm shifts because

of a new insight, this reality ultimately shifts, and new categories, relationships, and examples are established.

2. Lhermitte F (1983): Utilization behavior and its relation to lesions of the frontal lobes, *Brain* 106: 237–55.

3. For a very interesting discussion of this phenomenon and a contrarian critique of its significance, see Levy N, Bayne T (2004): A will of one's own: consciousness, control and character, *International Journal of Law & Psychiatry* 27: 459–70 (special issue on *Responsibility and Mental Impairment*).

4. See ibid. for a discussion of this notion.

5. Libet B (1999): How does conscious experience arise? The neural time factor, *Brain Research Bulletin* 50: 339–40. See also Van de Grind W (2002): Physical, neural, and mental timing, *Consciousness & Cognition* 11: 241–64.

6. Platt ML, Glimcher PW (1997): Responses of intraparietal neurons to saccadic targets and visual distractors, *Journal of Neurophysiology* 78: 1574–89. See also Platt ML, Glimcher PW (1999): Neural correlates of decision variables in parietal cortex, *Nature* 400: 233–8.

7. Libet B, et al. (1983): Time of conscious intention to act in relation to onset of cerebral activity (readiness-potential): The unconscious initiation of a freely voluntary act, *Brain* 106(3): 623–42.

8. For a discussion of this see Platt ML (2002): Neural correlates of decisions, *Current Opinion in Neurobiology* 12: 141–8.

9. Lau HC, Rogers RD, Haggard P (2004): Attention to intention, *Science* 303: 1208–10.

10. Engleman DM (2004): The where and when of intention, *Science* 303: 1144–6.

11. Lau et al. (2004): Attention to intention, 1210, showed that stronger connectivity occurred between the presupplementary motor area and the prefrontal cortex when the subjects were asked to pay attention to their intention to move.

12. Wegner DM (2002): *The Illusion of Conscious Will*, MIT Press, Cambridge, MA.

13. Dennett DC (2003): *Freedom Evolves*, Allen Lane, London.

14. Wegner (2002): *The Illusion of Conscious Will*, 318.

15. Ibid., 326. For a discussion of somatic marker theory, see Damasio AR (1999): *The Feeling of What Happens: Body and Emotion in the Making of Consciousness*, Harcourt, New York, 42.

16. Ibid., 327.

17. Hasson U, et al. (2004): Intersubject synchronization of cortical activity during natural vision, *Science* 303: 1634–40. See also Pessoa L (2004): Seeing the world in the same way, *Science* 303: 1617–18.

18. Davidson RJ (2000): Affective style, psychopathology, and resilience:

Brain mechanisms and plasticity, *American Psychologist* 55, 1196–214.

19. Imaging technologies such as computerized axial tomography (CAT scans), functional magnetic resonance imaging (fMRI), positron emission tomography (PET scans), and computerized electroencephalography (CEEG), to name a few.

20. Tancredi LR (1997): Science of the mind in the contexts of a culture; in Romanucci-Ross L, Moerman DE, Tancredi LR, eds., *The Anthropology of Medicine,* 3d ed., Bergin & Garvey, Westport, CT, 205–317.

21. Tobler PN, Fiorillo CD, Schultz WC (2005): Adaptive coding of reward value by dopamine neurons, *Science* 307: 1642–5. Note that midbrain dopamine neurons discriminate among schedule (size, etc.) of varying rewards.

22. Studies are revealing the presence of neural circuits for primary emotions. See Pelletier M, et al. (2003): Separate neural circuits for primary emotions? Brain activity during self-induced sadness and happiness in professional actors, *Brain Imaging* 14: 1111–16. See also Eugène F, et al. (2003): The impact of individual differences on the neural circuitry underlying sadness, *NeuroImage* 19: 354–64.

23. Damasio (1999): *The Feeling of What Happens,* 42 ff.

24. Herschkowitz FN, Herschkowitz EC (2002): *A Good Start in Life: Understanding Your Child's Brain and Behavior from Birth to Age 6,* Dana Press, New York, 201–2.

25. Ibid., 201. For further inquiry see Cassidy KW, Chu JY, Dahlsgaard KK (1997): Preschoolers' ability to adopt justice and care orientations to moral dilemmas, *Early Education & Development* 8: 419–34.

26. Herschkowitz & Herschkowitz (2002): *A Good Start in Life,* 171.

27. Ibid., 202. For further exploration, see Kochanska G, Casey FJ, Fukumoto A (1995): Toddlers' sensitivity to standard violations, *Child Development* 66: 643–56.

28. Wallis C, Dell K (2004): "What Makes Teens Tick," *Time* 163 (May 10): 56–65.

29. Gotay N, Giedd J, Rapoport JL (2002): Brain development in healthy, hyperactive, and psychotic children, *Archives of Neurology* 59: 1244–8.

30. Giedd J (1999): Brain development, IX: Human brain growth, *American Journal of Psychiatry* 156: 4–7.

31. Anderson SW, et al. (1999): Impairment of social and moral behavior related to early damage in human prefrontal cortex, *Nature Neuroscience* 2: 1032–7.

32. Note Moll JCA, de Oliveira-Souza R, Eslinger P (2003): Morals and the human brain: A working model, *NeuroReport* 14: 299–305. Researchers recognize the presence of specific cortical–subcortical loops that organize motivation, emotion, and social cognition to uniquely human experience

and behavior. Recognizing that they are unlikely to identify a specific "moral center" of the brain, they identified several regions that may be important: decoding by sensory systems; activation of basic emotional reactions by anteromedial temporal, brain stem, and basal forebrain structures; attachment of moral emotional relevance by orbital and medial prefrontal structures; and implementation and control of actions by the frontal lobes. There appears to be a corticolimbic network (i.e., one involving both the cortex and limbic structures) recruited during moral judgments: functional connectivity increases between the left frontopolar cortex (FPC) and the orbitofrontal cortex (OFC), the anterior temporal and anterior cingulate cortices, in addition to subcortical and limbic structures, such as the thalamus, midbrain, and basal forebrain during the performance of moral judgments.

33. De Waal FBM (1998): *Chimpanzee Politics: Power and Sex among Apes*, rev. ed., Johns Hopkins University Press, Baltimore, 235 ff.; Wright R (1994): *The Moral Animal: Why We Are the Way We Are*, Vintage Books, New York, 466 ff.

34. Brosnan SF, de Waal FBM (2003): Monkeys reject unequal pay, *Nature* 425: 297–9.

35. Ibid., 299.

36. It is important to note that "inequity aversion" is essential for cohesiveness in a society. One way one could argue that inequity aversion is supportive of cooperation is that it prevents to some extent the reasons for envy and jealousy, which are ultimately very destructive forces.

37. Brosnan & de Waal (2003): Monkeys reject unequal pay, 299.

38. Ibid., 297–9.

39. Gazzaniga MS (1992): *Nature's Mind: The Biological Roots of Thinking, Emotions, Sexuality, Language, and Intelligence*, Basic Books, New York, 2–7, 199–204.

40. *Interactionism* is a third way of looking at the nature–nurture debate. Advocates of this theory acknowledge that many basic qualities of human nature are in fact genetically determined, but that environmental influences can shape variations in such capacities. To the interactionist, therefore, the brain is seen as malleable, and capable of change through learning, but within well-defined limitations that are set by our genes.

41. Gazzaniga (1992): *Nature's Mind*, 2.

42. Jerne N (1967): Antibodies and learning: Selection versus instruction; in Quarton G, Melnechuk T, Schmitt FO, eds., *The Neurosciences: A Study Program*, Rockefeller University Press, New York, vol. 1, 200–5.

43. Broca P (1863): Localisation des fonctions cérébrales: Siège du langage articulé. *Bulletins de la Société d'Anthropologie* 4: 200–4.

44. Wernicke C (1874): *Der apasische Symptomkomplex*, Cohn & Weigert, Breslau, Germany.

45. Calvin WH, Bickerton D (2000): *Lingua ex Machina: Reconciling Darwin and Chomsky with the Human Brain,* MIT Press, Cambridge, MA.

46. Chomsky N (1957): *Syntactic Structures,* Morton de Gruyter, The Hague.

47. Chomsky N (1986): *Knowledge of Language: Its Nature, Origin, and Use,* Praeger, New York.

48. Chomsky N (2000): *New Horizons in the Study of Language and Mind,* MIT Press, Cambridge, MA.

49. Greene J (1972): *Psycholinguistics: Chomsky and Psychology,* Penguin Books, Harmondsworth, UK.

50. Pinker S (1997): *How the Mind Works,* W. W. Norton, New York, 165–92.

51. Gazzaniga (1992): *Nature's Mind,* 74–9.

52. Herschkowitz & Herschkowitz (2002): *A Good Start in Life,* 202–3.

53. Moll et al. (2003): Morals and the human brain, 303–5.

7. Sex and the Single Moral Code

1. Gray J (1993): *Men Are from Mars, Women Are from Venus.* Harper-Collins, New York.

2. Cahill L (2003): Sex-related influences on the neurobiology of emotionally influenced memory, *Annals of the New York Academy of Sciences* 985: 163–73; also see Giedd JN, et al. (1997): Sexual dimorphism of the developing human brain, *Neuropsychopharmacology and Biological Psychiatry* 21: 1185–201.

3. George MS, et al. (1996): Gender differences in regional cerebral blood flow during transient self-induced sadness or happiness, *Biological Psychiatry* 4: 859–71; also Goldstein JM, et al. (2001): Normal sexual dimorphism of the adult human brain assessed by in vivo magnetic resonance imaging, *Cerebral Cortex* 11: 490–7.

4. Baron-Cohen S (2003): *The Essential Difference: The Truth about the Male and Female Brain,* Basic Books, New York. See also Baron-Cohen S, Lutchmaya S, Knickmeyer R (2004): *Prenatal Testosterone in Mind: Amniotic Fluid Studies,* MIT Press, Cambridge, MA.

5. Baron-Cohen (2003): *The Essential Difference,* 26–7.

6. Ibid., 61.

7. Ibid., 61–2.

8. Ridley M (1996): *The Origins of Virtue: Human Instincts and the Evolution of Cooperation,* Penguin, London, 151–69; see also Mithen S (1996): *The Prehistory of the Mind,* Penguin, Harmondsworth, UK.

9. Baron-Cohen (2003): *The Essential Difference,* 96–9.

10. Baron-Cohen (ibid., 96–7) points out that studies of rats show that male rats are far superior at finding their path through a maze. He adds that males of various species from as early as two years of age have superior

accuracy over the females in throwing objects. This involves systemizing in understanding the basic rules involved in projecting, motion, and force.

11. Noe R (1992): Alliance formation among male baboons: Shopping for profitable partners; in Harcourt AH, de Waal, FBM, eds., *Coalitions and Alliances in Humans and Other Animals,* Oxford University Press, Oxford.

12. Ridley (1996): *The Origins of Virtue,* 151–4.

13. Testosterone increases relatively during menopause in women because of the decline of estrogen. One often sees at this time heightened sensual desire. See Fisher H (2004): *Why We Love: The Nature and Chemistry of Romantic Love,* Henry Holt, New York, 82–3.

14. Baron-Cohen (2003): *The Essential Difference,* 97–9; also see Michael RP, Zumpe D (1998): Sex difference in spatial abilities: Strategic and experiential correlates, *Development Neuropsychology* 14: 233–60.

15. For a discussion of testosterone levels in male children, see Ridley M (1993): *The Red Queen: Sex and the Evolution of Human Nature,* HarperCollins, New York, 255–8. Also see Zucker KJ (2003): Re: [Hrabovsky & Hutson (see note 17)] Androgen imprinting of the brain in animal models and humans with intersex disorders: Review and recommendations, *Journal of Urology* 169(6): 2306.

16. Ridley (1996): *The Origins of Virtue,* 99; see also Reinisch JM (1977): Prenatal exposure of human fetuses to synthetic progestin and estrogen affects personality, *Nature* 266: 561–2.

17. Hrabovszky Z, Hutson JM (2002): Androgen imprinting of the brain in animal models and humans with intersex disorders: Review and recommendations, *Journal of Urology* 168(5): 2142–8. See also Hines M (1998): Abnormal sexual development and psychosexual issues, *Bailliere's Clinical Endocrinology & Metabolism* 12: 173–89.

18. Berenbaum SA, Hines M (1992): Early androgens are related to childhood sex-typed toy preferences, *Psychol Sci* 3: 203.

19. Ehrhardt AA, Meyer-Bahlburg HF (1981): Effects of prenatal sex hormones on gender-related behavior, *Science* 211: 1312–18.

20. Hrabovszky & Hutson (2002): Androgen imprinting, 2143–4. Also see Imperato-McGinley J, et al. (1957): Steroid 5 alpha-reductase-deficiency in man: Imprinting and the establishment of gender role, *AMA Archives of Neurological Psychiatry* 77: 333; and Farkas A, Rosler A (1993): Ten years experience with masculinizing genitoplasty in male pseudohermaphroditism due to 17 beta-hydroxysteroid dehydrogenase deficiency, *European Journal of Pediatrics* 152 (Suppl. 2): S88–90.

21. Geschwind N, Galaburda AM (1985): Cerebral lateralization, biological mechanisms, associations and pathology, I: A hypothesis and a program for research, *Archives of Neurology* 42: 428–59.

22. *Note:* There seems to be ample evidence of this phenomenon in nature.

There are several medical conditions where either too little testosterone is produced prenatally, or there is a problem with the body's ability to utilize the testosterone that is produced, which results in male children who have problems with spatial ability and systematizing. See, for example, idiopathic hypogonadotropic hypogonadism (IHH), where there is a deficiency in the hormone that regulates the production and release of testosterone and other sex hormones, and androgen insensitivity syndrome (AIS; formerly known as testicular feminization), where normal sex hormones are produced but there is a genetic abnormality at the level of the cell, which is insensitive to the hormones. These males look like females but have no female organs and are not good at systematizing. [See Baron-Cohen (2003): *The Essential Difference,* 102.] Also see Masica D, et al. (1968): IQ, fetal sex hormones and cognitive patterns: Studies of the testicular feminizing syndrome of androgen insensitivity, *Johns Hopkins Medical Journal* 124: 34–43.

23. Martino G, Winner E (1995): Talents and disorders: Relationships among handedness, sex, and college major, *Brain and Cognition* 29: 66–84. See also Bryden M, McManus I, Bulman-Fleming M (1994): Evaluating the empirical support for the Geschwind–Behan–Galaburda model of cerebral lateralization, *Brain & Cognition* 26: 103–67.

24. Sapolsky RM (1997): *The Trouble with Testosterone: And Other Essays on the Biology of the Human Predicament,* Simon & Schuster, New York, 149–59. See also Baron-Cohen et al. (2004): *Prenatal Testosterone in Mind.*

25. Adolphs R (2003): Investigating the cognitive neuroscience of social behavior, *Neuropsychologia* 41: 119–26.

26. Adolphs R (2003): Is the human amygdala specialized for processing social information? *Annals of the New York Academy of Sciences* 985: 326–40. Studies confirm that the amygdala has a major role in modulating cognition as well as behavior "on the basis of a stimulus' motivational, emotional, and social attributes." The amygdala's primary function in lower animals may be domain-general processing of motivation. However, in primates and especially humans it may have reached the stage of specifically processing social information.

27. Adolphs R (2001): The neurobiology of social cognition, *Current Opinion in Neurobiology* 11: 231–9.

28. Rowe AD, et al. (2001): "Theory of mind" impairments and their relationship to executive functioning following frontal lobe excisions, *Brain* 124(3): 600–16.

29. Thomas KM, et al. (2001): Amygdala response to facial expressions in children and adults, *Biological Psychiatry* 49: 309–16.

30. Farrow TF, et al. (2001): Investigating the functional anatomy of empathy and forgiveness, *NeuroReport* 12: 2433–8.

31. Fletcher PC, et al. (1995): The mind's eye: Precuneus activation in memory-related imagery, *NeuroImage* 2: 195–200.

32. Baron-Cohen S, et al. (1999): Social intelligence in the normal and autistic brain: An fMRI study, *European Journal of Neuroscience* 11: 1891–8.

33. Chrétien RD, Persinger MD (2000): "Prefrontal deficits" discriminate young offenders from age-matched cohorts: Juvenile delinquency as an expected feature of normal distribution of prefrontal cerebral development, *Psychological Reports* 87: 1196–202.

34. Kiehl KA, et al. (2001): Limbic abnormalities in affective processing by criminal psychopaths as revealed by functional magnetic resonance imaging, *Biological Psychiatry* 50: 677–84.

8. Brain Biology and Sex

1. Karama S, et al. (2002): Areas of brain activation in males and females during viewing of erotic film excerpts, *Human Brain Mapping* 16: 1–13.

2. Beauregard M, Levesque J, Bourgouin P (2001): Neural correlates of conscious self-regulation of emotion, *Journal of Neuroscience* 21: RC 165.

3. Arnow BA, et al. (2002): Brain activation and sexual arousal in healthy heterosexual males, *Brain* 125: 1014–23.

4. Hull EF, et al. (1995): Extracellular dopamine in the medial preoptic area: Implications for sexual motivation and hormonal control of copulation, *Journal of Neuroscience* 15: 7465–71.

5. Meston CM, Frohlich PF (2000): The neurobiology of sexual function, *Archives of General Psychiatry* 57: 1012–30.

6. Pfaus JG, Kippin TE, Centeno S (2000): Conditioning and sexual behavior: A review, *Hormones & Behavior* 40: 291–321.

7. Pradham S, Singh MN, Pandey N (2998): Klüver Bucy syndrome in young children, *Clinical Neurology & Neurosurgery* 100: 254–8.

8. Terzian H, Dalle Ore G (1955): Syndrome of Klüver and Bucy reproduced in man by bilateral removal of the temporal lobes, *Neurology* 5: 373–80.

9. Freeman W (1973): Sexual behavior and fertility after frontal lobotomy, *Biological Psychiatry* 6: 97–104.

10. Meisel RL, Sachs BD (1994): The physiology of male sexual behavior; in Knobil E, Neill JD, eds., *The Physiology of Reproduction,* 2 vols., Raven Press, New York, vol. 2, 3–105.

11. Greenfield S (2000): *The Private Life of the Brain,* Wiley, New York, 4–7.

12. Fisher H (2004): *Why We Love: The Nature and Chemistry of Romantic Love,* Henry Holt, New York, 79–82.

13. Hamann S, et al. (2004): Men and women differ in amygdala response to visual stimuli, *Nature Neuroscience* 7: 411–16.

14. Ibid., 411–14.
15. Gottfried JA, O'Doherty J, Dolan RJ (2003): Encoding predictive reward value in human amygdala and ortibofrontal cortex, *Science* 301: 1104–7.
16. Thoughtful monkey sex, in Holden C, ed. (2004): Random samples, *Science* 303: 952.
17. Baron-Cohen S (2003): *The Essential Difference: The Truth about the Male and Female Brain,* Basic Books, New York, 110–11.
18. Rasia-Filho AA, Londero RG, Achaval M (1999): Effects of gonadal hormones on the morphology of neurons from the medial amygdaloid nucleus of rats, *Brain Research Bulletin* 48: 173–83.
19. Baron-Cohen (2003): *The Essential Difference,* 110.
20. Holstege G, et al. (2003): Brain activation during human male ejaculation, *Journal of Neuroscience* 23: 9185–93.
21. Ibid., 9189–91.
22. Sell LA, et al. (1999): Activation of reward circuitry in human opiate addicts, *European Journal of Neuroscience* 11: 1042–18. See also Brieter HC, et al. (1997): Acute effects of cocaine on human brain activity and emotion, *Neuron* 19: 591–611.
23. Seecof R, Tennant Jr FS (1986): Subjective perceptions to the intravenous "rush" of heroin and cocaine in opioid addicts, *American Journal of Drug & Alcohol Abuse* 12: 79–87.
24. Holstege et al. (2003): Brain activation, 9191.
25. Ibid., 9192. The researchers confirmed earlier studies in primates that the medial optic area and amygdala seem to show no role in arousal and ejaculations.
26. Hamann et al. (2004): Men and women differ, 413–15.
27. Hamann SB, et al. (2002): Ecstasy and agony: Activation of the human amygdala in positive and negative emotion, *Psychological Science* 13: 135–41.
28. Hamann et al. (2004): Men and women differ, 414–16.
29. Gold JI (2003): Linking reward expectation to behavior in the basal ganglia, *Trends in Neuroscience* 26: 12–14. Also see Schultz W (2000): Multiple reward signals in the brain, *Nature Reviews Neuroscience* 1: 199–207.
30. Holstege et al. (2003): Brain activation, 9192. Since the amygdala is activated by fearful stimuli, part of the enhancing effect of its deactivation might reflect the absence of confounding factors (i.e., fearful stimuli) during orgasm.
31. Larsson K, Ahlenius S (1999): Brain and sexual behavior, *Annals of the New York Academy of Sciences* 877: 292–308.
32. Ridley M (1993): *The Red Queen: Sex and the Evolution of Human Nature,* HarperCollins, New York, 247–9.

33. Gingrich BY, et al. (2000): D2 receptors in the nucleus accumbens are important for social attachment in female prairie voles, *Behavioral Neuroscience* 114: 173–83.
34. Kampe KK, et al. (2001): Reward value of attractiveness and gaze, *Nature* 413: 589.
35. Ibid.
36. Ibid.
37. Fisher (2004): *Why We Love,* 69–76. See also Rasia-Filho et al. (1999): Effects of gonadal hormones.
38. Fisher HE, Aron A, Mashek D et. al. (2002): Defining the brain systems of lust, romantic attraction, and attachment, *Archives of Sexual Behavior* 31: 413–19. See also Muskin P (2004): Imaging data uncover mysteries of love, *Psychiatric News* 39(8) (April 18): 73.
39. Fisher (2004): *Why We Love,* 62–4.
40. Ibid., 71.
41. Ibid., 73.
42. Ibid., 73–4.
43. Bartels A, Zeki S (2000): The neural basis of romantic love, *NeuroReport* 11: 3829–34.
44. Ibid., 3830.
45. Bartels A, Zeki S (2004): The neural correlates of maternal and romantic love, *NeuroImage* 21: 1155–66.
46. Diamond LM (2003): What does sexual orientation orient? A biobehavioral model distinguishing romantic love and sexual desire, *Psychological Review* 110: 173–92.
47. Greenfield (2000): *The Private Life of the Brain,* 1012–20.
48. Young LJ, Wang Z, Insel TR (1998): Neuroendocrine bases of monogamy, *Trends in Neurosciences* 21: 71–5.
49. Fisher (2004): *Why We Love,* 88; see also Wang ZZ, Ferris CF, De Vries GJ (1994): The role of septal vasopressin innervation in paternal behavior in prairie voles, *Proceedings of the National Academy of Sciences [USA]* 91: 400–4. Recent research on voles points to a gene for fatherhood. See Wade N (2005): DNA of deadbeat voles may hint at why some fathers turn out to be rats, *New York Times,* June 10: A12.
50. Fisher (2004): *Why We Love,* 90.
51. Greenfield (2000): *The Private Life of the Brain,* 1012–20.
52. Thomas A, Kim NB, Amico JA (1996): Differential regulation of oxytocin and vasopressin messenger ribonucleic acid levels by gonadal steroids in postpartum rats, *Brain Research* 741: 48–52.
53. Quinsey VL (2003): The etiology of anomalous sexual preferences in men, *Annals of the New York Academy of Sciences* 989: 105–17, discussion at 144–53.
54. LeVay S (1994): *The Sexual Brain,* MIT Press, Cambridge, MA.

55. Baron-Cohen (2003): *The Essential Difference*, 90–115.
56. Johnston VS (1999): *Why We Feel: The Science of Human Emotions*, Perseus, Reading, MA.
57. Bailey JM, Dunne MP, Martin NG (2000): Genetic and environmental influences on sexual orientation and its correlates in an Australian twin sample, *Journal of Personality & Social Psychology* 78: 524–36.
58. Quinsey (2003): The etiology of anomalous sexual preferences, 105–8. Also note: Researchers have recently discovered that one gene acting as a "master sexual gene" is able to affect the sexual behavior of the fruit fly (*Drosophila*). Females given the variant of the gene found in males acted just like males in the courtship process. Hence, this single gene in *Drosophila* determines the flies' behavior and sexual orientation. Among other things, this finding shows that instinctive behaviors like sexual preference can be determined by genetic programs and therefore seem "hardwired." See Rosenthal E (2005): For fruit flies, gene shift tilts sex orientation, *New York Times*, June 3: A1, A20. The *New York Times* report was based on the following articles in *Cell:* Demir E, Dickson B (2005): *fruitless* splicing specifies male courtship behavior in *Drosophila, Cell* 121: 785–94; and Stockinger P, et al. (2005): Neural circuitry that governs *Drosophila* male courtship behavior, *Cell* 121: 795–807.
59. Smith D (2004): Love that dare not squeak its name: Homosexuality among animals is common, *New York Times*, sec. Arts & Ideas, February 7: B7–B8.
60. Bailey et al. (2000): Genetic and environmental influences.
61. Quinsey (2003): The etiology of anomalous sexual preferences, 107.
62. Allen LS, Gjorski RA (1992): Sexual orientation and the size of the anterior commissure in the human brain, *Proceedings of the National Academy of Sciences [USA]* 89: 7199–202.
63. Robinson SJ, Manning JT (2000): The ratio of 2nd to 4th digit length and male homosexuality, *Evolution & Human Behavior* 21: 333–45.
64. Lippa RA (2003): Handedness, sexual orientation, and gender-related personality traits in men and women, *Archives of Sexual Behavior* 32: 103–14.
65. Wade N (2005): For gay men, different scent of attraction, *New York Times*, May 10: A1, A14, a report based on the following research: Savic I, Berglund H, Lindström P (2005): Brain response to putative pheromones in homosexual men, *Proceedings of the National Academy of Sciences [USA]* 102: 7356–61. See also Kovacs G, et al. (2004): Smelling human sex hormone-like compounds affects face gender judgment of men, *NeuroReport* 15: 1275–7.
66. Freund K, Kuban M (1993): Toward a testable developmental model of pedophilia: The development of erotic age preference, *Child Abuse & Neglect* 17: 315–24.

67. Quinsey (2003): The etiology of anomalous sexual preferences, 109.
68. Kafka MP (2003): The monoamine hypothesis for the pathophysiology of paraphilic disorders: An update, *Annals of the New York Academy of Sciences* 989: 86–94.
69. Ibid., 87.
70. Maes M, et al. (2001): Pedophilia is accompanied by increased plasma concentrations of catecholamines, in particular epinephrine, *Psychiatry Research* 103: 43–9.
71. Greenberg DM, Bradford JMW (1997): Treatment of the paraphilic disorders: A review of the role of the selective serotonin reuptake inhibitors, *Sexual Abuse: Journal of Treatment & Research* 9: 349–60.
72. Kafka (2003): The monoamine hypothesis, 88. See also Soubrie P (1986): Reconciling the role of central serotonin neurons in human and animal behavior, *Behavioural Brain Research* 9: 319–64.
73. Kafka (2003): The monoamine hypothesis, 90.

9. Deception

1. Piaget J (1965 [1932]): *The Moral Judgment of the Child,* trans. Gabim M, Free Press, Glencoe, IL; also see Vasek ME (1986): Lying as a skill: The development of deception in children; in Mitchell RW, Thompson NS, eds., *Deception: Perspectives on Human and Nonhuman Deceit,* Albany, NY, SUNY Press, 271–92.
2. Quek TK (2004): The truth about a child's compulsive lying (Web site): webhome.idirect.com/~readon/lies.html .
3. Ibid.
4. Lewis M (1993): The development of deception; in Lewis M, Saarni C, eds., *Lying and Deception in Everyday Life,* New York, Guilford Press, 90–105.
5. Forrest J, Feldman RS, Tyler J (2004): When accurate beliefs lead to better lie detection, *Journal of Applied Psychology* 34: 764–80.
6. Feldman RS (2001): "The Truth about Lying" (video interview about lying on ABC-TV's *PrimeTime,* air date March 15), Films for the Humanities & Sciences, Princeton, NJ. See also Hrubes D, Feldman RS, Tyler J (2004): Emotion-focused deception: The role of deception in the regulation of emotion; in Philippot P, Feldman RS, eds., *The Regulation of Emotion,* Laurence Erlbaum Associates, Mahwah, NJ, 227–49.
7. Carey B (2005): The secret lives of just about everybody, *New York Times,* sec. Science Times, January 11: F1. This article points out how frequent double lives are, mentioning famous figures such as Charles A. Lindbergh, who had three children by a second woman who was not his wife; architect Louis I. Kahn, who had a long-term relationship with a woman other than his wife; *New Yorker* editor William Shawn, who had

an ongoing affair with writer Lillian Ross; and oil heir Gordon P. Getty, who had two families – four sons in San Francisco with his wife, and three daughters with another woman in Los Angeles.

8. Feldman RS, Forrest JA, Happ BR (2002): Self-presentation and verbal deception: Do self-presenters lie more? *Basic & Applied Social Psychology* 24: 163–70.

9. DePaulo BM, et al. (1996): Lying in everyday life, *Journal of Personality & Social Psychology* 70: 979–95.

10. DePaulo et al. (1996): Lying in everyday life, 975–9.

11. Gilson É (1955): *History of Christian Philosophy in the Middle Ages,* Random House, New York, 77–81.

12. Kant I (1909 [1873]): *Critique of Practical Reason and Other Works on the Theory of Ethics,* trans. Abbott TK, 6th ed., Longmans, London, 16 ff.

13. Bok S (1978): *Lying: Moral Choice in Public and Private Life,* Pantheon, New York.

14. Taylor M, Lussier GL, Maring BL (2003): The distinction between lying and pretending, *Journal of Cognition & Development* 4: 299–324.

15. Vasek (1986): Lying as a skill, 271.

16. De Waal FBM (1996): *Good Natured: The Origins of Right and Wrong in Humans and Other Animals,* Harvard University Press, Cambridge, MA, 44.

17. Ibid., 75.

18. Patterson F, Linden E (1981): *The Education of Koko,* Holt Rinehart & Winston, New York.

19. Langleben D, et al. (2002): Brain activity during simulated deception: An event-related functional magnetic resonance study, *NeuroImage* 15: 727–32.

20. Ford E (in press): Lie detection: Historical neuropsychiatric and legal dimensions, *International Journal of Law & Psychiatry.*

21. Farwell LA, Donchin E (1988): Taking off the top of your head: Toward a mental prosthesis utilizing event-related brain potentials, *Electrocephalographic & Clinical Neurophysiology* 70: 510–23.

22. *Harrington v. State,* no. 122/01-0653 (Iowa Sup. Ct. 2003). In this case, the evidence was exculpatory.

23. Langleben et al. (2002): Brain activity during simulated deception, 730–1.

10. The Biology of Money

1. Schwartz JM, Begley S (2002): *The Mind and the Brain: Neuroplasticity and the Power of Mental Force,* HarperCollins, New York, 69.

2. Newberg A, D'Aquili E, Rause V (2001): *Why God Won't Go Away,* Ballantine Books, New York, 45.

3. David M, Whalen PJ (2001): The amygdala: Vigilance and emotion, *Molecular Psychiatry* 6: 13–34. See also Goosens KA, Hobin JA, Maren S (2003): Auditory-evoked spike firing in the lateral amygdala and Pavlovian fear conditioning: Mnemonic code or fear bias? *Neuron* 40: 1013–22.

4. Zalla T, et al. (2000): Differential amygdala responses to winning and losing: A functional magnetic resonance imaging study in humans, *European Journal of Neuroscience* 12: 1764–74.

5. Breiter HC, et al. (2001): Functional imaging of neural responses to expectancy and experience of monetary gains and losses, *Neuron* 30: 619–39. For understanding how reward signals impact on neurons, also see Schultz W (2000): Multiple reward signals in the brain, *Nature Reviews Neuroscience* 1: 199–207.

6. Thut G, et al. (1997): Activation of the human brain by monetary reward, *NeuroReport* 8: 1225–8.

7. Richardson MP, Strange BA, Dolan RJ (2004): Encoding of emotional memories depends on amygdala and hippocampus and their interactions, *Nature Neuroscience* 7: 278–85.

8. Newberg et al. (2001): *Why God Won't Go Away,* 45–8.

9. Scoville WB, Milner B (2000 [1957]): Loss of recent memory after bilateral hippocampal lesions, *Journal of Neuropsychiatry & Clinical Neurosciences* 12: 103–13. Scoville's study shows the critical role of the anterior hippocampus and hippocampal gyrus in retaining current experience, including ups and downs in stocks. See also Rosen JB, et al. (1992): Lesions of the perirhinal cortex but not of the frontal, medial prefrontal, visual, or insular cortex block fear-potentiated startle using a visual conditioned stimulus, *Journal of Neuroscience* 12: 4624–33. Rosen et al. show that lesions of the perirhinal cortex block fear-potentiated startle projects to the amygdala. This suggests that the perirhinal cortex may have a role in memory, and hence the startle effect of a falling stock market.

10. Hariri AR, et al. (2002): Serotonin transporter genetic variation and the response of the human amygdala, *Science* 297: 400–2.

11. Goldberg E (2001): *The Executive Brain: Frontal Lobes and the Civilized Mind,* Oxford University Press, New York, 35.

12. Ibid., 321–36.

13. Koechlin E, et al. (1999): The role of the anterior prefrontal cortex in human cognition, *Nature* 399: 148–61.

14. Note that patients with prefrontal cortex lesions deomonstrate impairment in planning and problem-solving tasks. See Colvin MK, Dunbar K, Grafman J (2001): The effects of frontal lobe lesions on goal achievement in the water jug task, *Journal of Cognitive Neuroscience* 13: 1129–47.

15. Rowe JB, et al. (2001): Imaging the mental components of a planning task, *Neuropsychologia* 39: 315–17.

16. Rogers RD, et al. (1999): Choosing between small, likely rewards and large, unlikely rewards activates inferior and orbital prefrontal cortex, *Journal of Neuroscience* 19: 9029–38.

17. Pribram KH, McGuinness D (1975): Arousal, activation, and effort in the control of attention, *Psychological Review* 82: 116–49.

18. Daffner KR, et al. (2000): The central role of the prefrontal cortex in directing attention to novel events, *Brain* 123: 927–9.

19. Gray TS (1999): Functional and anatomical relationships among the amygdala, base forebrain, ventral striatum and cortex: An integrative discussion, *Annals of the New York Academy of Sciences* 877: 439–44.

20. Bechara A, Damasio H, Damasio AR (2003): Role of the amygdala in brain function: Basic and clinical approaches, Part 6: Amygdala functions in emotion and memory in humans, *Annals of the New York Academy of Sciences* 985: 356–69.

21. Bechara A, et al. (1997): Deciding advantageously before knowing the advantageous strategy, *Science* 275: 1293–5.

22. Anderson SW, et al. (1999): Impairment of social and moral behavior related to early damage in human prefrontal cortex, *Nature Neuroscience* 2: 1032–7. Here the gambling task was applied to two patients who sustained injury to their prefrontal cortex before they were sixteen days old.

23. Bechara A, et al. (1997): Deciding advantageously, 1295.

24. Gomez-Beldarrain M, et al. (2004): Patients with right frontal lesions are unable to assess and use advice to make predictive judgments, *Journal of Cognitive Neuroscience* 16: 74–89. See also Sanfey AG, et al. (2003): Phineas gauged: Decision-making and the human prefrontal cortex, *Neuropsychologia* 41: 1218–29.

25. *Note:* In addition to the dorsolateral prefrontal cortex and the anterior cingulate cortex, other interconnected areas of the brain are activated to target stimuli. These areas include the insular cortex and the basal ganglia. See Huettel SA, et al. (2004): Dynamic and strategic aspects of executive processing, *Brain Research* 1000: 78–84.

26. Huettel SA, Mack PB, McCarthy G (2002): Perceiving patterns in random series: Dynamic processing of sequence in prefrontal cortex, *Nature Neuroscience* 5: 485–90. Also see Ivry R, Knight, RT (2002): Making order from chaos: The misguided frontal lobe, *Nature Neuroscience* 5: 394–6.

27. Huettel et al. (2002): Perceiving patterns in random series, 487.

28. The anterior cingulate gyrus and anterior middle frontal gyrus become more active on error trials that on trials that are correct, or predictive. See Huettel SA, McCarthy G (2004): What is odd in the oddball task? Prefrontal cortex is activated by dynamic changes in response strategy, *Neuropsychologia* 42: 379–86.

29. Ibid., 383–6. See also Huettel et al. (2004): Dynamic and strategic aspects of executive processing.

30. Lane RD, et al. (1998) Neural correlates of levels of emotional awareness: Evidence of an interaction between emotion and attention in the anterior cingulate cortex, *Journal of Cognitive Neuroscience* 10: 525–35.

31. Carter CS, Botvinick MM, Cohen JD (1999): The contribution of the anterior cingulate cortex to executive processes in cognition, *Reviews in the Neurosciences* 10: 49–57.

32. Richmond BJ, Liu Z, Munetaka S (2003): Predicting future rewards, *Science* 301: 179–80.

33. Munetaka S, Richmond BJ (2002): Anterior cingulate: Single neuronal signals related to degree of reward expectancy, *Science* 295: 1709–11.

34. Schwartz & Begley (2002): *The Mind and the Brain,* 64–7.

35. Goldberg (2001): *The Executive Brain,* 33.

36. McCoy AN, et al. (2003): Saccade reward signals in the posterior cingulate cortex, *Neuron* 40: 1031–40.

37. Cohen JD, Blum KI (2002): Reward and decision-making, *Neuron* 36: 193–8. See also "Sponsors' Foreword" (2002): Reward and decision making: Opportunities and future directions, *Neuron* 36: 189–92.

38. O'Doherty J (2003): Can't learn without you: Predictive value coding in orbitofrontal cortex requires the basolateral amygdala, *Neuron* 39: 731–3.

39. Roesch MR, Olson CR (2004): Neuronal activity related to reward value and motivation in primate frontal cortex, *Science* 304: 307–10. Researchers studying the macaque brain have shown that neuronal activity in the orbitofrontal cortex addresses the value of the expected reward. In contrast, neuronal activity in the premotor cortex shows the degree of motivation.

40. O'Doherty (2003): Can't learn without you, 731–2.

41. Knutson B, et al. (2001): Anticipation of increasing monetary reward selectively recruits nucleus accumbens, *Journal of Neuroscience* 21: RC 159.

42. Carelli RM, Ijames SG, Crumlin AJ (200): Evidence that separate neural circuits in the nucleus accumbens encode cocaine versus "natural" (water and food) reward, *Journal of Neuroscience* 20: 4255–66.

43. Zink CF, et al. (2004): Human striatal responses to monetary reward depend on saliency, *Neuron* 42: 509–17.

44. Zink CF, et al. (2003): Human striatal response to salient nonrewarding stimuli, *Journal of Neuroscience* 23: 8092–7.

45. Volkow ND, Fowler JS, Wang GJ (2003): The addicted human brain: Insights from imaging studies, *Journal of Clinical Investigation* 111: 1444–51; also see Volkow, ND, Fowler JS, Wang GJ (2002): Role of dopamine

in drug reinforcement and addiction in humans: Results from imaging studies, *Behavioural Pharmacology* 13: 355–66.

46. Yasgur BS (2004): The neurologic roots of addiction, *NeuroPsychiatry Reviews* 5: 20.

47. Zweig J (2002): Is your brain wired for wealth? *Money,* September 27, money.cnn.com/2002/09/25/pf/investing/agenda_brain_short/ .

48. Thut et al. (1997): Activation of the human brain by monetary reward.

49. Hitt J (2004): American kabuki: The ritual of scandal, *New York Times,* sec. 4 (Week in Review), July 18, 2004: 1, 3, at 3.

50. Ibid., 1, 3.

51. Sorkin AR (2005): Ex-Chief and Aide Guilty of Looting Millions at Tyco, *New York Times,* June 18: A1.

52. Shaffer HJ, Hall MN, Vander Bilt J (1999): Estimating the prevalence of disordered gambling behavior in the United States and Canada: A research synthesis, *American Journal of Public Health* 89: 1369–76.

53. Potenza MN, Kosten TR, Rounsaville BJ (2001): Pathological gambling, *Journal of the American Medical Association* 286: 141–4; see also Shaffer et al. (1999): Estimating the prevalence, 1370–4.

54. Sood ED, Pallanti S, Hollander E (2003): Diagnosis and treatment of pathologic gambling, *Current Psychiatry Reports* 5: 9–15.

55. Arehart-Treichel J (2005): As gambling problems grow, treatment options studied, *Psychiatric News* 40(6): 28–9. These problems are reportedly believed related to impaired impulse control, since brain areas crucial for impulse control – i.e., the ventromedial prefrontal cortex (including ventral anterior cingulate) – seem to activate less in pathological gambling.

56. American Psychiatric Association (1980): *Diagnostic and Statistical Manual of Mental Disorders,* 3d ed., American Psychiatric Association, Washington, DC, 312.31.

57. Arehart-Treichel (2005): As gambling problems grow, 28. Twin studies suggest problem gambling has a genetic component.

58. Nower L, Derevensky JL, Gupta R (2004): The relationship of impulsivity, sensation seeking, coping, and substance use in youth gamblers, *Psychology of Addictive Behaviors* 18: 49–55.

59. Potenza MN, Hollander E (2004): Pathological gambling and impulse control disorders; in Davis KL, et al., eds. *Neuropsychopharmacology: The Fifth Generation of Progress,* Lippincott Williams & Wilkins, Philadelphia, 1725–42.

60. Potenza MN (2001): The neurobiology of pathological gambling, *Seminars in Clinical Neuropsychiatry* 6: 217–26.

61. Zack M, Poulos CX (2004): Amphetamine primes motivation to gamble and gambling-related semantic networks in problem gamblers, *Neuropsychopharmacology* 29: 195–207.

62. Potenza et al. (2001): Pathological gambling, 142–3.

63. Ibid., 143–4.
64. Volkow et al. (2002): Role of dopamine, 355–6.
65. White NM (1996): Addictive drugs as reinforcers: Multiple partial actions on memory systems, *Addiction* 91: 921–46.

11. The Bad and the Mad

1. Tancredi LR (1997): Science of the mind in the contexts of a culture; in Romanucci-Ross L, Moerman DE, Tancredi LR, eds., *The Anthropology of Medicine,* 3d ed., Bergin & Garvey, Westport, CT, 205–317.
2. Simon B (1978): *Mind and Madness in Ancient Greece: The Classical Roots of Modern Psychiatry,* Cornell University Press, Ithaca, NY.
3. Ibid., 56.
4. Jaynes J (1977): *The Origin of Consciousness in the Breakdown of the Bicameral Mind,* Houghton Mifflin, Boston.
5. Simon (1978): *Mind and Madness in Ancient Greece,* 71.
6. Tancredi (1997): Science of the mind, 306.
7. See the work of Bowlby J (1980): *Attachment and Loss,* 3 vols., Basic Books, New York.
8. Bateson G, et al. (1956): Toward a theory of schizophrenia, *Behavioral Science* 1: 251–64. The term "schizophrenogenic mother" is thought to have originated with Fromm-Reichmann F (1948): Notes on the development of treatment of schizophrenics by psychoanalytic psychotherapy, *Psychiatry* 11: 263–73.
9. Lidz T, Fleck S, Cornelison AR (1965): *Schizophrenia and the Family,* International Universities Press, New York. See also the work of Lyman Wynne, who conceptualized the pseudomutual and pseudohostile communication in families. Here the child learns a specific verbal communication that does not apply in other circumstances with others. Wynne LC, et al. (1958): Pseudo-mutuality in the family relations of schizophrenics, *Psychiatry* 21: 205–20.
10. Kendler KS (2003): The genetics of schizophrenia: Chromosomal deletions, attentional disturbances, and spectrum boundaries, *American Journal of Psychiatry* 160: 1549–53.
11. Schulz B (1932): Zur Erbpathologie der Schizophrenie (On the hereditary pathology of schizophrenia), *Zeitschrift für die Gesamte Neurologische Psychiatrie* 143: 175–293; also see Kendler KS, Zerbin-Rudin E (1996): Abstract and review of "Zur Erbpathologie der Schizophrenie," *American Journal of Medical Genetics (Neuropsychiatric Genetics)* 67: 343–6.
12. Ketty S, et al. (1968): The types and prevalence of mental illness in the biological and adoptive families of adopted schizophrenics, *Journal of Psychiatric Research* 6: 345–62.

13. Shenton ME, et al. (2001): A review of MRI findings in schizophrenia, *Schizophrenia Research* 49: 1–52.
14. Sallet P, et al. (2003): Reduced cortical folding in schizophrenia: An MRI morphometric study, *American Journal of Psychiatry* 160: 1606–13.
15. Okugawa G, Sedvall GC, Agartz I (2003): Smaller cerebellar vermis but not hemisphere volumes in patients with chronic schizophrenia, *American Journal of Psychiatry* 160: 1614–17. Here the volume reduction has been shown to be prominent in the cerebellar vermis.
16. Genetic research seems more advanced recently for the schizophrenic range of mental illnesses, but studies are also being conducted for bipolar illness. See Geller B, et al. (2004): Linkage disequilibrium of the brain-derived neurotrophic factor val66met polymorphism in children with prepubertal and early adolescent bipolar disorder phenotype, *American Journal of Psychiatry* 161: 1698–700.
17. See the Irish Study of High-Density Schizophrenia Families (ISHDSF): Straub RE, et al. (2002): Genome-wide scans of three independent sets of ninety Irish multiplex schizophrenia families and follow-up of selected regions in all families provides evidence for multiple susceptibility genes, *Molecular Psychiatry* 7: 542–59. For a discussion of this, see Kendler (2003): The genetics of schizophrenia, 1552. Subsequent studies of twenty schizophrenia genome scans revealed agreement in these studies beyond what might have been expected by chance alone; e.g., Lewis CM, et al. (2003): Genome scan meta-analysis of schizophrenia and bipolar disorder, Pt. II: Schizophrenia, *American Journal of Human Genetics* 73: 34–48.
18. The chromosome detected with linkage to schizophrenia was "6p24-22"; see Schizophrenia Linkage Collaborative Group for Chromosomes 3, 6, and 8 (1996): Additional support for schizophrenia linkage on chromosomes 6 and 8: A multicenter study, *American Journal of Human Genetics (Neuropsychiatric Genetics)* 67: 580–94.
19. The DNA markers are in the gene DTNBP1 (dystrobrevin-binding protein 1, or dysbindin-1. See Straub RE, et al. (2002): Genetic variation in the 6p22.3 gene DTNBP1, the human ortholog of the mouse dysbindin gene, is associated with schizophrenia, *American Journal of Human Genetics* 71: 337–48. See also Bassett AS, et al. (2003): The schizophrenia phenotype in 22q11 deletion syndrome, *American Journal of Psychiatry* 160: 1580–6.
20. Wallace C, et al. (1998): Serious criminal offending and mental disorder: Case linkage study, *British Journal of Psychiatry* 173: 477–84.
21. Monahan J, et al. (2001): Violence and the clinician: Assessing and managing risk; in *Rethinking Risk Assessment: The MacArthur Study of Mental Disorder and Violence,* Oxford University Press, Oxford, 129–43. Also see Steadman HJ, et al. (1998): Violence by people discharged from

acute psychiatric inpatient facilities and by others in the same neighbor-hoods, *Archives of General Psychiatry* 55: 393–401.

22. Swanson JW, et al. (1990): Violence and psychiatric disorder in the com-munity: Evidence from the Epidemiologic Catchment Area surveys, *Hos-pital & Community Psychiatry* 41: 761–70.

23. Brennan PA, Mednick SA, Hodgins S (2000): Major mental disorders and criminal violence in a Danish birth cohort, *Archives of General Psy-chiatry* 57: 494–500.

24. Taylor P, Gunn J (1999): Homicides by people with mental illness: Myth and reality, *British Journal of Psychiatry* 174: 9–14.

25. Note that there seems to be a relationship between an allele encoding the low activity variant of catechol-O-methyltransferase (COMT) and aggressive behavior in schizophrenic patients. See Lachman HM, et al. (1998): Association between catechol-O-methyltransferase genotype and violence in schizophrenia and schizoaffective disorder, *American Journal of Psychiatry* 155: 835–7.

26. Modestin J (1998): Criminal and violent behavior in schizophrenic pa-tients: An overview, *Psychiatry & Clinical Neurosciences* 52: 547–54.

27. Hubl D, et al. (2003): Pathways that make voices: White matter changes in auditory hallucinations, *Archives of General Psychiatry* 61: 658–68.

28. Prasad KMR, et al. (2004): The entorhinal cortex in first-episode psychot-ic disorders: A structural magnetic resonance imaging study, *American Journal of Psychiatry* 161: 1612–19.

29. Ibid., 1618.

30. Roche T (2002): Andrea Yates: More to the story, *Time* "Web Exclusive," March 18, www.time.com/time/nation/article/0,8599,218445,00.html.

31. Liptak A (2005): New trial for a mother who drowned 5 children, *New York Times,* sec. National Report, January 7: A16. See also Roche (2002): Andrea Yates.

32. CNN – US News Year in Review – Susan Smith Trial – Dec. 28, 1995, www.cnn.com/EVENTS/year_in_review/us/smith.html; also *CNN Time Capsule: The Defining Moments of 1995* (CD-ROM).

33. Raine A, Buchsbaum M, LaCasse L (1997): Brain abnormalities in mur-derers indicated by positron emission tomography, *Biological Psychiatry* 42: 495–508.

34. Pietrini P, et al. (2000): Neural correlates of imaginal aggressive behavior assessed by positron emission tomography in healthy subjects, *Amer-ican Journal of Psychiatry* 157: 1772–81. See also Brower MC, Price BH (2001): Neuropsychiatry of frontal lobe dysfunction in violent and crim-inal behaviour: A critical review, *Journal of Neurology, Neurosurgery & Psychiatry* 71: 720–6.

35. Raine A, et al. (1998): Prefrontal glucose deficits in murderers lacking

psychosocial deprivation, *Neuropsychiatry, Neuropsychology & Behavioral Neurology* 11: 1–7.

36. Weaver ICG, Cervoni N, Champagne FA (2004): Epigenetic programming by maternal behavior, *Nature Neuroscience* 7: 847–54.

37. Raine A, et al. (2003): Corpus callosum abnormalities in psychopathic antisocial individuals, *Archives of General Psychiatry* 60: 1134–42.

38. Raine A, et al. (2000): Reduced prefrontal gray matter volume and reduced autonomic activity in antisocial personality disorder, *Archives of General Psychiatry* 57: 119–27.

39. Caspi A, et al. (2002): Role of genotype in the cycle of violence in maltreated children, *Science* 297: 851–4.

40. McBurnett K, et al. (2000): Low salivary cortisol and persistent aggression in boys referred for disruptive behavior, *Archives of General Psychiatry* 57: 38–43.

41. For a discussion of this, see Walsh AA (1979): The curious trial of "The Durham Boy," *Newport: The Magazine of the Newport College – Salve Regina* 2(2): 4–8.

42. Neal J (1835): The case of Major Mitchell, serialized on the front page of *New England Galaxy:* January 17 (no. 3), 24 (no. 4), 31 (no. 5), February 7 (no. 6), and 14 (no. 7). This extensive review contains a detailed description of the case.

43. Walsh AA (1976): Phrenology and the Boston medical community in the 1830s, *Bulletin of the History of Medicine* 50: 261–73, and Walsh AA (1976): The "new science of the mind" and the Philadelphia physicians in the early 1800's, *Transactions & Studies of the College of Physicians of Philadelphia,* 4th ser., 43(4): 397–415.

44. Editorial (1835): Phrenology vindicated, *New England Galaxy:* February 28 (no. 9): 1.

45. ALI test. Tancredi LR, Slaby AE, Lieb J (1975): *Legal Issues in Psychiatric Care,* Harper & Row, New York.

46. Greene JD, et al. (2004): The neural bases of cognitive conflict and control in moral judgment, *Neuron* 44: 389–400.

47. Greene JD, et al. (2001): An fMRI investigation of emotional engagement in moral judgment, *Science* 293: 2105–8.

48. Greene et al. (2004): The neural bases of cognitive conflict, 389, 392.

49. Ibid., 389–400.

50. Katz LD (2002): Toward good and evil: Evolutionary approaches to aspects of human morality; in Katz, LD, ed., *Evolutionary Origins of Morality: Cross-Disciplinary Perspectives,* Imprint Academic, Thorverton, UK, ix–xvi.

51. Damasio AR (1994): *Descartes' Error: Emotion, Reason and the Human Brain,* Grosset/Putnam, New York.

12. Creating a Moral Brain

1. For a detailed, complete discussion on the impact of neuroscience developments on law, see Jones OD, Goldsmith TH (2005): Law and behavioral biology, *Columbia Law Review* 105: 405–502.
2. Caspi A, et al. (2002): Role of genotype in the cycle of violence in maltreated children, *Science* 297: 851–4.
3. Camille N, et al. (2004): The involvement of the orbitofrontal cortex in the experience of regret, *Science* 304: 1167–70.
4. Libet B (1999): How does conscious experience arise? The neural time factor, *Brain Research Bulletin* 50: 339–40; Platt ML, Glimcher PW (1997): Responses of intraparietal neurons to saccadic targets and visual distractors, *Journal of Neurophysiology* 78: 1574–89, and Platt ML, Glimcher PW (1999): Neural correlates of decision variables in parietal cortex, *Nature* 400: 233–8.
5. Eagleman DM (2004): The where and when of intention, *Science* 303: 1144–5.
6. Gazzaniga MS (2005): *The Ethical Brain*, Dana Press, Washington, DC. Dr. Gazzaniga in this very recently published book uses the term "designer children."
7. Crowley A, Walsh V (2001): Tickling the brain: Studying visual sensation, perception and cognition by transcranial magnetic stimulation, *Progress in Brain Research* 131: 411–25.
8. Dudai Y (2004): The neurosciences: The danger that we will think that we have understood it all; in Rees D, Rose S, eds., *The New Brain Sciences: Perils and Prospects,* Cambridge University Press, Cambridge, UK, 167–80.
9. Musallam S, et al. (2004): Cognitive control signals for neural prosthetics, *Science* 305: 258–62. See also Nicolelis MAL (2003): Brain–machine interfaces to restore motor function and probe neural circuits, *Nature Reviews Neuroscience* 4: 417–22.
10. Valenstein ES (1986): *Great and Desperate Cures,* Basic Books, New York.
11. Dudai Y (2004): The neurosciences, 168–9.
12. *Kaimowitz* v. *Department of Mental Health for the State of Michigan,* no. 73-19434-AW (Cir. Ct., Wayne County, Mich., 1973), *Prison Law Reporter* 2.
13. Erikson KT (1966): *Wayward Puritans: A Study in the Sociology of Deviance,* John Wiley & Sons, New York.
14. Slaby A, Tancredi L (1975): *Collusion for Conformity,* Jason Aronson, New York.

Glossary

amygdala One of the limbic structures, this bilateral, almond-shaped brain structure is activated by emotional reactions – most particularly fear. The amgdala has close connections to the prefrontal cortex, as well as the autonomic and hormonal systems in the body, and it possesses the capacity to store emotional memory.

anterior cingulate cortex (ACC) This part of the human brain – the outer layer of the convoluted ridge known as the **anterior cingulate gyrus (ACG)** – acts like a limbic structure when it is associated with pain, fear, and emotions. When it is involved with detecting errors in thinking and the making of decisions, it functions like part of the frontal lobe.

anterior commissure One of three important bridges of fibers that cross from one hemisphere of the brain to the other. The anterior commissure is a main connection of the olfactory (i.e., associated with the sense of smell) portions of the hemispheres.

attachment mediating hormones Two neurochemicals – oxytocin and vasopressin – produced in the hypothalamus and gonads that have been shown to be involved in attachment (i.e., pair bonding and infant–caregiver attachment).

autonomic nervous system This system consists of sympathetic and parasympathetic nerves that regulate essential bodily functions such as respiration, sweating, blood pressure, temperature, urinary bladder function, and intestinal motility.

basal ganglia This refers to a subcortical structure (putamen, caudate nucleus, and globus pallidus) that is involved in cognitive, emotional, and motor functions.

Glossary

brain electrical activity mapping (BEAM) A type of CEEG that allows for the comparison of the electrical activity of a patient's brain with that of a healthy individual.

brain fingerprinting This device for the detection of lies uses an EEG to record event-related potentials induced during questioning of the subject. If the person knows the information asked and lies, he or she will produce a specific brain wave, a P300 pattern, which is emitted during recognition of a stimulus or object.

Broca's area This is the cortical area that is involved in language comprehension as well as in muscle movements for the production of speech.

caudate nucleus This nucleus (one in each hemisphere) is an elongated mass of gray matter located near the center of the brain. It consists of a swollen area (its "head") bulging into the front horn of the lateral ventricle. The remainder of the nucleus draws out into a slender "tail," which curves around in the shape of a horseshoe. By being involved in the detection and perception of a reward, as well as producing the motivation to actually obtain it, this region is part of the brain's "reward system."

central nervous system This is a general term for the spinal cord and the brain.

cerebral cortex This refers to the outer thin layer of the brain, which contains the cell bodies of neurons. This layer, also referred to as the "gray matter" (since this is where most of that lies), consists of specialized primary, secondary, and associational areas of the sensory and motor regions.

claustrum This is a thin plate of gray matter located along the side of the putamen and above and sideways from the amygdala. It is activated during sexual stimulation.

computerized electroencephalography (CEEG) A process that enhances the value of the traditional EEG by allowing greater specificity in the localization of abnormal brain waves. In addition, the computer provides for the easy recognition and correlation of these brain wave patterns with well-defined external stimuli to ensure that a basis will be established for detecting abnormalities. *Compare* brain electrical activity mapping.

corpus callosum The thick bundles of nerves that connect the two hemispheres of the brain.

electroencephalography (EEG) This is a technique for recording the electrical activity of the brain.

entorhinal cortex This cortex (one in each hemisphere) is located in the medial (inner) temporal lobe. It serves, among other things, as a relay station between the hippocampus and the prefrontal cortex. Recent studies are linking both the left and the right entorhinal cortices to the production of delusions and the psychotic process.

event-related potential (ERP) This is a measure of cortical electrical activity that is in response to stimulation.

emotional brain This refers to the part of the brain, mainly the limbic structures, that mediate emotional responses.

empathy This involves the capacity of an individual to intuit the attitude and mood of another person.

fontanels This refers to several soft, membranous spaces located at the angles of the cranial bones in an infant's skull.

frontal lobe This area of the human cortex located in the front of the brain is the site of cognition, emotions, and motion.

functional MRI (fMRI) An MRI technique modified to show the relative activation of areas of the brain when a particular activity is being performed.

gray matter The area of the brain, mostly the cerebral cortex, that consists of nerve cell bodies and is gray in appearance.

hemisphere The right or left half of the cerebrum, the two being joined by the corpus callosum.

hippocampus This subcortical structure is one of the limbic structures. It is involved with memory, mostly short-term memory, and works often in tandem with the amygdala.

hypothalamus One of the limbic structures (but *not* bilateral – there's only one), this functions as the regulator of the autonomic, immunological, and endocrine structures of the body.

insular cortex A region in the cerebral cortex (in both temporal lobes), this cortex – the outer layer of the triangular **insula** – collects information regarding bodily reactions, such as internal pain (e.g., the sensation of discomfort in the stomach), palpitation, and external temperature and touch. It also participates in the processing of emotions.

limbic structures This region of the brain comprises such structures as the amygdala, hippocampus, hypothalamus, and parts of the thalamus and of the cerebral cortex. It is involved in thinking, memory formation, emotional behavior, and the autonomic nervous system.

magnetic resonance imaging (MRI) A technique that uses magnetic fields to produce pictures of the structure of the brain. *Compare* functional MRI.

mentalism Refers to the concept derived from introspective psychology that the mind exists as a realm separate from the physical brain and that mental activity is responsible for and directs thinking and behavior. Mentalism operates under the "dualist" notion that both mental and physical spheres exist and are not "reducible" to each other.

mesodiencephalic transition zone This area of the brain, particularly several of its constituent structures – the medial and ventral thalamus, the midline, the subparafascicular nucleus, lateral central tegmental field (LCTF), zona incerta, and ventral tegmental area (VTA, *which see*) – is the most intensely activated during sexual stimulation and ejaculation.

mirror neurons These are neurons of a type responsible for learning by imitation.

neuron The neuron, or nerve cell, is the basic unit of the nervous system. It comprises a cell body, an axon (for electrical output signals), and dendrites (to receive incoming electrical signals).

neurotransmitters This refers to substances that act as chemical messengers, both allowing neurons to communicate with one another, and targeting organs for the activation of their functions. Examples of neurotransmitters are serotonin, norepinephrine, dopamine, and glutamate.

neuroplasticity The ability of the brain to adapt, by growing new neural connections or eliminating old ones, to changing conditions through learning, rehabilitation, and procedures such as transcranial magnetic stimulation.

nucleus accumbens (often called **ventral striatum**) This nucleus (one in each hemisphere) is a collection of neurons in the basal forebrain region. It connects to the globus pallidus (a pale-gray spherical area), which projects to the thalamus, and thereby to the prefrontal cortex – a major input to the nucleus accumbens, as is the ventral tegmental area (VTA). The nucleus accumbens plays an important role in pleasure, reward, and addiction.

peripheral nervous system The nervous system outside of the spinal cord and the brain.

pheromones These are chemical structures that an animal emits that serve to stimulate, largely through scent, behavioral responses in other animals of the same species.

physicalism This notion takes the position that mental things do not exist separate from the physical brain, that the brain essentially "makes" the mind, and that the brain, therefore, directs thinking and behavior.

positron emission tomography (PET) This imaging technique depends on the presence of rapidly decaying radioactive substances – like radioactive glucose – to produce pictures of functioning brain regions.

posterior cingulate cortex Present in both hemispheres, this is the back section of the cingulate cortex (the ACC is the front). It is responsible for updating the expectations of a reward in light of changes in circumstances.

prefrontal cortex This cortex is the anterior lobe of the frontal cortex. It functions in cognition, problem solving, and emotions.

premotor cortex This is an area of the cortex (in both hemispheres) of the frontal lobe that lies anterior to (i.e., in front of) the primary motor cortex. It is involved in sensory guidance of movement, as well as in activation of proximal and trunk muscles.

psychopathy The psychological state of a person who suffers from a mental disorder that manifests itself in abnormal social and violent behavior.

putamen This is the lateral zone of the lentiform nucleus, which is located in the white center in both hemispheres, between the insula and the caudate nucleus. The putamen is connected to the caudate nucleus by intervening bands of gray matter.

readiness potential (RP) The increase in electrical potential (i.e., voltage) on the scalp prior to voluntary action.

receptor This is the name for the docking site for a neurotransmitter on the receiving end of the synapse.

single-photon emission computed tomography (SPECT) A precursor of positron emission tomography scans that uses isotopes with longer half-lives, producing lower-resolution images than PET scans.

subcortical structure The name applied for structures of the brain that are located underneath the cortex.

superior temporal sulcus This refers to a fissure that begins in both hemispheres near the temporal pole, runs parallel to the lateral cerebral fissure, and terminates in the parietal lobe.

synapse The space between two nerve cells that acts as the place of connection. This connection can take place by means of an electrical impulse, or more directly via a neurotransmitter.

thalamus This structure (*not* bilateral – there's only one) is the primary relay center between the subcortical centers, including the limbic structures, and the cerebral cortex.

transcranial magnetic stimulation (TMS) A technology that stimulates the brain with the use of magnetic forces applied outside the skull. Depending on the TMS pulse rate, brain function will either be suppressed (slow pulse) or enhanced (fast pulse).

ventral striatum *See* nucleus accumbens.

ventral tagmental area (VTA) This is part of the brain reward circuitry that is rich in both norepinephrine and dopamine. The VTA – along with a structure in the limbic system, the nucleus accumbens (*which see*) – is activated strongly when addicts use cocaine or heroin. It also participates in enhancing focused attention, motivation, and feelings of elation.

Wernicke's area An area of the association region of the cerebral cortex that is involved in the comprehension of language.

white matter This refers to the myelinated (i.e., ensheathed in myelin, a white fatty substance) axons of neurons located under the cortex of the brain.

Index

Index

Index

Index

Index

Index